Counter-Terrorism, Aid and Civil Society

Non-Governmental Public Action

Series Editor: **Jude Howell**, Professor and Director of the Centre for Civil Society, London School of Economics and Political Science, UK.

Non-governmental public action (NGPA) by and for disadvantaged and marginalized people has become increasingly significant over the past two decades. This new book series is designed to make a fresh and original contribution to the understanding of NGPA. It presents the findings of innovative and policy-relevant research carried out by established and new scholars working in collaboration with researchers across the world. The series is international in scope and includes both theoretical and empirical work.

The series marks a departure from previous studies in this area in at least two important respects. First, it goes beyond a singular focus on developmental NGOs or the voluntary sector to include a range of non-governmental public actors such as advocacy networks, campaigns and coalitions, trades unions, peace groups, rights-based groups, cooperatives and social movements. Second, the series is innovative in stimulating a new approach to international comparative research that promotes comparison of the so-called developing world with the so-called developed world, thereby querying the conceptual utility and relevance of categories such as North and South.

Non-Governmental Public Action Series
Series Standing Order ISBN 978–0–230–22939–6 (hardback) and
978–0–230–22940–2 (paperback)
(*outside North America only*)

You can receive future titles in this series as they are published by placing a standing order. Please contact your bookseller or, in case of difficulty, write to us at the address below with your name and address, the title of the series and the ISBN quoted above.

Customer Services Department, Macmillan Distribution Ltd, Houndmills, Basingstoke, Hampshire RG21 6XS, England

Counter-Terrorism, Aid and Civil Society

Before and After the War on Terror

Jude Howell
Professor and Director of the Centre for Civil Society
London School of Economics and Political Science, UK

and

Jeremy Lind
Research Associate, Centre for Civil Society
London School of Economics and Political Science, UK

First published 2009 by
PALGRAVE MACMILLAN

Palgrave Macmillan in the UK is an imprint of Macmillan Publishers Limited, registered in England, company number 785998, of Houndmills, Basingstoke, Hampshire RG21 6XS.

Palgrave Macmillan in the US is a division of St Martin's Press LLC, 175 Fifth Avenue, New York, NY 10010.

Palgrave Macmillan is the global academic imprint of the above companies and has companies and representatives throughout the world.

Palgrave® and Macmillan® are registered trademarks in the United States, the United Kingdom, Europe and other countries.

ISBN-13: 978–0–230–22949–5 hardback

This book is printed on paper suitable for recycling and made from fully managed and sustained forest sources. Logging, pulping and manufacturing processes are expected to conform to the environmental regulations of the country of origin.

A catalogue record for this book is available from the British Library.

A catalog record for this book is available from the Library of Congress.

10   9   8   7   6   5   4   3   2   1
18   17   16   15   14   13   12   11   10   09

Printed and bound in Great Britain by
CPI Antony Rowe, Chippenham and Eastbourne

To families and friends

Contents

Acknowledgements

The research for this book has taken us well over three years. In the course of that time we have travelled to Afghanistan, India, Kenya, the US and Denmark. We have interviewed over 200 people, including development NGO and relief workers, government officials, human rights activists, civil society groups, lawyers, journalists, social commentators, scholars, security analysts, military representatives, and representatives of bilateral and multilateral donor agencies. We have had our notes copied in India, our pictures taken in Kenya and we were lucky to narrowly escape a rocket attack in Kabul.

We are indebted to many people for helping us to fathom the complex ways in which the War on Terror regime has intertwined with international development and civil society. We owe much to the stellar administrative support of Jane Schiemann, manager of the Centre for Civil Society at the London School of Economics and Political Science, who has trawled through endless receipts and chits of paper from around the world, looked after visitors and ensured that bureaucracy never stood too much in the way of us fulfilling our tasks. Similarly, we could not have done without the creative inputs of Christine Whyte, who designed policy briefs for our research, established a website, edited raw drafts of research papers and cast a meticulous eye over the final script.

We owe particular thanks to Abdul Basir and Elizabeth Winter for tirelessly explaining to us so much about the situation in Afghanistan, for introducing us to Mr Hashim Mayar and Anja de Beer of the Agency Coordinating Body for Afghan Relief (ACBAR) and for commenting on the draft Afghanistan chapter. ACBAR kindly hosted us during our research visit in 2006, providing us with much practical advice, expertise on the operational situation for NGOs in Afghanistan, and facilities to organise a round-table for our research. We are also grateful to Jos Van Mierlo and others at Christian Aid in Herat who were invaluable in facilitating our research visit there and hosting us during our stay. We learned much from our discussions with Sirajuddin Khalid, our research assistant in Kabul, and Niamattulah Ibrahimi. We are also grateful to the countless people in Kabul and Herat who were generous with their time and insights when discussing our research.

In Kenya, we are grateful to Elvin Nyukuri, our research assistant in Nairobi who did valuable background research prior to our visit. Henry Maina at the Legal Resources Foundation in Nairobi helped us to organise an initial round-table discussion in Nairobi to discuss our research questions in the Kenyan context. We also thank Mutuma Ruteere and Mikewa Ogada, at the time with the Kenya Human Rights Institute, for organising a final seminar in Nairobi where we presented our preliminary report. We benefited greatly from discussions with MUHURI in Mombasa, and key Muslim leaders in Nairobi such as Abdullahi Abdi, Abdul Slatch and Al Amin Kimathi. We also benefited from the scholarly insights into our work given by Paul Goldsmith, Musambayi Katumanga and Haroub Othman. Kate Longley graciously hosted us on several visits to Nairobi and we are grateful for her warm hospitality.

In India, we owe great thanks to Pooran Pandey, then head of the Voluntary Action Network India, who organised with us a round-table for our research in New Delhi. In addition to the many civil society groups, government officials and donor representatives we met in New Delhi and Ahmedabad, we thank Sushila Zeitlyn, Neera Chandhoke and Monica Banerjee for meeting with us at length to discuss the research.

We thank Mark Sidel at the University of Iowa, who invited us to present our research at an international meeting in Iowa City that he organised on counter-terrorism and civil society. We also thank Kay Guinane at OMB Watch in Washington, D.C., for organising a meeting with key civil society activists during our visit there in April 2008. In the UK we have benefited greatly from discussions with officials at the Charity Commission, DFID, Christian Aid, Oxfam and Islamic Relief, including Charles Abugre, Pauline Martin, Sarah Jane Digby, David Walker and Ed Cairns. We thank Eric Stobbaerts at MSF-UK, who worked with us in planning a round-table with humanitarian actors in London, at which our research was discussed. We also thank Roger Middleton and Sally Healy at Chatham House, who we worked with to organise a round-table to discuss our findings on Kenya and the Horn of Africa. We presented our findings at a seminar hosted by the National Council for Voluntary Agencies in London. We thank Karl Wilding and Veronique Jochum for giving us this opportunity.

We have also been assisted in our research by Nisrine Mansour, Chris Pallas and Melody Mohebi, doctoral students at the LSE Centre for Civil Society. Their conscientious ferreting through documents and websites and stewarding and assistance with organising meetings for the research in London were invaluable. Thanks are also due to Bob Benewick,

Armine Ishkanian and Ben Jones for reading the final draft and giving us their broad comments.

None of this work would have been possible without funding provided by the Economic Social Research Council (ESRC) as part of the ESRC Non-Governmental Public Action (NGPA) programme. Chris Wyatt, ESRC NGPA programme case-officer, and his predecessor Lyndy Griffin were both unstinting in their support for both the project and the programme. In addition, we are very grateful for funding we received from the Ford Foundation office in Nairobi, and particularly Tade Aina and Willy Mutunga, who took such a keen interest in our research.

There are countless others we have not mentioned by name who have offered their practical help, thoughtful insights, incisive analysis and encouragement, and to all of them we extend our gratitude and thanks.

Jude Howell and Jeremy Lind

List of Acronyms

ACBAR	Agency Coordinating Body for Afghan Relief
ATC	Anti-Terrorism Certificate
AusAID	Australian Agency for International Development
BJP	Bharatiya Janata Party
CDC	Community Development Council (Afghanistan)
CJTF	Combined Joint Task Force (Horn of Africa)
CSO	Civil Society Organisation
CTM	Counter-Terrorism Measure
DACAAR	Danish Committee for Aid to Afghan Refugees
DFID	Department for International Development
EC	European Commission
ESRC	Economic Social Research Council
EU	European Union
FATF	Financial Action Task Force
FCO	Foreign and Commonwealth Office
FCRA	Foreign Contributions Regulation Act
FY	Financial Year
GJLOS	Governance, Justice, Law and Order Sector
ICC	International Criminal Court
INGOs	International Non-governmental Organisations
ISAF	International Security Assistance Force (in Afghanistan)
MCOCA	Maharashtra Control of Organised Crime Act
MSF	Médecins Sans Frontières
NATO	North Atlantic Treaty Organisation
NGOs	Non-Governmental Organisations
NSP	National Solidarity Programme
ODA	Overseas Development Agency
OECD	Organisation of Economic Cooperation and Development
OEF	Operation Enduring Freedom
POTA	Prevention of Terrorism Act (of India)
POTO	Prevention of Terrorism Ordinance (of India)
PRT	Provincial Reconstruction Team
SIDA	Swedish International Development Agency
SIMI	Students Islamic Movement of India
SOT	Suppression of Terrorism Bill (of 2003, Kenya)

TADA   Terrorist and Disruptive Activities (Prevention) Act
UAPA   Unlawful Activities Prevention Act
UK   United Kingdom of Great Britain and Northern Ireland
UN   United Nations
UNDP   United Nations Development Programme
US   United States of America
USAID   United States Agency for International Development

1
Introduction

The United States will use this moment of opportunity to extend the benefits of freedom across the globe. We will actively work to bring the hope of democracy, development, free markets, and free trade to every corner of the world. The events of September 11, 2001, taught us that weak states, like Afghanistan, can pose as great a danger to our national interests as strong states. Poverty does not make poor people into terrorists and murderers. Yet poverty, weak institutions, and corruption can make weak states vulnerable to terrorist networks and drug cartels within their borders.[1]

> George W. Bush, comments in foreword to
> the US National Security Strategy, 2002

The threat comes because, in another part of the globe, there is shadow and darkness where not all the world is free... where a third of our planet lives in poverty... and where a fanatical strain of religious extremism has arisen... and because in the combination of these afflictions, a new and deadly virus has emerged. That virus is terrorism...

> Tony Blair, then prime minister of UK in a
> speech given to the Congress on 17 July 2003

Within days of his inauguration as President of the United States in January 2009, Barack Obama declared an end to some of the most controversial aspects of the 'War on Terror'[i] he inherited from his predecessor.[2] Marking a bold break with post-9/11 Bush doctrine, Obama resolutely announced that the 'language we use matters'. It was no longer about a 'war' but a 'strategic challenge'.[3] It was no longer about the civilised West confronting the forces of evil and barbarism, as expressed so vividly in Tony Blair's speech to the US Congress in July 2003. Bush based the War on Terror on a template of good versus evil in which the enemy was simplified as an undifferentiated mass of militants and dissenting voices opposed to the civilising, liberal ideals of Western democracies. Throughout his successful presidential campaign, Obama was careful to pledge his complete support for fighting terrorism while at the same time seeking to define the enemy more strategically. In his first White House televised interview with the Dubai-based Al Arabiya news network, Obama was careful to distinguish between those groups committed to destroying America, those disillusioned with US foreign policies and those holding different positions and values to America.[4]

Obama's swift use of his executive authority to shut the Guantanamo Bay detention facility, to close secret CIA prisons overseas, and to ban torture suggested to some that the War on Terror was over. Yet Obama signalled an intensified military campaign in Afghanistan and in February 2009 committed an additional 17,000 US troops, a substantial increase on the existing 36,000 troops that were already there.[5] In the initial weeks of his presidency, Obama opted to retain counter-terrorism tactics devised by the Bush administration. He created a task force to study rendition policy, but by removing other anti-terror mechanisms at the government's disposal, counter-intelligence officials suggested that the use of renditions might actually expand in coming years.[6] Further, the new director of the Central Intelligence Agency (CIA), Leon Panetta, opened a loophole in the other restrictions that Obama introduced on interrogation techniques.[7] Unquestionably, the struggle against terrorism remains a key focus of US domestic and foreign policy, although it is also the case that the US is adopting a more measured approach. Obama has suggested that there is a need to redress the imbalance between security and rights and civil liberties as well as a

---

[i] Quotation marks are used here to stress the authors' misgivings with respect to the War on Terror, both as a discourse and as an assemblage of counter-terrorism structures that were introduced in the aftermath of the 11 September 2001 attacks in the US. They are also used to underline the deeply politicised nature of this phrase, which has seeped into everyday political usage.

Subsequently from this point onwards, quotation marks are not used.

renewed commitment to international cooperation and starting a new dialogue with Muslim populations. However, although there is a distinctive change in the tone of US counter-terrorism policy under the Obama administration, the tenor remains very much the same in relation to defeating global jihadi networks. As Obama exhorted in one of the presidential debates during the election campaign in 2008, 'We will kill Bin Laden. We will crush Al Qaeda.'

This book will show that although the Obama administration has taken important steps towards modifying some of the strongly denounced aspects of the War on Terror, the counter-terrorism regime constructed in the aftermath of the September 11 attacks remains deeply entrenched in a thick web of regulations, policies, laws, institutional arrangements and bureaucratic practices. The focus of this book is on how this War on Terror regime has affected development, aid policy and civil society. We argue that the War on Terror has consolidated and intensified currents in security thinking and practice that incorporate aid and civil society more deeply and strategically. The post-9/11 global security regime uses coercion, co-option and cooperation to build a network of political actors spanning the public and private, governmental and non-governmental, commercial and charitable, and north and south. The War on Terror is a mobilising discourse first invoked by Bush and subsequently by America's allies to legitimise and pursue an assortment of military and political objectives. It expresses a polarising vision of the world, which pits modernity against backwardness, civilisation against barbarism and freedom against oppression. It is militaristic in content, reflected both in the choice of words such as 'war' and 'terror' and in its shorthand justification for pre-emptive military intervention. It denotes a global political post–Cold War re-ordering that creates new alliances and divisions amongst states and non-state actors of varying stripes and hues. It constitutes a new set of global and national institutional arrangements and policy and legal instruments that seek to link up the input of disparate, compartmentalised agencies and departments around a common purpose of defeating terrorism. To this end, it draws on 'hard' military, security and policing responses alongside new 'soft' measures that aim to dominate the ideological battlefield.

We refer to this as a 'regime' rather than merely a political discourse or set of policies associated with a particular administration. The use of 'regime' also infers that the policies, laws, bureaucratic regulations and practices, and institutional arrangements that have been formed in support of global counter-terrorism cooperation will endure beyond the political actors that hastened their emergence. The shift in political discourse in the US, although significant, is insufficient in and of itself to deconstruct and remove the regime. This would require a complete overhaul of the legal, policy, regulatory and institutional aspects of the regime. Though the new Obama administration has gone some way towards redefining the nature of the terrorist threat with more precision and regard for the multifarious voices within Islam, unravelling the War on Terror regime would be a necessarily long process requiring the expenditure of significant political capital and the activation of a social movement demanding such change. This book critically assesses how post-9/11 counter-terrorism structures have intersected with and shaped development aid policies and practices as well as the spaces and actors of civil society. Thus, it makes an important contribution to efforts to weigh up the impacts of the War on Terror regime, and the extent of change that will be required to undo some of its damaging effects.

The book is based on three initial propositions, which we return to in the conclusion. First, we propose that the War on Terror regime has deepened and intensified relations between development and security actors. This has led to the securitisation of aid and development. By the securitisation of aid and development we are referring to the absorption of global and national security interests into the framing, structuring and implementation of development and aid. Specifically, the interlocking of development and security has extended beyond the confines of conflict and post-conflict settings to the realm of development aid policy and practice in general. This can be observed along several dimensions: increased aid flows to frontline states in the War on Terror such as Afghanistan and Iraq; the greater prominence given in aid policy and rhetoric to national and global security objectives, the role of development in achieving these and the hardening of normative assumptions around the positive relation between development and security; the expansion of multilateral and bilateral counter-terrorist assistance and the development of programmes and projects devoted to countering terrorism and radicalisation; a thickening of interactions between ministries of defence, foreign policy, development and domestic affairs as governments develop networked institutional architecture and coordinating structures to enhance the coherence and effectiveness of interventions; and expanding military competencies on issues of social development.

Second, we argue that the deepening and intensification of ties between development and security has had significant consequences for civil society that merit investigating and documenting and which hitherto have received little attention, before or since 2001 (Caparini,

2005). The global War on Terror regime has brought civil society further into the gaze of security institutions, leading governments and donors to adopt a more circumspect approach towards civil society based on a view of 'good' and 'bad' non-governmental actors. There have been ambiguous impacts of new counter-terrorism structures and cooperation efforts on civil society. While civil society is a specific focus of concern in post-9/11 security thinking, and many governments have moved to merge their regulation of civil society with new counter-terrorism structures, the War on Terror has also created opportunities for 'good' civil society to cooperate with government departments and agencies. Thus, government approaches to civil society in the context of counter-terrorism efforts relate not only to the assessment that civil society could be misused by terrorist networks but also to the expectation that non-governmental public actors can lend legitimacy to counter-terrorism responses and strategy.

At this point we should clarify that 'civil society' is a much contested concept.[8] We use the term in this book to refer to the arena where people deliberate upon, organise and act around shared purposes and concerns. As an ideal type, it is distinct from government, market and family, though in practice the boundaries between these spheres are blurred and interwoven to varying degrees. Civil society is populated by organisations that vary in their degree of formality and typically includes associational forms such as trades unions, social movements, virtual networks, campaigns, coalitions, faith groups, direct action groups, peace groups, human rights organisations and so on. Whilst liberal democratic interpretations of civil society emphasise its plural and essentially harmonious nature, this book starts from the premise that civil society is a site of contestation and conflict as much as it is a site of unity and consensus. In other words, it is a battlefield upon which different values, ideas and political visions are debated, contended and struggled over. As such it is also a site that is used instrumentally by different actors, whether within the civil society realm or without, for different ideological, political and organisational purposes.

Third, we suggest that how the development/security nexus unfolds and how it affects aid policy and practice, domestic and foreign policy and civil societies in different places will be contextually specific. Important determining factors include whether a country is locked in war or emerging out of conflict; where a country sits along a spectrum of democratic–authoritarian regimes; the nature of state–civil society relations; and the relative strategic importance of a particular country to US and allies' interests in the War on Terror. To understand the particular contours of the War on Terror, we thus have to follow its course in specific and contrastive contexts. In brief, we argue that linkages between development and security have become generalised in the post-9/11 context, with consequences for aid programming and practice and donor and government approaches to civil society. The linkages between the War on Terror regime and civil societies in different parts of the world are neither neat nor uniform. Hence, the impacts of post-9/11 counter-terrorism structures on the spaces and actors of civil society have been nuanced and contextually varied.

The analysis in this book reflects several concerns implicit in recent assessments of the War on Terror, civil society and aid. Though human rights lawyers, activists and scholars have challenged the actual and potential effects of counter-terrorist legislation, policies and measures on civil liberties,[9] there has been far less written on the consequences of the War on Terror regime for aid policy and civil society. There is a nascent but growing body of work examining the effects of post-9/11 counter-terrorist legislation on civil society.[10] Complementary works have critically assessed the impacts of the War on Terror on development and humanitarian aid policy and practice.[11] The Dutch NGO Cordaid and the US non-profit group OMB Watch were pivotal in establishing a global network to monitor and advocate on the effects of the War on Terror regime on civil societies.

This emerging literature has tended to highlight the restrictive and negative effects of counter-terrorist legislation. Furthermore, it has relied more often on anecdotal evidence rather than in-depth research, often because the imperative to raise the issue for public debate was often greater than the desire or possibility to seek and amalgamate in-depth evidence. The focus of civil society has also been to resist aspects of new counter-terrorism structures rather than making a coherent political argument on the role and contribution of civil society to political and social change. The emphasis on the 'hard' measures of the War on Terror regime has thus neglected the subtle workings of 'soft' measures which are intended not to prohibit or restrict non-governmental actors but rather to encourage their cooperation. It is only by recognising this dual-pronged dynamic that we can fully grasp the politics of the War on Terror regime and its contradictory and ambiguous impacts on and implications for aid policy and civil society.

A related concern is that the strategic engagement by governments and donors with civil society both prior to and since the War on Terror has depoliticised and tamed sections of civil society that have depended on aid and government contracts for their survival.

Neo-liberal approaches towards civil society that underline civil society's role in enhancing state effectiveness and legitimacy through delivering services and providing social welfare permeate the discourse, policy and practices of bilateral and multilateral development agencies and other government departments. This perspective draws on intellectual currents in Western political thinking, particularly in the American context, that conceptualise civil society as a key ingredient in well-functioning liberal democracies and market economies. It contrasts with an alternative genealogy of civil society that emphasises the values of solidarity, mutuality and social justice rather than individualism, system maintenance or negative liberties (Howell and Pearce, 2001). The muted responses of 'mainstream' civil society groups to counter-terrorism efforts have exposed the depoliticising effects of government and donor financing of this part of civil society. Mainstream civil society refers here to the government- or donor-funded sector within civil society that is engaged in service delivery, social welfare provision and the technical implementation of governance reforms. This part of civil society is often referred to as NGOs or the 'voluntary sector', 'non-profit sector', or 'third sector'. This is not to say that government or donor funding need always have such an effect or that mainstream civil society organisations do not advocate on particular issues. Instead, as the analysis here will show, the pressures of resource competition, bureaucratic procedures and increasing scrutiny of charities in the War on Terror have led mainstream groups to focus on their own survival and interests rather than speak out in support of defending the spaces and actors of civil society, especially those working within 'suspect' communities. This in turn reflects the encapsulation of civil society into neo-liberal governance approaches. Civil society is not exclusively or always on the periphery of governing power. Rather, in some cases it contributes directly to the constitution of that power.

The other underlying concern relates to the re-absorption of development assistance into national security agendas and the consequences of this for aid policy and practice and for civil societies. The end of the Cold War heralded, perhaps optimistically in hindsight, a period during which developmental assistance was relatively freed of ideological shackles and poverty criteria became more important in targeting some types of aid. Not only has the War on Terror regime taken development backwards to a position of subordination to national and global security objectives, but it has also catapulted it forwards by integrating it more systematically with security goals, institutions and policies. A consequence of this is to affirm the strategic importance of poverty reduction and social inclusion to global and national security strategies.

Development/Security Nexus and Civil Society Intertwine

Development assistance has always been used in foreign policy as a tool to leverage support from governments. During the ideologically laden period of the Cold War contending superpowers directed aid towards geo-strategically important countries and regions to gain and maintain political alliances. With the end of the Cold War aid institutions were freed of ideological imperatives and able to prioritise development issues such as poverty reduction, health and education provision. The seeming supremacy of liberal democracy and markets coupled with the demise of any alternative political ideology created a context within which development institutions could focus attention on shaping governance structures and processes in aid-recipient countries.

The end of the Cold War gave development actors a new lease of relative autonomy to pursue development objectives. In the conflict and post-conflict settings of the so-called New Wars of the 1990s such as Kosovo, Sierra Leone and Bosnia, development and security actors also started to interact in new and overlapping ways in processes of peace-building and humanitarian relief. Observers of these processes pointed to the emergence of a development/security nexus, where security and development institutions began to intervene respectively in each other's once traditional domains. Writers such as Mark Duffield (2001), too, warned of the resulting 'securitisation' of aid as the agendas, objectives and operations of development and security institutions became increasingly interwoven in conflict and post-conflict settings. This closer encounter between security and development institutions created tensions and dilemmas. On the one hand, security actors such as national militaries and UN peace-keeping forces began to engage in reconstruction work and governance reforms. For non-governmental humanitarian agencies, expanding military engagement in relief and development posed crucial issues for them around principles of neutrality, independence and impartiality. On the other hand, bilateral development agencies pursuing governance reforms in the so-called 'fragile and post-conflict states' sought to apply standards of transparency and accountability to security institutions. For security institutions this inevitably threatened principles of secrecy that were deemed central to maintaining security.

The period of the 1990s saw not only the convergence of development and security in post-conflict settings but also the gradual strategic encounter between development and civil society. Non-governmental organisations (NGOs) concerned with development and 'Third World' issues mushroomed from the late 1970s onwards. Though governmental and inter-governmental development institutions were aware of their practical field operations and advocacy activities, there was little strategic policy thinking about how these new players either contributed to development processes or dovetailed with official development assistance (ODA). The development debate remained fixed around the ideologically polarised axis of whether the state or the market should be the main driver of growth and development.

Dissident intellectuals in Eastern Europe resurrected the idea of civil society to express their opposition to authoritarian socialism and to imagine alternative systems of governance. Throughout the 1980s democracy activists across the globe pushed for regime change, causing what Samuel Huntington described as a Third Wave of democratisation (Huntington, 1992). In doing so they also used the idea of civil society as a mobilising and liberating discourse. With the end of the Cold War political leaders sought alternative paths to development that were not hamstrung by the ideological debates around state and market. A new triadic paradigm emerged that posited state, market and civil society as essential, mutually compatible forces for liberal democratic and capitalist development. It was within this context that development agencies discovered civil society as a key agent in processes of development.

Guided by aims of democracy promotion and poverty reduction, donors began to design strategies for developing and strengthening civil society, established new civil society units and appointed specialist civil society advisors. The prevailing consensus was that civil society contributed positively to processes of democratisation and poverty reduction. Though donors recognised that civil society included a diverse range of actors and institutional forms, in practice they still tended to engage primarily with development and governance NGOs. In contexts where such formal NGOs did not exist or lacked the bureaucratic skills required by funding agencies, donors created NGOs to work on issues such as democracy, gender, human rights, HIV/AIDs and so on. The manufacturing of civil society by donor agencies generated a stratum of NGOs that were located in capital cities, weakly rooted in their societies and increasingly adept at adjusting their agendas to donor priorities (Howell, 2000).

By the end of the 1990s civil society had become an established part of development discourse, policy and practice. However, there was little analysis of or strategic thinking about the role civil society played in conflict situations or in promoting security. There were three main ways in which civil society intersected with the development/security nexus in the 1990s. The first was in the context of peace-building and post-conflict reconstruction, where NGOs encountered the increasing presence of militaries engaged in delivering relief and/or implementing development projects and often faced the dilemma of whether and how to work with military actors. The second field in which non-governmental development and security actors began to encounter each more closely was in the reform of security sector institutions. Here bilateral donors looked towards civil society organisations to demand and monitor accountability and transparency in security institutions. The third way in which civil society played a role in the emerging nexus was in advocating for an alternative conceptualisation of security that gave priority to the broader idea of human security rather than a narrower concern with state security.

By the start of the millennium, civil society, development and security institutions had accumulated considerable experience of working with each other. Some of the tensions and dilemmas that these relatively new encounters engendered had begun to surface. Multilateral and bilateral development institutions, parliamentarians and political leaders expressed concerns about the accountability, representativeness and transparency of NGOs. They queried the effectiveness of the relatively small-scale operations of NGOs and noted the transaction costs of dealing with so many different small organisations and groups. Observers and actors in the development/security field were also questioning the effectiveness of this approach, the added value brought by the different actors to each other's traditional terrains, and the dilemmas of increased military intervention in development.

All this took place against a backdrop of heightening expectations about what aid could deliver, as reflected in the launch of the Millennium Development Goals, and growing concern about problems of donor coordination, sustainability and aid modalities. International development institutions began to review existing aid modalities, including their engagement with civil society. As some bilateral donors shifted towards budgetary support and sector-wide approaches and in the process passed decisions about engaging with civil society organisations to national governments, support for and contact with civil society became more indirect. It is against this background of shifting aid goals, modalities and policies, emerging doubts around the develop-ment/security nexus and concerns about how to engage effectively with civil society that the effects of the War on Terror regime on civil societies and aid have to be understood.

Development and Civil Society post-9/11

The launch and pursuit of the War on Terror changed the global political context within which international development institutions and civil societies operated. As this book will demonstrate, the global political context of the War on Terror has accelerated and intensified the conver-gence of development, security and civil society, affecting the way aid policy is conceived and operationalised and how international devel-opment institutions engage with civil societies. There are differences, however, in how specific donors connect development and security and how they operationalise this. The emerging development/security nexus of the 1990s transforms into the development/security/civil soci-ety nexus of the early millennium. The encounter of these three terrains is generalised beyond the 'exceptionality' of post-conflict settings to the broad mainstream of development policy, discourse and practice. More-over, the intertwining of development, security and civil society is not accidental or wholly unintended but an integral strategic element of the War on Terror regime. This is because civil society, as a crucial actor in the constitution of political power and authority to govern, has been identified as a strategic battlefield on which the War on Terror will be won or lost.

Like the Cold War regime, the new War on Terror regime needs to subordinate foreign assistance to its objectives and priorities in order to secure and reward its allies. However, the 'golden era' of the 1990s gave aid institutions greater leeway to forge their own goals and agen-das and thus made them more willing and able to negotiate the roles they might play in the War on Terror. How aid institutions negotiated their positions, priorities and autonomy has contributed to the varying levels and ways in which donor agencies have cooperated in the pur-suit of the political objectives of the War on Terror. The post-9/11 global security regime also needs to identify and remove threats that lurk in the crevices and folds of civil society as well as mobilise and manipulate the 'good' parts of civil society so as to dominate the ideological battle-field. In this changing global political context, civil societies come under the scrutiny of governments and international development and secu-rity institutions. New elements are brought into the gaze of donors and governments as they try to control, familiarise themselves with and discipline unknown as well as hidden parts of civil society such as Muslim groups, mosques and Islamic centres.

Organisation of the Book

The accelerating and deepening convergence of security, development and civil society is the main theme of Chapter 2. Here we analyse the changing global political context post-9/11, which sets the stage for the global War on Terror regime and the increasing securitisation of aid. We trace the gradual encounter of development and aid policy with civil society from the 1950s through to the end of the Cold War and then up to the 9/11 attacks. We examine the gradual convergence of development and security in the 1990s and how civil society actors became drawn into the orbit of security institutions. We then look at how these relationships intensify and deepen in the post-9/11 context and the broad impact this has had on aid goals, policies and programmes as well as donor outlooks on civil society.

In Chapter 3 we examine the effects of the War on Terror regime on government–civil society relations in donor countries, focusing on the US, the UK and the EU. Though recent literature on the effects of the War on Terror regime on civil society has tended to highlight the negative aspects, here we suggest that the effects have been ambiguous and contradictory. On the one hand, governments have introduced various 'hard' measures to crack down on 'bad' elements in civil society, such as shutting down charities and freezing their assets, scrutinising international money transfers to some charities, increasing the vetting of grantees including checks of NGO personnel, and requiring other due diligence checks both by grant-making agencies and by the groups they support. On the other hand, governments have pursued various 'soft' measures including increased dialogue with some non-governmental actors, engaging with perceived 'moderate' Muslim leaders and representative bodies, and new funding for groups contributing to donors' counter-radicalisation aims. Hence, the interest of political leaders in civil society has expanded beyond a primary concern that they contribute to service delivery to encompass what contribution they can make to achieving the political goals of counter-terrorism.

In Chapter 4 we examine how the War on Terror regime has affected development aid objectives, policies and programmes, drawing out some of the differences between the United States Agency for International Development (USAID), the UK Department for International

Development (DFID), the Australian Agency for International Development (AusAID) and Swedish International Development Agency (SIDA). Overseas development assistance has always been a key part of foreign policy. During the Cold War period both the 'communist' Soviet Union and the 'capitalist' West used international development assistance to foster and reward allies in Africa, Latin and Central America, and Asia. In the post-9/11 context aid, too, has been drawn into the web of the War on Terror, with substantial increases in military and development assistance to frontline states such as Pakistan, Iraq and Afghanistan. The harnessing of international development assistance into the prosecution of the War on Terror has not been limited to increased resource allocations to strategic states. It has also required a shift in development priorities, greater engagement between development and security institutions, the expansion and creation of new programmes promoting security interests and an explicit ideological linking of development with counter-terrorism and security. We also assess how post-9/11 counter-terrorism laws have affected bureaucratic practices within international donor agencies and charitable foundations with respect to their partnerships with NGOs and groups.

In Chapters 5, 6 and 7 we explore the effects of the securitisation of aid on civil societies with reference to three case studies, namely Afghanistan, Kenya and India. A key assumption of the research is that civil society actors in more established democratic polities such as India will mount a more robust response to incursions upon the spaces of civil society, particularly as these relate to marginalised groups and social groups linked discursively with the War on Terror. In contrast, in countries where the state is fragile and civil society is weak, such as in Afghanistan, or in newly democratising countries such as Kenya, the ability of civil society actors to resist the implementation of counter-terrorism structures will be considerably weaker. The chapters demonstrate how the specific historical and political contexts of each country, their relations with the US and their engagement with donor agencies shape the way the securitisation of aid and the effects of the War on Terror regime on civil societies play out. As will be shown, the failure of mainstream civil society in established democracies in speaking out against counter-terrorism measures, practices and discourses challenged our initial assumption that in such contexts non-governmental actors would robustly defend and protect the spaces for civil society to organise, including for groups that work on or within 'suspect' populations.

The Afghanistan case is particularly instructive because it is the first theatre of attack in the War on Terror and the subsequent site of contradictory efforts to simultaneously fight terrorism and promote a neo-liberal democracy and market economy. We explore the emergence of a civil society debate and the proliferation of particular organisational forms of civil society following the demise of the Taliban regime. We examine the heated debates around the involvement of foreign militaries in development as part of a counter-insurgency strategy to win hearts and minds. We also analyse the development of a neo-liberal model of state and state–society relations in the post-Taliban period and the implications of this for civil society.

The Kenya chapter begins by sketching the geo-political significance of Kenya and more generally the Horn of Africa to US foreign policy. Kenya has come under international pressure to introduce counter-terrorist legislation. Human rights lawyers and activists along with key Muslim associations and leaders mounted a campaign against the Suppression of Terrorism Bill, which the Kenyan government ultimately withdrew in 2003. The response of Kenyan civil society to this Bill challenged our original proposition that civil society actors in newly democratised states would be less able to counter the pressures of the War on Terror regime. However, as elsewhere, opposition was confined to human rights activists, lawyers and Muslim groups, with most mainstream groups and churches remaining silent on the issue. The Kenyan case also highlights the vulnerability of historically marginalised groups such as Kenya's substantial Somali and Muslim populations to counter-terrorist discourses and practices. Here too, mainstream groups have been mostly indifferent to counter-terrorism operations in Muslim neighbourhoods and the rendition of Kenyan Muslims abroad, a pattern that echoes experiences elsewhere in the world. The chapter also examines the broader dynamics of aid in a shifting and volatile political context in which civil society has fragmented around discrete regional, ethnic and religious interests.

Compared to Afghanistan and Kenya, India is the iconic example of a long-established developing country democracy. We would expect that civil society actors would be able to resist more effectively the effects of repressive measures instituted in response to terrorism. The chapter examines how the discourses of War on Terror, Islamic terrorism and extremism have become appropriated into the language of political leaders and struggles in India. It considers the responses of civil society actors to the detention of suspects under India's counter-terrorist legislation and more generally to the subtle linking of Islam to the idea of terrorism. We find that the response of civil society to these ideas has been muted. It is yet again human rights organisations that have taken the lead in challenging counter-terrorist activity and raising concerns about the abuse of vulnerable groups through this legislation. The chapter also explores the position of Muslims in Indian society. It focuses on responses to the publication of the 2006 Sachar Committee report on Muslims and the reactions of civil society groups to the construction of Muslims as problematic and linked to terrorism. The case of anti-Muslim attacks backed by political leaders in the state of Gujarat in February 2002 is particularly instructive in understanding the contours of these issues. Finally, the chapter looks at the engagement of donors with civil society, the importance of global security issues in their agendas and the introduction of programmes aimed at addressing perceived extremism and terrorism.

The concluding chapter draws together the key findings of each chapter and reflects upon the original propositions that guided the research. It considers the theoretical and policy implications of the findings for conceptualising civil society, not only as a site of unity and harmony but also as an arena of autonomy from the state and global forces. It reflects on the implications of the research for how we understand the politics of donor engagement with civil society and the effects of donor support on the organisational terrain and autonomy of civil society. It also examines the implications of the findings for how we understand the politics of development and its relation to security. The findings suggest that this may be an opportune moment for governments, policy-makers and international institutions to scrutinise their inheritance from the Bush administration and to craft a new strategy of global engagement that prioritises issues of justice, equity, peace and inclusion. It is also an opportune moment for civil society actors, and in particular those courted by donors and governments, to reflect more critically on their political positions and to recover some of the passion and sense of justice that once drove their activities.

In reviewing the key findings it thus weighs up the effects of the War on Terror and the changes that governments and civil societies need to make if the War on Terror regime is to be unravelled and consigned to history.

Notes

1. The National Security Strategy of the United States of America. September 2002. http://www.state.gov/documents/organization/15538.pdf. Accessed 22 February 2009.
2. 'Bush's "War on Terror" Comes to a Sudden End.' *The Washington Post.* 23 January 2009.

3. 'After the War on Terror'. *The New York Times*. 29 January 2009.
4. Ibid.
5. 'Putting Stamp on Afghan War, Obama Will Send 17,000 Troops.' *The New York Times*. 17 February 2009.
6. 'Obama Preserves Renditions as Counter-Terrorism Tool.' *The Los Angeles Times*. 1 February 2009.
7. 'Obama's War on Terror May Resemble Bush's in Some Areas.' *The New York Times*. 18 February 2009.
8. For a useful discussion of different disciplinary approaches to the idea of civil society see White (1994). Other useful treatments of civil society include Keane (1988), Taylor (1990), Hann and Dunn (1996) and Gellner (1994).
9. See, for example, Amnesty International's 2007 annual report, which explores the trade-off between security and human rights. As the Secretary-General Irene Khan wrote in her foreword, 'In recent years heightened fears about terrorism and insecurity have reinforced repression – or the risk of it – in a variety of ways' (2007, p. 6).
10. These include works by Mark Sidel (2004), Daniel Stevens (2009), Joshua Rubongoya (2009), Alison Dunn (2008), Conor Gearty (2003, 2007), Alex Colas (2009), John Cosgrave (2004), Jude Howell (2006), Jo Beall (2006) and Beth Elise Whitaker (2007), among others.
11. See Macrae and Harmer (2003), Christian Aid (2004), Cosgrave (2004), Fowler (2005), Woods (2005) and Moss (2005). There has also been a general burgeoning of literature on terrorism since 2001. Post-9/11 literature on terrorism will account for over 90 per cent of all studies on terrorism if current trends continue, according to Professor Silke, University of East London (Shepherd 2007).

2
Theorising the Securitisation of Aid and Effects on Civil Societies

> Not only are development, security and human rights all imperative: they also reinforce each other... While poverty and denial of human rights may not be said to 'cause' civil war, terrorism or organised crime, they all greatly increase the risk of instability and violence.... we will not enjoy development without security, we will not enjoy security without development.
>
> Section IB, paragraphs 16 and 17, UN General Assembly 2005, 'In larger freedom: towards development, security and human rights for all' Report of the Secretary-General. A/59/2005, March

International development assistance has always been a key part of foreign policy. During the Cold War period both the 'communist' Soviet Union and the capitalist West used international development assistance to foster allies in Africa, Latin and Central America, and Asia. In the post-9/11 context, too, international development and military aid have been deployed as tools to reward and persuade. The harnessing of international development assistance into the prosecution of the War on Terror has not been limited to increased resource allocations to strategic front-line states such as Iraq, Pakistan and Afghanistan. It has also required a shift in development priorities, in greater engagement between development and security institutions, the expansion and creation of new programmes promoting security interests, and an explicit ideological linking of development with counter-terrorism.

This intensification of the relations between international development assistance and national security interests has had consequences for civil societies post-9/11. International donor agencies and foundations have come under pressure to scrutinise their relations with Southern partners as the latter became suspect in harbouring terrorists. Similarly, Muslim charities, organisations, mosques and centres have come under the gaze of security agencies, political leaders and the media as being particularly vulnerable to manipulation by Islamic terrorists and as potential sites for the 'breeding of terrorists'. Civil society becomes not only the target of suspicion in the War on Terror, but also increasingly recruited into combating anti-radicalisation and preventing terrorism. Multilateral and bilateral aid agencies as well as foreign policy institutions have all, since September 2001, sought to varying degrees to engage more resolutely with Muslim communities, establishing projects and programmes focussing on Muslim groups identified as particularly vulnerable to radicalisation.

These changes in relations between development, security and civil society post-9/11 did not happen abruptly; rather they were a continuation, deepening and extension of trends that were already evolving over the 1990s, as detailed by Duffield (2001, 2007), Macrae and Harmer (2003, 2004), the Reality of Aid (2006), Stewart (2003) and Tujan *et al.* (2004). In this same period bilateral and multilateral aid agencies began to strategise around how to engage effectively with civil society so as to advance democracy and reduce poverty. In post-conflict settings civil society was drawn into the web of security through security sector reforms and conflict prevention strategies and projects.

This chapter traces these encounters between development, security and civil society over the 1990s, which laid the seeds for the intensification and deepening of these relationships post-9/11. It begins by examining the changing conceptualisation of the relationship between development and security from the late 1980s up to 2001, the discursive shifts around the concept of security and the absorption of certain extended meanings into aid rhetoric, policy and practice. It observes the rise of a human security agenda that becomes embedded in the policy rhetoric and documentation of international institutions. The next section traces the gradual encounter of development with civil society throughout the 1990s, the emergence of dedicated civil society strengthening programmes and units, and the gradual incorporation of civil society through civil society strategies. Whilst these strategies were concerned primarily with engaging civil society in relatively stable contexts, there is also a parallel process of strategic thinking around the contribution of civil society in post-conflict settings to conflict prevention and state-building. It was in these contexts that civil society first became absorbed in a strategic way into the security domain. The final section examines how by the end of the decade doubts and tensions surrounding both the development/security nexus and the encounter between development and civil society started to swell. These contributed in the changed global political climate post-9/11 not only to a deepening and intensification of these relationships but also to renewed affirmation of the strategic importance of aid, poverty reduction and civil societies to global and national security goals.

Encounter of security and development

National security concerns have always related indirectly to developmental assistance as a complement to diplomacy. Foreign aid has always been part of donor states' soft approach to pursuing foreign policy, military and commercial objectives (Cassen, 1994; German and Randel, 1995; Belgrad and Nachmias, 1997; Reusse, 2002). In the Cold War era security concerns and aid policy were embedded in a global political framework of ideological and geopolitical superpower rivalry. Though development assistance formed part of Cold War strategies, aid and security were separate policy and institutional domains that intersected occasionally and episodically. It is only after the end of the Cold War that strengthening global and national security became an objective of development in its own right and a focus within development studies. Conversely, although 'hearts and minds' development work had been a component of counter-insurgency strategies previously, it was only after the Cold War that militaries intervened more systematically in the field of development.

The crystallisation of a development–security nexus during the 1990s has been the result of converging impulses from both the fields of development and security. Its roots lie in the end of the Cold War, which created opportunities for changing the scope and mandate of development agencies, for greater multilateral intervention in conflict-ridden, collapsed and post-conflict states, and for expanding the role of the UN in peace-building and reconstruction processes. It was in the conflict/post-conflict settings of the 'New Wars' that had erupted in the aftermath of the Cold War, such as in Kosovo, Sierra Leone, East Timor and Zaire, that development and security encountered each other more closely. The rise of a governance agenda and the expanding role of the UN in peace-making and peace-building ploughed the fields on which development and security began to court each other. Development actors advanced into the traditional territory of security actors through the vehicle of security sector reforms and conflict prevention work, whilst security actors advanced into the terrain of development through the field of peace-keeping and peace-building.

The end of the Cold War and the apparent supremacy of liberal democracy and markets gave rise to a new development agenda of 'good governance'. In the early 1990s aid was made conditional upon states meeting criteria of good governance such as respect for human rights, rule of law, transparency and accountability (Moore, 1993). This focus on the processes of governing steered attention, inter alia, towards the role of state security institutions and legal agencies in upholding 'good' practices or otherwise. Though the Brandt report of 1980 had criticised excessive military expenditure in the so-called Third World, Cold War powers were reluctant to act upon this as they needed to retain the alliance of client states, not least through the sales of arms. In the early 1990s donors began to raise concerns about the relationship between military expenditure and development, leading some governments such as Germany and the UK and international institutions such as the World Bank and the International Monetary Fund (IMF) to link development aid to reductions in military expenditure (Ball and Brzoska with Kingma and Wulf, 2002, p. 22). However, aware that this approach was not leading to greater security for the poor or lower military spending or indeed higher levels of development, donors began to focus on ensuring that security expenditures were used efficiently and effectively and that security institutions were more open and accountable. In a lecture given at the World Bank in 1999, former UN Secretary General Kofi Annan highlighted the importance of applying the notion of good governance to the security sector.[1]

During the Cold War security institutions were neither a concern for bilateral, multilateral or non-governmental development agencies nor open to scrutiny by citizens and civil society organisations (CSOs). With Cold War superpower rivalries no longer dominating relations between development agencies and aid-recipients, development actors could pay closer attention to problems of poor governance in state security institutions without the risk of losing a Cold War ally. A new field of development programming, practice, discourses and institutions began to grow around security sector reforms. Using the leitmotiv of 'good governance', donors to varying degrees sought to make security institutions more open to public scrutiny. They supported projects and programmes that attempted to strengthen the capacity of non-state actors to demand transparency and accountability from state security institutions, and to foster civilian oversight over military and security entities. In this way security sector reforms came to encompass not just those core institutions with the authority and capacity to use force to protect the state and civilians, such as militaries, police, and intelligence services, but also organisations that manage and monitor the sector such as parliament, ministries, and civil society and rule of law institutions such as the judiciary, local and traditional justice systems and prisons (Anderlini and Conaway, 2004, p. 31).

Whilst the rise of the governance agenda afforded a fertile terrain upon which development could court security, the increasing engagement of the UN in peace-building in conflict and post-conflict situations laid the ground for further interaction between the worlds of security and development. Boutros Boutros Ghali's 'An Agenda for Peace' in 1992 spelled out the new opportunities for UN peace-keeping and peace-building made possible by the end of the 'adversarial decades of the Cold War' (p. 1). In the 'Supplement to an Agenda for Peace' in 1995 the concept of peace-building was extended from referring to post-conflict settings in 1992[2] to the whole conflict cycle in 1995,[3] covering before, during and after conflicts. This not only expanded the scope of the UN's work but also extended the scope of humanitarian work, and with it NGOs, bilateral and multilateral development agencies, beyond relief work to wholesale intervention in the processes of state-building and societal reconstruction.

Throughout the 1990s development donors sought to promote the role of non-state actors in conflict prevention and peace-building at local, national and regional levels. The conflagration of 'New Wars' caused considerable concern among donor and aid agencies surrounding their seeming intractability, impacts on development and humanitarian consequences. Not only did these conflicts outnumber international conflicts but they increasingly took their toll upon civilians, leading to civilian deaths, internal displacement and refugee flows.[4] One thread of concern was the possible impact of development on feeding into conflict dynamics and the importance of development actors to 'do no harm' (Anderson, 1999). A separate thread of concern emerged around the possibility of conflict as being caused by underdevelopment (Cramer, 2006). Thus, development came to be seen as having an important contribution to make in preventing conflict and peace-building. Conflict prevention emerged as a distinct area of programming and thinking in the field of development. This encompassed new aid policies and strategies for working on conflict, including commitments to minimise the impact of development on the causes of conflict, and new programming that sought to link development activities to reducing the underlying causes of conflict. Examples of programming included efforts to promote a 'culture of peace' at the community level, often involving the creation of an infrastructure of decentralised peace committees, work with youth groups and incorporating the participation of women. A further thread was concerned with the failure of 'Track I' type peace processes in overcoming the intractable nature of 'New Wars' that involved non-state actors, complex trans-boundary linkages, and violence against civilian populations. 'Track II' peace processes sought to work beyond the limited confines of 'Track I' official diplomacy by involving eminent personalities, peace activists and civil society groups in leading dialogues and crafting peace proposals. Dedicated conflict analysis NGOs such as International Alert, Conciliation Resources, the International Peace Research Institute, Oslo and the United States Institute for Peace also emerged as influential actors in their own right by providing detailed analysis of conflict dynamics and actors.

By 2001 the term 'peace-building' was broadened again to also cover addressing the causes of conflict and thereby brought development and democracy promotion within the scope of peace-building[5] (Hanggi, 2005, pp. 10–11). As UN peace-keeping missions increased and took on new dimensions such as human rights, policing and the rule of law, so too bilateral and multilateral development agencies and NGOs engaged increasingly in activities such as disarmament, demobilisation and reintegration and security sector reforms in post-conflict situations. As the need to address the structural as well as operational causes of conflicts gained increasing attention, so development policies were pushed to the centre stage of conflict prevention agendas (Hurwitz and Peake, 2004, p. 2). This gave rise not only to new fields of policy, operations and practice but also to new sub-fields of academic research on conflict and development and peace-building within development studies, security studies and international relations.

Peace-building in conflict and post-conflict situations provided the terrain in which development and security agendas intersected most deeply. Donors advanced towards security through the vehicle of security sector reforms and conflict prevention, drawing security agencies into their net, whilst security actors, particularly militaries, ventured towards development through the extended mandates of UN peace-keeping missions and military intervention in humanitarian working, thereby drawing development agencies into their web. This convergence of development and security actors particularly in the terrains of conflict prevention and security sector reforms not only fostered and consolidated implicit assumptions about the relationship between development and security but also challenged the orthodox concept of security as state security. The interlocking of development and security throughout the 1990s brought to the surface various implicit assumptions about this relationship that were guiding policy and practice. The liberal perspective on war that dominates development thinking is that conflict and development are incompatible. This perspective is well illustrated by the quote at the start of this chapter. Hence where there is conflict and instability, there can be no development; where there is violence there can be no development; without state security and the physical security of citizens there is no freedom from harm, violence and abuse, so there could be no development. Peace, stability and security were thus preconditions of and a starting point for development.

This liberal perspective trickles through into the field of security sector reforms, where well-governed state security institutions are seen as crucial to preventing conflict and fostering state stability. Writers on security sector reforms point out how unaccountable security sector institutions constrain development. Hurwitz and Peake (2004, p. 5), for example, state, 'An unaccountable and un-impugned security sector impinges directly upon development: it disenfranchises communities, contributes to poverty, distorts economies, creates instability and stunts political development. Consequently reform to security sector institutions is a critical element of conflict prevention and peace-building strategies.' Similarly, Ball and Brzoska with Kingma and Wulf, 2002 underlines the importance of 'participatory decision-making processes' and therefore CSOs to effective state security institutions.

Prior to the 1990s there was no specific theorisation of how security and development were interlinked. Security, conflict and violence were not themes in development studies, policy or practice; nor was development a key theme in security studies, policy or practice. Indeed, peaceful and stable conditions were presumed in most development strategies and programming. However, this does not mean that security concerns, violence and conflict were not integral to development processes. Marxist and neo-Marxist analyses of colonialism, post-colonialism and imperialism have exposed the violent, exploitative and conflictual aspects of colonialism and 'development'. Development theories such as world systems theory and dependency theory have underlined the unequal and exploitative power relations between the so-called 'developed world and developing countries' (Frank, 1966; Cardoso and Faletto, 1979; Wallerstein, 1979). More recently, Christopher Cramer (2006, pp. 7–10) has challenged liberal perspectives on war in developing countries, which present these as symptomatic of development failure, a lack of modernisation and fundamentally deviant. Cramer argues that such a position can be sustained only through historical amnesia. Contrary to the liberal perspective that 'war is development in reverse', Cramer suggests that development may not be possible without often violent conflict (p. 10).

Not only did the increasing convergence of security and development entrench implicit normative liberal assumptions about the relationship between security and development but it also unsettled orthodox notions of security. The opening up of the idea of security began to challenge the conventionally narrow focus on security as national and state security. Over the 1990s the concept of security extended in three main ways.[6] First, in the post–Cold War era there was a growing recognition that threats to security arose not only from military aggression but also from transnational economic, environmental and societal sources (Hanggi, 2005, p. 6). In particular, poor countries and countries in conflict were increasingly constructed in donor documentation during the 1990s as threats to regional and global security. For example, the DFID 1997 White Paper on Development not only underlines the negative impact of conflict on development but also reflects an image of poor, conflict-ridden countries as a threat to regions: 'Violent conflict generates social division, reverses economic progress, impedes sustainable development and frequently results in human rights violations. Large population movements triggered by conflict threaten the security and livelihood of whole regions' (DFID, 1997, p. 67 quoted in Duffield, 2001, p. 37). Similarly, the Swedish International Development Cooperation Agency (SIDA) published a Strategy on Conflict Management and Peacebuilding (1999).

Second, in the post–Cold War era the concept of security was extended to cover not only the security of states and elites but also that of individuals and communities (Ball and Brzoska with Kingma and Wulf, 2002, p. 6). Internal wars and the often concomitant breakdown of states as captured in terms such as 'failed states', 'collapsed states' and 'crisis states' drew attention to the impact of insecurity on a wider range of actors than just the state. By the turn of the millennium the re-definition of security as referring not only to the security of the state but also to the people had become commonplace in international institutions.[7] This extension of the term beyond states and elites led to new concepts of security such as 'societal security'[8] and 'human security'.

The concept of human security has gained considerable currency in policy and academic discourse. The rising currency of human security in the 1990s related to concerns around the interconnectedness of threats, or the 'underbelly of globalisation', as detailed above. Its position in development policy discourse was established with the publication of the 1994 Human Development Report of the United Nations Development Programme (UNDP), which highlighted the idea of human security. Emphasising the human-centred focus of the human security concept, the report states that 'human security is not a concern with weapons – it is a concern with human development and dignity' (UNDP, 1994, p. 22). Human security recognises a range of threats to people's security such as hunger, disease, unemployment, environmental degradation and repression and the need to protect people from such threats. Since then it has been used variously in a broad sense that equates human development with human security and in a narrower sense that highlights protecting individuals and groups against violence (Ball and Brzoska with Kingma and Wulf, 2002, p. 6). In this latter sense human security and human development are treated as distinct but complementary concepts, a position that is underlined in the 2003 Report of the Commission on Human Security.[9] The Canadian government, which made human security a cornerstone of its foreign policy in the 1990s, defined human security as 'freedom from pervasive threats to people's rights, safety or lives', and encompassing approaches to prevent conflict, protect civilian populations, and increase state capacities to ensure security for their populations (Government of Canada, 2002, p. 3).

The third dimension along which the orthodox concept of security has been stretched relates to inclusivity. Whilst in the Cold War era security concerns were deemed a matter for security institutions, and political elites, since 1989 there has been a growing recognition that state security institutions can be effective only if a wider range of actors are involved in making, overseeing and monitoring security policies, legislation and institutions. In some contexts such as Guatemala, where security sector reforms had been underway since the signing of the Peace Accords in 1996, the concept of 'democratic security' or 'security in democracy' emerged to capture the idea of a more inclusive, democratic approach to security that was not premised on a trade-off between state security and 'the security of the people' (Pearce, 2006, pp. 28–29).

By the turn of the millennium the development–security nexus had become institutionalised and routinised through recurring and increasingly dominant discourses, specific programmes, specialist staff and a body of policy documentation. It was by now generally accepted that noty only was security a matter of concern for a wider range of actors than just political elites and militaries[10] but also that state security and people's security were mutually interdependent. For example, an OECD study stated that 'the security of states and the security of people should be seen as mutually reinforcing, suggesting that unmet social, political and economic needs may provoke popular unrest and opposition to government, ultimately making them more vulnerable to internal and external threats' (OECD, 2001, p. 42). Similarly, the Canadian government's foreign policy on human security notes, 'human security reinforces state security by strengthening its legitimacy and stability' (GoC, 2002, p. 2).

The concern for human welfare and social development implied in the human security agenda meant that issues such as climate change, food shortages and disease pandemics were cast as 'security' problems owing to their destabilising impacts on economies and societies in an interconnected world. The human security agenda promoted a notion of shared security and mutual responsibility for addressing assorted environmental, health and economic problems in the south. Responding to HIV/AIDS, food insecurity, and environmental degradation in developing countries was seen to be important because they undermined human welfare and development and threatened international security. The human security agenda uncovered the connectivity between north and south and proposed global approaches to address particular human insecurities. The achievements of the human security agenda in this regard would become apparent in the signing of international environmental agreements, the creation of the Global Fund on HIV/AIDS, Tuberculosis and Malaria, and international commitment to achieving the Millennium Development Goals.

Thus, the success of the human security agenda in raising the political profile of human welfare and development became evident in the increasingly interventionist and internationalist approaches to what were considered to be 'global security' issues. Although the language of the human security agenda was to fade in the new millennium, elements of the human security agenda were to be absorbed in the new global security regime post-9/11. The notion of connectivity and the need for global approaches implicit in the human security agenda were to be harnessed for the purposes of a new global fight against terror.

Development's foray into security gave rise to new programmes, projects, specialist units and staff, and dedicated resource flows. For example, in 2000 a new foundation was established, namely the Geneva Centre for the Democratic Control of Armed Forces, to promote security sector reforms. New conflict and post-conflict units employing specialist staff mushroomed in bilateral and multilateral development institutions. For example, the World Bank established a Post-Conflict Unit in

1997; the Department for International Development set up a special conflict unit known as Conflict and Humanitarian Assistance and Development (CHAD) in the mid-1990s, which later became the Conflict, Humanitarian and Security Department (CHASE). Conflict prevention has been a significant focus of Sweden's development co-operation since the 1990s when it established a programme on Peace, Democracy and Human Rights. It sought to mainstream conflict prevention across its development programming, an effort that was enshrined as policy in its Strategy on Conflict Prevention and Management (1999). This was superseded in 2005 with the publication of its policy on *Promoting Peace and Security through Development Cooperation*. In 2001, UNDP established the Bureau for Crisis Prevention and Recovery to bridge relief and development through work on conflict prevention and building the foundations for sustainable peace and recovery. These new units have been the laboratories for new programmes concerned with promoting security sector reforms such as reform of military and police structures, the training of the police and military in human rights, the strengthening of civilian oversight mechanisms and the building of a civil society capacity to monitor security institutions. They have also supported civil society to work on addressing societal tensions and the causes of conflict.

On the security side, UN peace-keeping missions have increasingly appointed staff and established programmes concerned with the rule of law, policing and human rights protection. This ties into the recommendations of the Brahimi Panel on UN Peace Operations (2000), which proposed 'a doctrinal shift in the use of civilian police and related rule of law elements in peace operations'. Other recommendations included ensuring that budgets of complex peace operations included disarmament, demobilisation, and reintegration programmes and making it easier for heads of UN peace operations to fund 'quick impact projects'. Illustrative of these changes, in February 2003 the civilian police division of Department of Peace-Keeping Operations established a criminal law and judicial advisory unit (Hurwitz and Peake, 2004, p. 7).

The steady increase in military engagement in humanitarian and development work throughout the 1990s became part of 'normal practice' in conflict and post-conflict situations. Growing concerns over this engagement have prompted ad hoc joint military–NGO groups and meetings between security and civilian actors. Within academia new fields of research concerned with the development–security nexus have emerged within development studies, international relations and security studies. The positive associations between development and peace, the importance of development to addressing conflict issues, and the need to improve the governance of security sector institutions through reforms had gained considerable acceptance amongst security and development actors by the end of the decade. In the next section we trace the contours of the encounter between development and civil society over the 1990s and the gradual recruitment of civil society into the security domain in post-conflict settings.

Development encounters civil society

In the Cold War period, competing ideologies of capitalism, social democracy and communism informed development theory, aid policy and practice. The main axis of theoretical and policy debate revolved around the relative role of the state and market in processes of development. For advocates of statist approaches to development, the rise of the Newly Industrialising Countries of South Korea, Hong Kong, Singapore and Taiwan provided evidence of what developmental states could achieve. However, for neo-liberal economists, the success of these 'Four Tigers' was due to market forces, not state interventionism. Within this dichotomous and polarised development paradigm the relevance of non-governmental actors to processes of societal, economic and political change was considered to be relatively marginal. In humanitarian situations NGOs such as the International Red Cross or Oxfam were acknowledged to make an important contribution in providing relief. However, the solidarity NGOs supporting liberation struggles and revolutionary political projects in Namibia, Cuba, China, Mozambique and Angola or the new social movements mobilising around women's, green, apartheid or Third World issues neither sought to co-operate operationally with official development agencies, nor were sought by the latter as 'partners' in development. The rise of the basic needs agenda in the late 1970s created new spaces where established development NGOs could develop their operational activities and, importantly, experiment with new ways of doing development that were small-scale, community-based and needs-focussed.

From the mid-1970s, gradual disillusion with the role of the state as an agent of accumulation, development and economic distribution swung the ideological barometer towards a fervent celebration of the market. The failure of many so-called Third World States, especially in sub-Saharan Africa, to foster sustainable growth, the growing costs of the Western European welfare states and the economic stagnation and political oppression characterising actually existing socialist states in the Soviet Union, Eastern Europe and Africa combined to reinforce and justify the rise of neo-liberalism in the late 1970s and 1980s. Parallel to this, the number of developmental NGOs continued to grow. Some of these sought to raise awareness about global inequities and the distorting effects of colonialism on the Third World. In doing so they promoted alternative visions of development and developmental assistance, drawing on different theoretical and ideological perspectives rooted in Marxism, liberation theology and anarchism. Some sought to intervene operationally through raising funds, providing technical assistance, volunteering and experimenting with alternative ways of doing development such as small-scale technology and consciousness-raising literacy programmes. As these diverse non-governmental actors accumulated experience on the ground, they not only contributed to a growing critique of official development assistance but also created new models of development such as Schumacher's 'small is beautiful' and the idea of participation in development projects. In this way they emphasised values of solidarity, mutuality and equality and gave priority to the voices of the grass-roots over that of urban-based political elites.

As NGOs became more visible both operationally in the so-called Third World and discursively in their increasingly informed critiques of official development assistance, they also attracted greater attention from official development agencies. The UNDP was one of the earliest donor agencies to engage more systematically with NGOs. Already in 1975 the UNDP administrator issued guidelines on strengthening collaboration with NGOs to all its staff and resident representatives (UNDP, 1995, pp. 2–3). The UNDP saw NGOs not only as an important way to strengthen self-reliance at the community level but also as important contributors to policy advocacy and change. After the Rio de Janeiro conference on the environment the UNDP adopted a policy in 1986 to collaborate more closely with NGOs in the fields of poverty alleviation and environmental sustainability. This was followed in 1986 with the establishment of a special Division for NGOs in the Bureau for Programme Policy and Evaluation. In 1988 the UNDP launched its Partners in Development Programme, which provided direct support for small-scale activities of NGOs and community-based organisations such as income-generation projects. At a later stage other donors such as the then UK Overseas Development Agency (UK ODA), SIDA, and Norwegian Agency for Development Cooperation (NORAD) began to channel more resources towards NGOs to implement projects in health, literacy and education.

As neo-liberal policies took hold across industrialised and developing countries, the opportunities for NGOs to engage operationally in development expanded. Whilst development agencies such as the UNDP valued NGOs because of their distinct approach to development, which resonated with their organisational values and objectives, other agencies focussed on the benefits NGOs could bring against the backdrop of neo-liberalism. Structural adjustment programmes called for cutbacks in public expenditure, leading to the gradual dismantling of public welfare provision. Welfare was left in the hands of private sector agencies, families and communities and NGOs. It was within this context that donors turned more systematically to NGOs to implement donor-sponsored targeted welfare programmes. In the 1980s NGOs were being absorbed into donor policy agendas in contradictory ways: on the one hand, for the alternative approaches to development they offered; and on the other hand, as vehicles for the implementation of neo-liberal policies.

However, some international institutions were reluctant to court NGOs. The relationship between NGOs and international institutions such as the International Monetary Fund and the World Bank was fraught with tension and mutual suspicion. The Multilateral Development Bank campaign, which was launched in 1983, mounted a strident critique of the World Bank's role in development, raising particular issues around International Development Association (IDA) loans for large-scale dam construction, environmental impact and human rights (Fox and Brown, 1998, p. 4). In 1994 it organised the '50 Years Enough Campaign', which again criticised the development programmes of multilateral agencies, in particular the World Bank. For much of the 1980s the World Bank responded defensively to pressure from NGOs, conceding some limited space for dialogue and consultation, the establishment in 1982 of the NGO–World Bank Committee being a prime example thereof (World Bank, 1996, p. 5). As demands by NGOs for greater accountability from the World Bank resonated with internal pressures for reform, the World Bank instituted channels for public grievances and for greater participation. In 1989 it established the NGO Unit, ostensibly with the goal of providing support to NGOs but also as a public relations exercise to dampen criticism of the World Bank, particularly in light of its promotion of structural adjustment programmes.

By the mid-1980s the growth in development NGOs and their increasing visibility had spawned a new field of research that highlighted and tended to laud the role of NGOs in development processes. Numerous case studies were published, documenting the pioneering work of NGOs and asserting their comparative advantages over official development agencies such as their responsiveness to local needs, their flexibility and their proximity to the grass-roots (Frantz, 1987; Landim, 1987; Fowler, 1988, 1991; Corvalan, 1992; Bebbington and Farrington, 1993; Pearce, 1993; Van Rooy, 1998). These research and consultancy studies enhanced the legitimacy of NGOs as credible actors in the field of development.

The growing presence of NGOs in field operations and in development debates coupled with official development agencies' incremental experiences of working with NGOs led donors to establish more formalised mechanisms for supporting NGOs. In the late 1980s, for example, the UK ODA began to directly fund NGOs through the Joint Funding Scheme. Bilateral donors set up ad hoc working groups, committees and forums to engage in dialogue with non-governmental actors who were criticising official development assistance policy. They also began to seek their informal input into the design and evaluation of official development policy. Throughout the 1980s multilateral and bilateral development agencies interacted primarily with Northern humanitarian and developmental NGOs as opposed to southern NGOs or other actors in civil society and used the language of 'NGOs' to describe these developmental actors.

Whilst NGOs proliferated and grew in strength throughout the 1980s, several other trends were emerging that were to radically shift the paradigm of development from a dualistic, ideologically informed focus on the state/market to a triadic paradigm that placed state, market and civil society as equal players in the development game. By the end of the 1980s it was already apparent that the structural adjustment programmes promoted under the neo-liberal Washington Consensus had failed to trigger growth in the developing world. Indeed growth rates in sub-Saharan Africa were even lower than in the previous decade. Furthermore, the sharp cuts in public expenditure and the introduction of user fees for basic services such as water, health and education had sharpened inequalities and made the poor even poorer (Cornea *et al.*, 1987). Political pressure grew to swing the pendulum back from the market to the state, whilst keeping nevertheless within the frame of a capitalist model of development. At the same time democratic movements were sweeping across the world, usurping dictatorial and authoritarian regimes. Described by Samuel Huntington (1991) as 'the Third Wave of democracy', these democratic uprisings in Africa, Latin America and Eastern Europe drew attention to the role of civil actors in processes of social and political change. In the Soviet Union intellectual critics such as the Czech writer Vaclav Havel and Adam Michnik in Poland resurrected the language of civil society to express their

opposition to authoritarian rule and their vision of an alternative democratic society. Democratic activists in other continents appropriated this
emancipatory language of civil society to articulate their aspirations for
a more democratic and participatory government.

With the end of the Cold War and the ideologically informed
approach to international development assistance, the way was paved
for a new approach to aid. The new tripartite paradigm that emerged
at the dawn of the 1990s not only posited three key agents of development, namely state, civil society and market, but also portrayed these as
partners rather than antagonists in processes of economic and political
change. This tripartite approach that emphasised partnership, consensus and stability provided the framework within which the new 'good
governance' agenda arose. This sought not only to promote and consolidate democratic transitions but also to improve the effectiveness
of aid by strengthening the democratic functioning of government.
Civil society came into force here in its liberal roles as watchdog of
the state, demanding accountability and transparency, and as alternative or supplementary provider of welfare services, depending on state
capacities.

The language of civil society that had been a mobilising force for
East European dissidents, Latin American and African activists was now
absorbed into the policy and practice of multilateral and bilateral development agencies. The term 'civil society' provided a language that
development policy-makers could use to conceptualise, operationalise
and justify their deeper engagement with non-governmental actors in
development. However, the idea of civil society that has come to dominate donor policy is a liberal one that has been heavily influenced by
American experience and history, not the more radical idea of civil society that was articulated by East European dissidents, democracy activists
in Latin America or left-leaning groups in Europe. Given that the US has
been the main funder of civil society–strengthening programmes, the
US perspectives on its own historical experiences of democracy, its analysis of the contemporary decline in civic engagement in the US and its
concerns to maintain its global supremacy have strongly shaped the way
the idea of civil society has entered donor discourse.

Four major US influences have steered the discourse around civil
society, development and democracy (Howell and Pearce, 2001). The
nineteenth-century writings of the French political thinker Alexis de
Tocqueville on democracy in America underlined the importance of
associationalism for balancing liberty and equality, nurturing a democratic culture and protecting the individual against despotism or the

will of the majority. In the 1950s and 1960s the maintenance of political order and stability was a key concern for political scientists, including those researching political development in the Third World. The classic work of Gabriel Almond and Sydney Verba (1989) on civic culture in five countries concluded that trust, tolerance and associationalism underpinned well-functioning democracies such as the US and the UK and noted the weakness or absence of these in the Third World. Robert Putnam (1993a,b) drew on Almond and Verba's work in his studies of social capital in North and South Italy and on Tocqueville's work on associationalism but drew the conclusion that social capital, which is produced through networks of reciprocity and civic engagement, was not just a product of democracy but also a precondition for political development. As he connected the conclusions of his detailed Italian study to a contemporary analysis of declining political participation and civic engagement in the US, Putnam's influence in the US grew and the notion of social capital was enthusiastically embraced by development institutions such as the World Bank and the United States Agency for International Development (USAID), looking for ways of promoting democracy. The final major US influence on discourse around civil society and development is the body of knowledge produced by Lester Salamon and colleagues (1992, 1999) at Princeton University. By measuring and quantifying the 'Third Sector' Salamon provided rigorous evidence of the economic and social contribution of non-profit organisations. This gave empirical substance to the notion that the tripartite paradigm of development was the way forward for rich and poor countries. These four influences have shaped the debate around civil society, development and democracy and legitimised a paradigm of development that emphasises partnership, consensus and system maintenance.

This contrasts with another genealogy of civil society which emphasises the emancipatory potential of civil society, the values of mutuality and solidarity rather than individual rights and interests, and the need to find ways to reconcile the imbalance in liberal democracy between political equality and socio-economic inequalities. This has its roots in the radical continental European discussion of civil society and democracy found, for example, in the writings of Jean Jacques Rousseau and Karl Marx, in the work of Antonio Gramsci (1971, 1978) that was revitalised in the 1970s in Europe, and in Juergen Habermas' groundbreaking exploration of the conditions for rational and critical debate of public issues (Habermas, 1992). Gramsci's writings on civil society have drawn attention to the power relations and inequalities that run through associationalism, and the strategic importance of using the spaces of civil society to challenge dominant ideologies. Habermas' work on the public sphere and deliberative democracy has renewed interest in participatory forms of democracy and provided a discourse to legitimise radical practical initiatives such as participatory budgeting. It was to these more radical political perspectives that grass-roots campaigners, East European dissidents and democracy activists turned to analyse issues of inequality and injustice, to articulate their demands and to develop their alternative visions of civil society, democracy and development.

As the liberal discourse of civil society seeped into development jargon, donor agencies set up new civil society units and civil society working groups and appointed civil society liaison officers (Howell and Pearce, 2001, pp. 89–100). Throughout the 1990s donor agencies began to develop civil society strategies and provide rationalisations for their strategic engagement. For example, in 1994 USAID set up a new Center for Democracy and Governance, which had as one of its four strategic objectives the development of a 'politically active civil society'. The World Bank set up the NGO unit in the early 1990s and later renamed this as the NGO and Civil Society Unit. With the rise of New Labour in the UK in 1997 the newly named Department for International Development (DFID) absorbed the language of civil society both to express its intention to engage with a wider range of actors than just Northern NGOs and to work more strategically with non-governmental actors within the frame of the new tripartite paradigm of development. Replacing the NGO Unit with the Civil Society Unit in 1998 and establishing the Civil Society Challenge Fund were key moments in this discursive shift towards civil society. The reasons for engaging with civil society varied across donors, the foremost reasons being democracy promotion and poverty reduction. Agencies such as USAID developed a sophisticated civil society strategy as part of their democracy promotion work. Other agencies such as DFID placed their approach to civil society within their broad development remit of poverty reduction. By the end of the decade most development agencies had issued civil society strategy papers of varying degrees of detail and sophistication, which rationalised and justified their engagement with and distribution of resources to civil society.

As donors developed their civil society strategies, they also set up specific projects and programmes aimed at strengthening civil society so that they could contribute more effectively to democratisation and poverty reduction processes. These included activities such as supporting governments and civil society to develop; enabling legal and regulatory frameworks for civil society to operate; capacity-building of NGOs; fostering the development of CSOs in particular thematic and policy areas such as election monitoring, accountability and transparency, rights work, environmental advocacy, women's rights and HIV/AIDS. It is difficult to estimate the amount of aid directed towards civil society building and strengthening as these resources were usually hidden within broader accounting categories such as governance. Available figures suggest that these flows increased considerably from the late 1980s onwards (Van Rooy, 1998, pp. 33–36).

In developing strategies, projects and programmes for engaging with civil society, donor agencies used empirically broad definitions of civil society that specified not only development and humanitarian NGOs as key components thereof but also other civil society actors such as faith-based groups, trades unions, business and professional associations, virtual networks, human rights groups, environmental groups, parents–teachers associations. This suggested a growing awareness amongst donors that processes of development required not just governments, markets and NGOs but also a host of other non-governmental public actors both in the North and in the South. In this way donors broadened the nominal field of non-governmental actors with whom they engaged in dialogue and to whom they provided support.

However, the instrumental approach of donors to civil society and the gradual bureaucratisation and routinisation of their relationships with civil society have tended to privilege partnerships with certain types of CSOs, namely formal organisations that can adapt to and comply with the bureaucratic requirements of multiple donor agencies. Such organisations invariably take the form of developmental and humanitarian NGOs; indeed, donors have created such organisations where 'civil society' was deemed to be absent. The problem with this approach is that focussing on only a subset of civil society risks losing sight of the matrix of non-governmental public actors that is crucial to processes of social and political change. In many East European and Central Asian countries there is now a layer of newly established NGOs dealing with issues such as women's rights, health, governance, HIV/AIDS, which are not firmly rooted in their societies and are heavily dependent on aid. The introduction of participatory poverty reduction strategy papers (PPRSP) in the late 1990s went some way towards involving a wider set of actors than formal NGOs. Nevertheless, later studies of PPRSPs revealed that these failed to draw in the perspectives of marginalised groups such as the rural poor, illiterate people, and people living in remote areas (Booth, 2003). The absorption of a civil society discourse into development policy and practice and its routinisation, regularisation and institutionalisation through civil society strategies, civil society–strengthening programmes and specialised personnel dealing with civil society led gradually to the depoliticisation and technicisation of the idea and the reduction again of civil society to NGOs.

Though strategies for closer donor engagement with civil society related primarily to stable, peaceful contexts and countries undergoing democratic transition, CSOs were also being brought more systematically into policies and programmes in post-conflict settings. In the conflict/post-conflict contexts of the 1990s CSOs entered the fields of security sector reforms, conflict prevention and peace-building, a terrain upon which civil society actors hitherto had trodden warily. During the Cold War, as Pearce (2006, p. 7) notes, the realpolitik of national security was used to justify closing off security institutions to public scrutiny, human rights monitoring and citizen participation in security-related policy-making. The preoccupation with national security and secrecy meant that security concerns and institutions were closed to public scrutiny and civil society engagement. Moreover, many CSOs deliberately kept a distance from intrusive and repressive security agencies, which often had a history of dealing brutally with dissidents and protestors. The collapse of the Soviet Union had put a lid on the idea that socialism or communism or developmental states could be viable alternative routes to development. Similarly, the notion that the non-aligned Third World might provide another model to capitalist paths to development had long been put to rest.

In this context where left-wing, radical and alternative groups in the North and South no longer posed a serious threat to liberal capitalism, global political order and stability, the possibility for engaging non-governmental actors in the realm of security opened up. Though security sector reforms focused largely on reforms to state security institutions, the shift in discourse towards extending matters of security beyond the confines of the state paved the way for citizens and civil society actors to become involved in the security realm. The role for civil society actors was to act as watchdogs on state security institutions, as advocates for reform and as sources of technical expertise both for states with weak capacity and for civil societies starting to engage in security sector reform work. By demanding access to information, transparency and accountability CSOs could ensure to some degree that security agencies did not act with impunity. Moreover, civil society actors with specialist knowledge could put forward alternative perspectives on security issues, propose alternative policy options and alternative ways of including diverse interests into security discussions (Caparini, 2005, pp. 72–73).

Development agencies increasingly recognised the importance of involving citizens in decision-making processes concerning security and thereby the fundamental role of civil society in making security institutions effective (Ball and Brzoska with Kingma and Wulf, 2002, p. 9). Donor support for civil society in the security sector promoted a layer of civic organisations that were concerned with issues of transparency, human rights and accountability of security institutions, civilian oversight of security institutions, the monitoring of defence budget allocations, lobbying for community policing, re-integrating de-mobilised soldiers, and human rights training and awareness. Despite donor support for civil society involvement in security sector reforms, deep historical mistrust between security institutions and civilians has meant that CSOs continue in practice to be excluded from, or do not take up opportunities to participate in, such reform processes (Anderlini and Conaway, 2004, p. 34; Caparini, 2005, p. 82).

Though non-governmental humanitarian organisations had long played a vital role in providing relief in disasters and wars, the outbreak of internal conflicts after the end of the Cold War and the increasing engagement of development agencies in conflict prevention work not only made the work of these humanitarians more visible but also drew them further into the strategies of development agencies. As the interest of international institutions expanded from the immediate aftermath of conflicts to maintaining the peace in post-conflict settings, the role of civil society widened to include conflict mediation especially at the community level, reintegrating de-mobilised soldiers into the economy and society, facilitating transitional justice processes, and addressing violence against women. Donors supported these processes by building the capacity of civil society actors, bringing them into dialogue with funders, government, militaries and the UN, and nurturing the development of new NGOs to take on these roles. By the end of the 1990s the role of civil society in security sector reforms and peace-building was widely recognised and reaffirmed in the policy documents of bilateral and multilateral agencies. In UN Secretary-General Kofi Annan's report (p. 1) on the prevention of armed conflict to the UN Security Council in 2001 he states, 'The primary responsibility for conflict prevention rests with national Governments, with civil society playing an important role.'[11]

The donor rationale for supporting CSOs in these fields related not only to conflict prevention but also to broader agendas of governance, state-building and democratic consolidation. However, there was no systematic conceptualisation of the relationship between civil society, security and peace-building. The civil society strategies that were being developed in country-offices of donor agencies in the 1990s were formulated essentially for contexts of peace and stability. Moreover, the dominance of a neo-Tocquevillian perspective on civil society, particularly in the US, gave prominence to a normative view of civil society as an arena of harmony, peaceful civic engagement and unproblematic pluralism. It was assumed that civil society was an agency of peace and good, of conflict mediation, reconciliation and bridge-building, of humanitarianism and solidarity, a premise that had its roots in a line of political thinkers going back to the late eighteenth century, who positioned civil society as a benign force in opposition to coercive states. Violence and civil society were seen as inimical; the one naturally excluded the other. Hence armed rebel groups, criminal gangs, or any citizen organisations using violence to achieve their objectives would not be part of civil society. Concomitantly, the 1990s gave rise to a body of literature which painted women and women's groups as building peace and harmony and bringing together divided communities, myths that were later challenged by some feminist writers (Jacobs *et al.*, 2000; El Bushra, 2007). The complex relations between civil society, violence and conflict were, however, rarely conceptualised. The consequences of a normative donor agenda towards civil society that assumes civil society is a force for reconciliation, compromise and dialogue are observed in the case of Bosnia, where channelling funds towards nationalist ethnic elites undermined the potential role of civil society in peace-building and reconciliation (Belloni, 2001, p. 166 quoted in Caparini, 2005, p. 84).

Thus the liberal perspective on civil society that dominated development policy and practice in the 1990s also permeated donor engagement with civil society in security sector reforms and peace-building. Moreover, it dovetailed neatly with the liberal perspective on security and development where violence, war and insecurity were counterposed to development. In the next section we examine some of the dilemmas, tensions and doubts around civil society, security and development that emerged towards the end of the millennium and informed these relationships after 9/11.

Development, security and civil society: Dilemmas, tensions and doubts

By the turn of the millennium there were already doubts and tensions emerging around the complex relationships between military actors, aid agencies, civil society and private sector. The rationale for the increasing intersection of development and security agendas, policies and programmes was being questioned. There were several concerns raised. Critics questioned the validity and utility of the human security concept and its relationship to state security, suggesting that the concept was too broad to be useful and difficult to operationalise. The list of potential insecurities was unending, creating unrealistic expectations of what international institutions and national governments could achieve. Though UN policy documents underline the complementarity of human security and human development, defining clearly where one begins and the other ends has proven challenging, particularly for field workers. The relationship between conventional notions of security and the new expanded meanings remains unclear. Does and should state security take precedence over economic, political and environmental security concerns? Is state security prior to the task of addressing other non-military threats to society? Whose security interests should and do in the end prevail?

The liberal assumption that development and security were positively related was also coming under question. In what ways do development agencies contribute to conflict and violence, albeit unwittingly? The IMF-sponsored structural adjustment programmes of the 1980s are a case in point. There is now a considerable body of work that demonstrates the negative impact of such programmes on poor communities, thereby increasing inequalities and the potential for conflict (Cornea *et al.*, 1987; Potts and Mutambirwa, 1998). A seminal text on the development–security nexus by Duffield (2001) relates the convergence of development and security to the radicalisation of development and the reconstitution of security in the post–Cold War era. The blurring of civilian and military boundaries in the liberal peace reflects one of several complex strategic networks of global liberal governance that bring together diverse and multiple actors such as military, civilian, government and non-governmental, public and private actors. Duffield (2001, p. 12) proposes that these networks are most sharply defined 'on the borders of global governance' such as the New Wars in Kosovo and Somalia, where strategic actors encounter values, systems, norms and social structures that are very different to those of global liberal governance. As will be discussed throughout the book, we suggest not only that the effects of the global War on Terror regime on aid policy and civil societies are most pronounced in the front-line states of the War on Terror such as Afghanistan and Iraq but that the effects of this pervade domestic and foreign policies across the world.

There was also mounting unease amongst humanitarian workers about the increasing role of military actors, whether under UN, North Atlantic Treaty Organisation (NATO) or otherwise, in development and humanitarian work. Debates centred on the blurring of military–civilian lines and the dangers this posed to humanitarian workers in the field. It also fuelled a continuing discussion about how military engagement in humanitarian work is undermining humanitarian principles of independence, neutrality and impartiality. This debate has, however, focused on the impact of military intervention on the security and principles of humanitarian workers rather than on the more general impact on CSOs, refugees or civilian populations. Issues also began to arise around the resourcing of these activities, and in particular whether such engagement should be supported from military or developmental aid funds. Distinguishing the activities that should be categorised as military as opposed to official development assistance has become increasingly complex since the UN began peace-keeping operations in the 1990s. Key areas of controversy in the Organisation of Economic Co-operation and Development (OECD) relate to the training of security forces in human rights and principles and the proposal of a blanket ban on using overseas development assistance for any military activity, even where it is in practice non-military. Similarly, proposals to include the financing of peace-keeping missions from the European Development Fund for African, Caribbean and Pacific countries, which would require revising eligibility criteria, have also raised concerns about the intermeshing of development, foreign policy and security objectives (Tujan *et al.*, 2004, p. 59). There were also other questions about the general effectiveness of the development–security nexus. Participants at an International Peace Academy conference held in 2003 in New York on assessing the development–security nexus since the 1990s lamented the gap between the goals and objectives of policy and the outcomes on the ground, a gap which they attributed to the lack of co-ordination amongst donors and security actors, the absence of local participation and insufficient resources and capacity (Hurwitz and Peake, 2004, pp. 8–9).

Tensions and doubts arose not only in relation to the development–security nexus but also regarding the encounter between development and civil society. The 1990s turned out in retrospect to be the heyday of civil society as donors courted NGOs, human rights groups, women's groups and advocacy networks, channelled resources to them and developed civil society–strengthening programmes. However, this honeymoon period was already beginning to wane by the turn of the millennium. By then donors had accumulated experience of the challenges of working with relatively small-scale actors such as NGOs. They better understood the limits of what they could achieve and raised concerns about the transaction costs of working with a large number of disparate organisations ranging in capacity, size, scope and sectoral domains. There was also growing concern about the accountability and legitimacy of NGO actors, not only in the field of aid but also more generally in global and domestic politics. As NGOs increased their advocacy work relating to international institutions and conferences such as the Earth Summit in Rio in 1992 and its follow-up, the World Summit on Sustainable Development in Johannesburg in 2002, some parliamentarians challenged claims by NGOs to represent 'the poor' or 'the South', arguing that they themselves were democratically elected and therefore had a mandate to represent. Critiques of the PRSP processes highlighted issues of legitimacy and representation and the exclusion of marginalised groups from dialogues and events. A backlash against civil society was underway (Carothers, 2006; Howell *et al.*, 2007). Alert to the need to clarify the role of non-governmental actors in global governance processes, Kofi Annan, then UN Secretary-General, established a panel of eminent persons to carry out a global consultation and devise recommendations for the desired relationship between the UN and civil society. Their report – published in June 2004 and entitled 'We the Peoples: Civil Society, the United Nations and Global Governance' – led to some modest re-ordering of UN–civil society relations.

The academic literature on NGOs had also burgeoned, providing contradictory findings on the role of NGOs in development. Studies of NGOs in Africa, Central Asia, Central America and Latin America have highlighted the problem of aid dependency. Donor support to civil society fostered the development of new CSOs that resembled in form and function the developmental NGO-prototypes seen in donor countries. Support for training and capacity-building had cultivated these new organisational forms and practices. However, as research and consultancy studies increasingly revealed, these new NGOs often lacked a social base in their countries and therefore any legitimacy (Clayton, 1996; Howell and Pearce, 2001). There were also important doubts raised over the sustainability of donor-funded NGOs and a legitimate concern that these new organisations would collapse without outside funding since they lacked adequate local support in many instances. At the same time donors questioned whether the innovative work of NGOs could be easily replicated elsewhere. Thus, debate ensued around the possibilities for scaling up the work of NGOs.

These simmering tensions and doubts over the development–security nexus and the encounter between development and civil society should be examined within a broader context where the effectiveness of aid was becoming a major concern for donors towards the end of the 1990s. The new millennium presented a moment for donors, governments and international institutions to reflect on aid and compelled them to set grander goals and expectations of what it could achieve. The launch of the Millennium Development Goals, a set of targets for improving human development indicators in eight key areas, at the signing of the UN Millennium Declaration in September 2000 was a major catalyst for addressing past weaknesses in the aid system. This in turn provoked a reassessment of the direction of aid, its scope and processes and, specifically, renewed a focus on states to manage and direct development processes instead of supporting stand-alone projects implemented by NGOs and community groups. As donors looked afresh at how best to implement aid resources and strengthen state capacities, they sought to change aid modalities by supporting sector-wide programmes and extending direct budget support to 'good performers'. This entailed a focus on strengthening state capacities. Concerns over the lack of donor co-ordination coincided with this shift in emphasis to the state and led to efforts to promote aid harmonisation and coherency, culminating in the signing of the Paris Declaration on Aid Effectiveness in March 2005.

Conclusion

Beginning in the 1980s, the groundwork was laid for heightened connectivity and co-ordination between development and security actors. A new field of development programming, practice, discourses and institutions began to grow around security sector reforms as donors sought to make security institutions more open to public scrutiny. At the same time, the role of non-state actors in peace-building and conflict resolution was increasingly encouraged. These trends dovetailed with the emergence of the aid-driven good governance agenda in the 1990s. Civil society came to be seen as a development panacea that could transcend otherwise complex governance problems and obstacles. Donors developed new programming around civil society, sought expert opinion on civil society and channelled significant resources through CSOs, often bureaucratic-type organisations, especially NGOs. However, this golden era for civil society was already beginning to wane by the late 1990s as concerns arose around the probity, legitimacy and representativeness of civil society. Some of the assumptions underlying the development–security nexus also came to be questioned. All the while, expectations of aid shifted with agreement on the UN Millennium Development Goals, which required the greater involvement of states in delivering greater developmental outcomes.

The launch of the War on Terror in September 2001 brought all these issues to a head. These sources of tension and doubt as well as some of the positive assumptions and experiences of these encounters contributed to the shaping of the development–security nexus post-9/11. As will be seen in subsequent chapters, the trend towards a convergence of development and security has intensified and deepened after the attacks on the Twin Towers in New York in September 2001 with consequences for both how aid policy and practice are framed and operationalised and also how donors engage with civil society. The strategic bifurcation of civil society into 'good' and 'bad' parts, as mentioned in the preceding chapter, through the discourses and practices of the global War on Terror regime becomes reflected in aid policy, strategy and practice towards civil society.

In the next chapter we look at the effects of the global War on Terror regime on government–civil society relations in the post-9/11 era, focussing on the US, the UK and the EU, which have been major players in producing and perpetuating the new post-9/11 security regime. We suggest that the post-9/11 global security regime has brought civil society actors more firmly into the gaze of security institutions. Against a backdrop of growing concern about the legitimacy and accountability of NGOs, the post-9/11 security regime has further contributed towards greater circumspection on the part of governments in their engagement with civil society both domestically and internationally. In particular, the new layers of counter-terrorist and related legislation and regulation essentially bifurcates civil society into 'good' and 'bad' parts, just as Muslims, as Mamdani (2005) argues, have been turned into 'good' and 'bad' Muslims. It has created both threats to the spaces of civil society as well as new opportunities for civil society and different parts of civil society to engage with formal development, security and government agencies.

Notes

1. In his words, 'Good governance, of course, means much more than democratisation in a formal political sense. Another very important aspect is the reform of public services – including the security sector, which should

be subject to the same standards of efficiency, equity and accountability as any other public service' (quoted in Ball and Brzoska with Kingma and Wulf, 2002, p. 5).

2. See paragraph 21 of Ghali's Agenda for Peace report, 1992.
3. See paragraph 46, 'Supplement to an Agenda for Peace', 1995.
4. Between 1993 and 2003 intra-state conflicts accounted for 7 million deaths, of which over 75 per cent were civilians (Hurwitz and Peake, 2004, p. 1).
5. This was spelled out by the then President Said Ben Mustapha in his 'Statement by the President of the Security Council', 2001:

> The Security Council recognizes that peace-building is aimed at preventing the outbreak, the recurrence or continuation of armed conflict and therefore encompasses a wide range of political, developmental, humanitarian and human rights programmes and mechanisms. This requires short and long-term actions tailored to address the particular needs of societies sliding into conflict or emerging from it. These actions should focus on fostering sustainable institutions and processes in areas such as sustainable development, the eradication of poverty and inequalities, transparent and accountable governance, the promotion of democracy, respect for human rights and the rule of law and the promotion of a culture of peace and non-violence.

6. For an excellent overview of the some of the key discursive shifts around security in the 1990s, see Pearce (2006, pp. 8–10).
7. For example, an OECD study on security development issues published in 2001 stated that 'the security of states and the security of people should be seen as mutually reinforcing...', quoted by Hurwitz and Peake (2004, p. 1).
8. The concept of 'societal security' was introduced by Barry Buzan (1991, 1993, 2007) against the background of an increase in internal wars after the Cold War and refers to threats to the identity of a society where society might be defined in terms of national, religious or ethno-national identities.
9. The 1994 UNDP Human Development Report (p. 23) makes clear that human security is not the same as human development, the latter being a broader concept referring to 'a process of widening the range of people's choices'. Human security is thus a narrower but related concept where people can 'safely and freely' exercise those choices. The complementarity and distinctiveness of the terms is again underlined in the 2003 Report of the Commission on Human Security (p. 2): 'Human security complements state security, enhances human rights and strengthens human development.'
10. Illustrative of this is the definition of the security sector given by the OECD Development Assistance Committee in 2001:

> the security forces and the relevant civilian bodies and processes needed to manage them and encompasses: state institutions which have a formal mandate to ensure the safety of the state and its citizens against

acts of violence and coercion (e.g. the armed forces, the police and paramilitary forces, the intelligence services and similar bodies; judicial and penal institutions) and the elected and duly appointed civil authorities responsible for control and oversight (e.g. Parliament, the Executive, the Defence Ministry etc.):

> (OECD/CAD, 2001, pp. 22–24, quoted in Pearce, 2006, p. 8,
> and originally in Ball and Brzoska with Kingma
> and Wulf, 2002, p. 7)

11. He reiterates this several times throughout the report, for example on p. 2: 'The UN is not the only actor in prevention ... member states ... the private sector, non-governmental organisations and other civil society actors also have very important roles to play in this field.'

3
Government–Civil Society Relations Post-9/11

> We can address directly three of the most dangerous sources of terrorist finance – the abuse of charities, the abuse of money service businesses and the abuse of financial transactions. We know that many charities and donors have been and are being exploited by terrorists.[1]
>
> Gordon Brown, Chancellor of the Exchequer,
> October 2006

Since 9/11 government and donor approaches to civil society have become more circumspect. As discussed in Chapter 2, by the turn of the millennium governments, international institutions and development agencies were beginning to adopt a more critical and strategic stance towards civil society, and especially towards advocacy organisations and funded NGOs. This more cautious engagement arose from concerns over the accountability, legitimacy, probity of civil society organisations as well as the bureaucratic costs of working with a compendium of small groups. Concurrently, there were concerns over aid effectiveness and donors were devising new ways of channelling aid to achieve the greater expectations of what development should deliver. This involved directing greater support through aid-recipient governments with a resulting de-emphasis on civil society support. Hence, government and donor strategies towards civil society were undergoing considerable changes prior to the emergence of security concerns and suspicions of civil society in the context of the War on Terror.

In this chapter we examine how post-9/11 security concerns have shaped further changes in the engagement of governments and international institutions with civil societies, focussing on the US, the UK and the EU. The chapter argues that governments and international institutions have adopted a dual approach towards civil society since 2001, which is based on the distinction governments are making between 'good' and 'bad' elements of civil society. This dual approach is also evident in the changing strategies of bilateral and multilateral donors, as will be explored in Chapter 4. On the one hand, states and multilateral institutions have adopted a 'hard' approach towards non-governmental actors suspected of associating with terrorists and extremists. This involves proscribing organisations that are alleged to finance terrorists, surveillance of suspect groups and enhanced regulation of civil society generally. These measures to crack down on 'bad' civil society have been coupled with 'soft' counter-terrorism approaches that seek to involve non-governmental actors in preventing radicalisation and promoting dialogue with 'suspect' communities, including Muslims, youth and refugees. Therefore, states combine a politics of eradicating assistance to terrorist organisations with the liberal management of the fear that terrorism generates.[2]

We explore the changing relations between civil society and governments and multilateral institutions post-9/11 through the cases of the US, the UK and the EU. The US is the avowed leader and principal architect of the War on Terror and to this end has exerted economic, military and political pressure on other states and international institutions to ally for this cause. As a close ally in this endeavour, the UK has been deeply implicated in the perpetration of the War on Terror. Both countries have gone furthest in promulgating new legislation, regulations and practices to address security concerns related to the War on Terror and specifically that charities might be misused in support of terrorism. Along with the EU, both countries are significant providers of development assistance.[3] The EU has also sought to strengthen its counter-terrorism structures and, specifically, to increase oversight over NGOs. These efforts arise from suspicion of civil society since 9/11 and the pressure to adopt a tough stance towards alleged abuses of charitable organisations. There are significant differences in the approaches adopted by the US, the UK and the EU towards suspicion of links between civil society and terrorism. Whilst the US has adopted a harder approach that emphasises proscription, regulation and surveillance, the UK has relied more on persuasion, co-option and ideology. This in part reflects the particular role played by the independent charity regulator, the Charity Commission of England and Wales. Encumbered by its burgeoning bureaucracy and having to negotiate the conflicting positions of different member states, the EU has acted much more slowly on both the soft and the hard approaches.

The chapter begins by outlining the key dimensions of the dual strategy towards civil society, before examining the contrasting approaches taken in the US, the UK and the EU. The final section considers the varied responses of different civil society actors to the shifting stance of governments and highlights some of the fissures within civil society that the changing context of 9/11 exposes.

The two-pronged approach to civil society post-9/11

The dawn of the new millennium heralded a comprehensive re-appraisal and 'tidying-up' of government and donor relations with civil society. As discussed in the previous chapter, the role of civil society in governance and development processes was increasingly being called into question towards the end of the 1990s. In general, the thrust of this new regulatory impulse was to tighten control over NGOs. Whilst in some contexts the demand for accountability and the pursuit of this through regulation was justified, in other more authoritarian contexts, where governments were intolerant to criticism from non-state actors, such regulation was used to introduce even tighter controls on NGOs.

The launch of the War on Terror added yet another layer of pressure onto civil societies and provided a powerful justification for greater scrutiny and caution towards non-governmental public actors. It was this particular pressure that drew civil society more forcefully into the realm of security in multiple and overlapping ways on both the domestic and the international fronts. Concerns around civil society that were emerging in the 1990s related to improving donor engagement with civil society, identifying any disreputable partners and terminating funding of groups that were either too small or lacked credibility. The declaration of the War on Terror was an additional impetus to these ongoing efforts to cement partnerships with 'good' sections of civil society while cutting off support for 'bad' groups.

For the purpose of the discussion here, 'good' civil society comprises organisations, networks, and associations that are registered, transparent in their operations and have formal internal procedures to promote accountability and good stewardship. 'Good' civil society promotes or at least embodies liberal values such as democracy, rights, gender, racial, ethnic and political equality. 'Good' civil society is an essential ingredient in a liberal democracy. To this end it advocates on behalf of minority interests, holds governments to account, demands transparency, promotes liberal values and provides a training ground for future leaders. 'Good' civil society is non-violent, tolerant of diversity and difference, self-regulating and basically harmonious and benign. In the field of development and aid 'good' civil society shares similar aims, values and principles to Western democratic governments and international institutions. Moreover, it cooperates with governments, donors and international institutions to achieve development priorities such as poverty reduction and spreading democracy.

In contrast, 'bad' civil society is unaccountable, opaque in its operations, and lacks internal governance procedures to ensure accountability and due diligence. This is thought to make such groups vulnerable to abuse by terrorists or criminal groups for purposes such as money-laundering or giving cover to terrorist organising. Undesirable civil society groups promote extremism, radicalism, illiberal and undemocratic values and attitudes, and hence are a problem for liberal democracies. Such groups claim to represent 'suspect' populations such as Muslims and populations on the margins of society. Further, they provide a training ground for radicals, extremists and terrorists. Unlike 'good' civil society it promotes and sometimes deploys violence and foments conflict and unrest. It may also subvert directly or indirectly the development priorities of official aid and undermine the activities of liberal, Western development and humanitarian NGOs.

This distinction between 'good' and 'bad' is inferred from the polarising language of the War on Terror, statements by political leaders around the world that raise suspicions of civil society while also seeking to embrace 'moderate' non-governmental actors, as well as official rationale for changing donor policies and strategies on civil society. The designation of particular groups as 'bad', 'uncivil' and 'suspicious' is deeply political. Political activity by civil society encompasses opposition and resistance and similarly underpins strategies of political subversion. Raising suspicions about certain groups is a time-old tactic to discredit dissident groups and secessionist movements and, hence, justify repressive measures. For example, opposition leaders and democracy and governance groups in Uzbekistan, Zimbabwe and Uganda have been labelled as 'terrorists' (Rubongoya, 2009; Stevens and Jailobaeva, 2009). The designation of groups as either 'bad' or 'good' depends on a country's politics and social divisions and how these intersect with regional and global politics. The fall-out of the War on Terror has been to raise particular suspicion around Muslim organisations and charitable networks while also giving governments an excuse to crack down on any group they deem to be threatening.

Non-governmental public action is important to political organisation and that is why governments have sought to expand their regulation of civil society while also seeking to co-opt particular non-governmental groups into strategies of liberal governance and counter-radicalisation. So, for example, some Muslim groups and leaders have cultivated ever-closer ties with Western donors and diplomats, who in turn have sought contacts with Muslim communities as part of their counter-radicalisation efforts. As will be seen in Chapter 6, this has sometimes led to fraught relations between Muslim advocacy groups and Western governments.

Governments, donors and multilateral institutions have increasingly relied on a dual-pronged approach to civil society. One approach centres on the use of 'hard' measures to crack down on 'bad' non-governmental actors. These include banning organisations, designating certain groups as 'terrorist organisations', increasing surveillance of suspect groups, and enhanced regulation in general. The second approach ties into 'soft' counter-terrorism strategies that co-opt civil society groups into preventing radicalisation and terrorism, promoting liberalism and encouraging dialogue with populations that have come under suspicion as being susceptible to terrorist recruitment. Each of these approaches is explained in turn below.

Hard measures refer to a range of legislation, regulations, policies and practices that aim to make the environment for terrorists more difficult to operate in. The hard measures can be divided into first-order measures, which are specifically tailored to counter terrorism, and second-order measures. These are amendments covering counter-terrorism to legislation, policies and regulations that have been conceived of for other purposes. The 2001 US Patriot Act, the 2001 UK Anti-Terrorism, Crime and Security Act and the EU 2005 Counter-Terrorist Strategy are examples of first-order measures. Other key first-order measures include the extension of surveillance; proscription of suspected terrorist organisations and the creation of official terrorist lists; extended powers to detain suspects without trial; wiretapping phones and electronic communication; monitoring the Internet and international money transfers; and bilateral and multilateral agreements to cooperate in the sharing of information for security purposes, such as airline passenger lists. They also include military intervention to thwart terrorism as in Iraq and Afghanistan; targeted military operations on terrorist cells, such as has occurred inside Somalia and Pakistan; renditions of terrorist suspects; the creation of detention facilities such as Guantanamo Bay to interrogate terrorist suspects; and the use of torture. They may also require the establishment of new counter-terrorist structures such as dedicated counter-terrorist police units, government working groups and committees.

Second-order hard measures include policies, directives, measures that spin off from these first layers and infect institutions, legislation and policies that are not directly related to countering terrorism such as aid policies, refugee and asylum policies, community development and the regulation of charities. A prominent example of a second-order hard measure is the Special Recommendations on Terrorist Financing of the Financial Action Task Force (FATF)[4], which it issued in the wake of the 9/11 attacks. Special Recommendation VIII (SR VIII) applied specifically to non-profit organisations, which FATF considered to be 'particularly vulnerable' to terrorist financing. It called upon countries to review their laws and regulations to 'ensure that they [non-profits] cannot be misused'.

Statements by Western political leaders alluding to links between terrorism and charities fed into a climate of opinion demanding tighter regulation of NGOs, leading to a spate of new and amended regulations governing NGOs. The FATF special recommendation gave cover to governments to intensify regulation of non-governmental actors, often in the absence of clear evidence that charities were being systematically misused. The new NGO Act in Afghanistan, for example, contains a clause on counter-terrorism. The government of Uzbekistan has used the pretext of terrorism to introduce banking controls over foreign funding of NGOs (Howell, 2006; Stevens, 2009). Furthermore, the casual and widespread use of language linking Islam and Muslims to terrorism, such as 'Islamic terrorism' and 'Muslim extremists' in the media and political discourse, has constructed Muslims as problematic and Islam as an extremist religion. This in turn has, along with the FATF SR VIII, cast suspicion upon Muslim charities, mosques, community centres and madrassas, drawing them into the surveillance web of intelligence agencies.

Other second-order measures include immigration and asylum policies amended to prevent counter-terrorism. In 2006 the UK Immigration, Asylum and National Act was amended to include additional measures relevant to counter-terrorism.[5] The British government also used the climate of fear generated after the 9/11 attacks, the March 2004 Madrid bombings and the London 7/7 bombings to resuscitate debates around identity cards, seeking to justify these in terms of counter-terrorism. In Denmark counter-terrorism and immigration have been linked through the Regions of Origin policy. The policy aims to stem the inflow of asylum seekers with the intention of limiting social alienation and extremism, which are widely thought to have been imported into Denmark from abroad.[6]

Governments have sought the contribution of civil society actors to 'soft' counter-terrorism approaches, which aim to undermine popular support for terrorist organisations by winning hearts and minds. Some of these measures include building alliances with 'moderate' groups and leaders in Muslim communities; preventing the 'breeding of terrorism' through anti-radicalisation programmes; promoting inter-faith dialogue and 'acceptable' interpretations of Islam; de-radicalisation programmes in prisons; and registration and training of imams. Soft measures are about ideology, persuasion and co-option. They aim not only to blunt the sharp edges of hard counter-terrorism measures but also to encourage popular buy-in to security measures. In particular, they seek to drive a wedge between terrorist organisations using Islam to justify their actions and moderate Muslims, who abhor terrorist activities. Aware of the gaps in knowledge about Islam and the Middle East amongst government administrators and the general public, many Western governments have channelled resources into Arabic language training, Middle Eastern studies and research on Islam. They have also used foreign assistance and political pressure to leverage reform of madrassas and have increased investment in education in countries with large Muslim populations such as Pakistan and Kenya.

Below, we analyse the different approaches taken in the US, the UK and the EU to suspicions that terrorist networks misuse civil society. We also examine the incipient responses of civil society to these enhanced concerns and subsequent regulatory scrutiny.

The United States: A broad offensive on 'bad' civil society

As the leading proponent of the War on Terror, the US government has charted many new legal and regulatory controls on the spaces and actors of its vast civil society. Counter-terrorism is the precept of new restrictive requirements for due diligence by US non-profit groups as well as the rationale for increased surveillance of suspect organisations and the closure of some Muslim charities. These controls arise from a singular view of civil society organisations as potential financiers and recruiters for terrorist groups. Acting on the 'one percent doctrine' – that is, if there is a 1 per cent chance that suspicions are true, then you act on them – the Bush administration has advanced these controls on the basis of security concerns but with little evidence and few actual examples of charities that have been misused in support of terrorists.[7] Indeed, the 9/11 Commission found that the attacks on New York and Washington were funded through illicit activities, smuggling and criminal activity and not primarily through the misuse of charitable groups. It concluded that rather than seizing the assets of terrorists, the US government should shift its focus to following the money trail as a strategy to disrupt plots (Weiss, 2005).

Still, the US government has continued to seize and freeze assets to block terrorism funding, including those assets allegedly misused through charities. President Bush has used extraordinary powers to expand and ease the freezing of assets of terrorist organisations and their financiers, which the administration claims includes charities (Sidel, 2007). In so doing it has adopted the same enforcement regime for charities and foundations that apply to organised crime and drug barons (OMB Watch/Grantmakers without Borders, 2008). Adopted in October 2001, the Patriot Act imposed other new regulatory requirements on American non-governmental actors such as penalties for providing material support to terrorist organisations. It gave powers to the executive branch to freeze the property or assets of persons or organisations suspected of committing or supporting terrorist acts. The material support statutes contained in the Patriot Act ban the provision of 'intangibles', including providing services, training and expertise to designated organisations (Sidel, 2007). US non-profit groups working overseas have argued that the wide meaning of what constitutes 'material support' threatens their work because it is uncertain what types of assistance may run foul of the law. Crucially, there is no exception for humanitarian assistance in the material support statutes beyond medicine and religious materials. The Humanitarian Law Project, a US non-profit group that provides human rights training to the Kurdistan Workers Party, which is on the 'designated' list, challenged the prohibition in the Patriot Act on any provision of 'expert advice or assistance'. In 2004 a federal judge struck down the provision as unconstitutional (Sidel, 2007).

Bush released Executive Order 13224 in October 2001, which gave the Secretaries of State and Treasury the authority to designate individuals and organisations as terrorists and terrorist supporters and to freeze their assets (Billica, 2006). The Order created a new category and named 27 'Specially Designated Global Terrorists' resulting in a significant expansion of the Specially Designated Nationals list. The Office of Foreign Assets Control (OFAC) publishes and periodically updates the master list of suspect individuals and organisations. The designation is made administratively with little scope for judicial review and without considering an organisation's intent in establishing its guilt.[8] OFAC is empowered to act on 'reasonable suspicion' to make a designation. The Patriot Act authorises stiff civil and criminal penalties for organisations found to be supporting terrorism (Billica, 2006). The Treasury Department has shut down and designated seven US charities and foundations as supporters of terrorism but to date only three have faced criminal prosecution and none have been convicted (OMB Watch/Grantmakers without Borders, 2008). Nearly all of the US non-profits that have been shut are Muslim. A charity lawyer that has represented some of the suspected organisations explained that this contributes to an impression of a targeted crackdown on Muslim civil society groups: 'the [anti-terror] laws are so wide in scope that they could be used to imprison any of us. They could shut down any business or NGO but they are not, because they are not Muslim. This is a policy that specifically targets Muslims.'[9]

There are few safeguards for groups that are being investigated. The law does not require that criminal charges be filed prior to administrative confiscation of an organisation's assets. Further, there is not an administrative requirement to inform the group being investigated that its assets will be seized. OFAC also is not required to provide a statement of reasons for either the designation or the investigation (OMB Watch/Grantmakers without Borders, 2008). The lack of due process protections reflects the hard approach the US government has adopted to the perceived misuse of civil society organisations. Designated groups are prohibited from presenting their own evidence in courts and from knowing and thus challenging secret evidence. So far, the courts have deferred to OFAC's judgment on grounds of national security (OMB Watch/Grantmakers without Borders, 2008). Civil society critics have argued that these onerous and harsh restrictions are partially explained by the fact that OFAC normally oversees compliance with economic embargoes against nations and criminal money-laundering laws targeting drug traffickers and organised crime (OMB Watch/Grantmakers without Borders, 2008). Thus, it lacks knowledge and expertise in non-profit law and regulation, which are normally the remit of the Exempt Organizations Division of the US Treasury. But this has been marginalised in enforcing the counter-terrorism financing provisions of the Patriot Act (Sidel, 2007).

The other manifestation of civil society scrutiny in the US is the *Anti-Terrorist Financing Guidelines: Voluntary Best Practices for US-based Charities*. These were devised by the Treasury Department but without consulting non-profit groups. They comprise extensive recommended governance, transparency, and grant-making practices. Among these is the suggestion that organisations that work overseas collect extensive information about recipient organisations and individuals, board members of grantee organisations and individuals or organisations with which grantees conduct business (Billica, 2006). But much of this information is often difficult to obtain (Sidel, 2007).

The guidelines pose numerous threats to non-governmental public action, and have awakened a broader response by American civil society to how counter-terrorism measures (CTMs) create difficulties for their work. Debate has turned on the exceptionally broad language of the guidelines, which also holds for the material support statutes. For example, the guidelines defined 'terrorist abuse' to include 'exploitation of charitable services and activities to radicalize vulnerable populations and cultivate support for terrorist groups and networks' (quoted in Arulanantham, 2008, p. 8). Civil society critics in the US have also argued that the guidelines require burdensome investigation by charities into their partners or grantees, which entails high administrative costs. While smaller foundations have found it difficult to adhere to the 'best practices' in the guidelines, larger organisations have adapted their practices and procedures to comply.[10]

In late 2005, the Treasury Department revised the guidelines in response to the vocal concerns of American civil society. In 2007, it released a companion tool to the Guidelines entitled *Risk Matrix for the Charitable Sector* (Sidel, 2007). However, Sidel notes that there is continuing criticism that the updated guidelines suggest that charitable organisations are agents of the government, require even greater data collection and amount to law-making by stealth. Besides these fundamental concerns, the guidelines are also ineffective against terrorism as terrorists have financed their operations through other means such as drug dealing and credit card fraud. Moreover, the cost of terrorist operations is insignificant, the London 7/7 bombings requiring just £8,000 to execute.[11]

Billica (2006) notes that the Treasury Department guidelines in particular have created 'an environment of fear and confusion in the philanthropic community'. Private grant-makers and foundations such as the United Way, and the Ford, Rockefeller, Koret and Macarthur Foundations regularly check designation lists and have inserted new language into their grant agreement letters. This has troubled some grantees. In April 2004, the provosts of nine major universities wrote to the Ford and Rockefeller Foundations opposing the transfer of the due diligence burden to grantee institutions and called the new grant language 'vague'

(Sidel, 2007). The Vice Chancellor of the University of California commented on the new language in grant agreement letters: 'While the University of California certainly does not condone terrorism, violence, or bigotry, we are concerned about the overbreadth and vagueness of the language being used by the foundations. We are troubled that the conditions...may be construed broadly to apply to protected speech of individuals who are part of the university "organization," including faculty and students.' The American Civil Liberties Union (ACLU) opted to decline further funding from the Ford and Rockefeller Foundations due to concern about the impacts funding agreements would have on the civil liberties of the organisation and its grantees.[12]

The due diligence requirements of post-9/11 anti-terror laws and measures have influenced new bureaucratic practices of control by federal US government agencies and private grant-makers. USAID has introduced a certification system that requires its grantees to sign Anti-Terrorism Certificates (ATCs) that commit them to undertaking checks on their partners. Recently, USAID has introduced requirements that its grantees submit highly personal information about key personnel and leaders that are checked against an intelligence database.[13] Following its implementation in its Palestine programme, USAID is rolling out the Partner Vetting System (PVS) across all its programming regions. Grantees will be required to complete a form that requires information on key personnel including dates and places of birth, citizenship, phone numbers and passport numbers. The information will be entered into USAID's database and checked by the USAID Office of Security against a secret intelligence database.[14] American NGOs objected that the use of this personnel information is shrouded in secrecy and that there is no procedure for USAID to report why it has rejected a group.[15] Other concerns that were voiced were that the PVS would compromise the civil rights of non-profit groups, undermine their programme effectiveness and endanger their staff members as well as the staff of their local partners.[16]

There is a sharp political edge to the execution of restrictive measures taken against US civil society groups and the impacts have been felt unevenly. Whereas the pressures have been acute for Muslim groups, dissenting groups and overseas agencies operating in conflict zones, most civil society organisations (i.e. non-Muslim groups) have experienced little, if any, impact.[17] Relief agencies have worried that they might lose foundation and government funding if they continue working in conflict areas where it is often difficult in practice to work around designated terrorist entities and associated charities (OMB Watch, 2005). Arulanantham (2008, p. 7) notes, 'material support laws put aid workers in the untenable position of having to choose between providing assistance, which exposes them and their organisations to the risk of exclusion from the United States, deportation, civil forfeiture or even criminal prosecution on the one hand, and abandoning the desperate victims of war and natural calamity in their hour of greatest need on the other'.

Anti-terror measures have also been used to target and intimidate dissenting voices of Bush administration policies. The FBI has monitored political groups with no clear association to designated terrorist organisations, including peace groups and civil rights organisations.[18] In April 2005, the ACLU launched its Spy Files Project and uncovered an intricate system of domestic spying on US civil society groups that was sanctioned by expanded powers granted under the Patriot Act (OMB Watch/Grantmakers without Borders, 2008). While there is a record of US intelligence agencies monitoring domestic NGOs – notably peace groups during the Vietnam War – this was not authorised legally or procedurally.[19] However, amendments to the Foreign Intelligence Surveillance Act under the Patriot Act expanded the authority of federal agencies to conduct warrantless electronic surveillance if there is 'reasonable belief' that one of the parties is overseas and suspected of involvement with Al Qaeda (WMD/ICNL, 2008). Since then it has emerged that telephone communication between Islamic organisations and their US lawyers has been monitored (Keefe, 2008).

The Bush administration has also curtailed the rights of public employees in the name of national security.[20] For example, political leaders in Bush's Republican Party demonised as unpatriotic public employees who did not accept significant wage and benefit cuts (Lafer, 2004). After 9/11 Bush denied unionisation rights to baggage screeners at US airports. Bush gave the Secretary of the Department of Homeland Security (DHS) the unilateral authority to waive civil service, anti-discrimination, whistleblower and union protections to the department's 170,000 employees who had enjoyed these rights while performing the same jobs under previous management before the creation of DHS.

Civil society responses to counter-terrorism legislation and measures affecting their work were slow to emerge. Partially this reflected the political atmosphere after 9/11, the patriotic impulse and pressure to conform to War on Terror policies. The few dissenting voices in the immediate aftermath of the 9/11 attacks have since then grown more vocal. Debate has centred on opposing the use of governmental power. However, there is still a lack of debate about the War on Terror, the need for CTMs, or indeed the causes of terrorism. An official of a well-known human rights organisation in the US commented, 'A lot of the work I do has been reactive, that is responding to legislation that we don't like. I'm working on stopping torture, restoring habeas corpus, closing Gitmo. A lot of our work is pushing back, righting the wrongs of the past seven years (since 9/11). We're not at the point yet where we talk about the causes of terrorism. That is important though for showing how ineffective CTM have been. There is an unfortunate lack of consideration of these issues.'[21]

Muslim and civil rights organisations and small pressure groups have led civil society in opposing the US government's counter-terrorism legislation, measures and bureaucratic practices that affect its work. However, wider civil society has been sluggish in its response. Sidel (2007, p. 109) notes, 'the nonprofit community responded to human, social, and economic needs after September 11 but failed to respond to the political dangers that September 11 also represented to itself.' Sidel (2007) explains that the broader nonprofit sector in America hoped that enforcement of counter-terrorism statutes would be limited to Muslim charities and that most non-Muslim groups would be unaffected. It was only when enforcement efforts began to impinge upon and threaten the autonomy of overseas charities such as Oxfam and CARE and private foundations like Rockefeller and Gates that the sector began to respond. Sidel (2007, p. 120) observes, 'the nonprofit sector's failure to effectively monitor and seek improvements in the government's approaches bespeaks a relative timidity, a willingness to let certain Muslim charities fall in the hope that other parts of the sector will remain untouched'.

Belatedly, US non-profit groups have instigated a more coherent and forceful response to counter-terrorism structures that have affected their abilities to organise, fund-raise and work with overseas partners. In 2005, the Treasury Guidelines Working Group of Charitable Sector Organisations and Advisors released the *Principles of International Charity* (Principles) as an alternative to the Treasury Guidelines (OMB Watch/Grantmakers without Borders, 2008). The Principles stress not only compliance with American law but also the independence and autonomy of charitable organisations. Private foundations have also published the 'Handbook on counter-terrorism measures: What US non-profits and grantmakers need to know' as a way of promoting compliance.

The advocacy infrastructure in Muslim communities has strengthened in response to the pressures on Muslim organisations and the suspicion of Muslims in general. Groups such as the Council for Islamic Relations and the US Arab Anti-Discrimination Committee have grown stronger than before. Private philanthropies such as Atlantic Philanthropies and the Open Society Institute have also looked to this as a new area for programming, providing support to strengthen groups representing the interests of Muslims, Arabs and south Asian peoples in the US.[22]

There are signs of renewed vigour within the community of civil rights and civil liberties groups as well. The membership of the ACLU has doubled since 9/11 and it has been able to make up funding it forfeited from big foundations through increased support from small donors. There are signs that people are standing up against the abuse of power. An official with a leading US-based human rights organisation commented, 'it is not surprising that the pendulum has shifted (away from unquestioning support for counter-terrorism). The initial response (to the 9/11 attacks) was knee-jerk and arose out of fear. It was counter-productive and went against the rule of law. The American public recognises this and has begun operating from a more rational perspective. To a large extent, these measures were justified by 9/11 but that is slipping into the background now. People are stepping back and assessing how these measures are not congruous with principles of the law that Americans hold proud.'[23]

Counter-terrorism and civil society in the UK

The UK has a history of terrorist attacks dating back to the Northern Ireland conflicts.[24] For this reason, prior to 9/11, it had dedicated intelligence services, elite special forces and temporary terrorist legislation. Despite the peace settlement in Northern Ireland agreed in April 1998, the new Labour administration sought to retain terrorist laws to ostensibly deal with new international terrorist threats. In 2000 the Labour government introduced the Terrorism Act, the UK's first permanent anti-terrorist legislation (Gearty, 2007b). This law proscribed 45 international terrorist organisations, including 14 organisations in Northern Ireland. Ironically, even in the darkest days of the Northern Ireland conflict, governments would have approached the act of proscribing an organisation with much caution and anxiety.[25]

In aligning himself closely with Bush, former British Prime Minister Tony Blair made the UK a top target for global jihadists. Since 2001, the UK has introduced a repertoire of hard and soft measures to deal with terrorist threats and acts. After the 9/11 attacks in the US, the government introduced the Anti-Terrorism Crime and Security Act of

2001, which included a clause permitting the detention of foreign terror suspects without trial (Wadham, 2002; Shabi, 2004). The House of Lords ruled against this clause so the government then introduced control orders under the Prevention of Terrorism Act (2005), which became law in March 2006. This Act created several new offences such as inciting terrorism through statements that 'glorify the commission or preparation . . . of such [terrorist] acts or offences'.[26] The vagueness of this phrase caused considerable alarm amongst human rights lawyers, the media and academics, who argued that it amounted to a retreat from habeas corpus. In 2007 the government presented a draft terrorism bill, which again provoked sharp divisions amongst parliamentarians and intense debate in the media. A key area of controversy was the number of days a terrorist suspect could be detained without trial. Under the 2006 Terrorism Act, this period was extended from 14 to 28 days, making this the longest maximum period of detention without charge in Western Europe (Morris, 2007).

Since 2001 legislation has been amended to give the police, security and intelligence agencies stronger powers to investigate terrorist activity, such as allowing police authorities to obtain information on suspects from telecommunication companies and government files, and extra powers for questioning, surveillance and arrest. It has also sought to introduce biometric passports and identity cards. In spite of official denials, the UK government has been complicit in facilitating the rendition of terror suspects to third party countries and, allegedly in some cases, to Guantanamo Bay (Norton-Taylor, 2009). By 2008 the government had spent over £2.25 billion annually on counter-terrorism, surveillance and resilience, double the figure before 2001 (Home Office website (www.security.homeoffice@gov.uk), accessed August 2008).

The use of hard measures has not only provoked outrage amongst human rights lawyers, scholars and activists but also had a negative impact on Muslim communities. Between 9/11 and March 2007 there were 1,228 arrests under the Terrorism Act. High-profile raids in predominantly Muslim neighbourhoods have contributed to the perception of Muslims as suspect. Islamic bookshops, mosques and community centres have been under surveillance and the sermons of imams have been monitored. Muslim charities have been accused of having linkages with militant groups abroad, particularly in Pakistan and the Occupied Palestinian Territories. This suspicion has fuelled an image of Islam as a religion enjoying a unique affinity with terrorism. Unsurprisingly, the civil liberties of individuals of Asian descent have been infringed. Figures released by the Home Office in July 2004 showed a threefold increase in police use of stop-and-search powers against British Asians compared to a twofold increase for white people (Shabi, 2004). The Muslim Council of Britain claimed in a parliamentary select committee report in 2005 that Muslim communities perceived community relations to have worsened since 2001, recounting a rising number of Islamophobic incidents (House of Commons, 2005, p. 25). The report criticised the role of the media in perpetuating the misconception that Muslims, Islam and asylum-seekers were by default associated with terrorism because of the government's response to the threat of terrorism.

Hard measures have also affected charities, especially Muslim charities. In line with the new FATF special recommendation on terrorist financing, the UK has introduced counter-terrorist clauses into national Anti-Money-Laundering legislation and increased pressure on commercial and financial institutions to monitor large and unusual international money transfers. It has raised due diligence requirements for alternative remittance systems, causing some disruption in the transfer of remittances by diaspora communities. In October 2006 the then Chancellor, Gordon Brown, announced that the Treasury would use closed-source evidence to freeze the assets of bogus charities and foreign exchange bureaux acting as fronts for terrorist money (Elliott, 2006). The listing of charities under FATF SR VIII has put pressure on charities to increase scrutiny of money transfers to international partners and to make their procedures more transparent and accountable. Unlike the US, UK charities and donor organisations such as the DFID have not introduced specific anti-terrorist clauses into their aid agreements such as the ATC. Nor have they introduced any partner vetting system, as USAID has done.

The Charity Commission of England and Wales has played a key role in investigating the possible links of charities to terrorism. By May 2002 it reported having investigated ten charities since September 11, closing two of these and freezing the assets of one (Morris, 2002). One such case was the International Islamic Relief Organisation, which was accused of being linked to terrorist groups. The formal enquiry established that the charity was inactive and had no assets or funds in the UK and so removed it from the register. It has followed up various cases of charities that appear on the US list of designated terrorist organisations such as the Revival of Islamic Society, which was cleared of any links with terrorism. The Charity Commission has undertaken three separate investigations into Interpal (Palestinians Relief and Development Fund), which the US has designated as a terrorist organisation. The first two investigations cleared the charity's name. A third enquiry was launched in December 2006 and concluded in February 2009. During the course of the enquiry the National Westminster Bank closed Interpal's accounts following court action by victims of Hamas suicide bombings in Israel on the grounds that the bank transferred funds through Interpal accounts to Hamas (Sidel, 2008, p. 32). The enquiry recommended, inter alia, that the trustees introduce proper due diligence and monitoring procedures to ensure that their partners had no links with designated entities. It also recommended that the charity renounce its membership and association with the Union of Good, given the potential for linkage to be made between Interpal and designated entities associated with the Union (Charity Commission, 2009, pp. 31–35).

In recent years, the British media has covered several other high-profile cases of Muslim charities that have been alleged to be front organisations for terrorists. In 2006 the UN added the UK-based charity Sanabel Relief agency to its list of designated terrorist organisations for alleged links to the Libyan Islamic Fighting Group (Fickling, 2006). Around the same time, the Israeli government accused Islamic Relief, a well-established British charity that receives substantial government funding from DFID, of transferring funds to Hamas. It detained the programme director in the West Bank for over three months before releasing him without charge (McGreal, 2006).[27] The case raised diplomatic tensions between Israel and the UK. In August 2006, two British charities, Jamaat ud Dawa (Association of the Call to Righteousness) and Crescent Relief, were accused of diverting donations for the earthquake relief operations in Pakistani Kashmir to terrorists involved in planning an attack on transatlantic flights originating from the UK (Filkins and Mekhennet, 2006; Timmons, 2006). As these cases show, Muslim charities have so far borne the brunt of bureaucratic pressure arising from a discourse that asserts the vulnerability of charities to being misused by terrorist groups.

There has continued to be considerable pressure on UK charities despite the fact that there have been very few cases of charities having verifiable links with terrorist groups.[28] The quote at the start of this chapter expresses the prevailing suspicion cast over charities. In February 2006 the Home Office and Treasury initiated a review into charities and terrorism. This was followed by the preparation of the Charity Commission's own counter-terrorism strategy that was unveiled in July 2008. The Commission's approach relies on emphasising the benefits of charities to governments rather than highlighting their risk of misuse by terrorists.[29] This approach stands in sharp relief to the hard approach taken by US authorities. As an interviewee from the Commission put it, 'Our approach is light touch regulation that will be effective, which does not overburden the sector. It is a risk-based approach. Our approach is miles away from the sledgehammer approach in the US, where, if there is doubt, you just take out the charity.' By the middle of 2008, the Charity Commission had found only two registered charities to have any proven links with terrorism, namely the Tamil Relief Organisation and the Finsbury Park Mosque in North London. In a further case involving a trustee of the Tamil Students Union who appeared on a designated list, rather than banning the charity the Commission suspended the trustee and authorised the charity to continue its work.[30]

Following the London 7/7 bombings in 2005, the UK government began to focus more concertedly on the ideological aspects of counterterrorism and 'soft' measures. Former UK Prime Minister Tony Blair emphasised in a speech to the World Affairs Council in Los Angeles in August 2006 that 'We will not win the battle against this global extremism unless we win it at the level of values as much as force...' (Wintour, 2006). The government then launched a comprehensive raft of 'soft' measures to prevent radicalisation, foster alliances with 'moderate' Muslim communities, and seek their assistance with intelligence-gathering. Immediately after the 7/7 bombings, the government established seven community-led working groups to formulate recommendations on preventing extremism. However, the process was criticised as too rushed and reliant on prominent figures who did not represent Muslim communities. Moreover, the government's reluctance to countenance the view that the UK's foreign policy in Iraq might have aggravated feelings of alienation made dialogue difficult. Government efforts to build relations of trust with Muslim communities have also been hindered by an inconsistent approach. Some Muslims have questioned the sincerity of the government's outreach when the police have continued to launch raids on suspects in Muslim neighbourhoods, notably the bungled police raid in Forest Gate in east London in 2006.

As part of this new emphasis on the ideological aspects, in December 2006 the government announced that it was abandoning the term War on Terror, which it deemed to be counterproductive, creating tensions with British Muslims and the Islamic world (Regan, 2006). In March 2007, former Prime Minister Blair declared that 'hearts and minds' work would be at the core of the government's approach towards violent extremism. In this context the UK Department for Communities and Local Government has been charged with working with communities to prevent radicalisation and terrorism. It provided £6 million to local authorities to work with communities against violent extremism. Indicative of the new strategic approach, the former head of MI6, Sir Richard Dearlove, stated in a speech at Lloyd's of London that 'the policy has to change'. He admitted that despite initial sympathy with special renditions and hostile interrogation techniques, such tactics were counterproductive (Laville, 2007). Unsurprisingly, some Muslims have criticised these efforts, not only because funded groups may be used for intelligence-gathering but also because such groups may not be representative of the community.

A further dimension of the government's 'soft' approach has been to fund research through the ESRC into the causes of radicalisation. The government supported the placement of academics in the Research, Information and Communications Unit (RICU) set up within the Home Office in 2007, which has publicised research by the MI5 that challenged common stereotypes of terrorists as being illegal immigrants (Travis, 2008a). RICU has also developed a strategy for undermining the narratives of Al Qaeda and circulating messages to the UK media. The RICU was influential in advising the government to avoid 'aggressive' language and terms such as the War on Terror and to refer instead to 'violent extremism', and similarly to use the idea of 'shared values' rather than 'a battle of ideas' (Travis, 2008b). By 2008 annual spending on counter-terrorism, intelligence and resilience was expected to reach £2 billion, double the value prior to 9/11 (HM Government, 2006, p. 3).

Civil society responses to these assorted measures have been mixed. The human rights community and Muslim leaders and organisations have most consistently challenged the government's counter-terrorist measures. For example, the Amnesty International 2007 annual report noted that discrimination against Arabs, Asians and Muslims had intensified due to counter-terrorism. Civil society actors along with some parliamentarians have queried the legal basis of the Iraq invasion, the detention without trial of British terrorist suspects in Guantanamo Bay and Belmarsh prison in the UK, and the use of UK air-facilities for the rendition of suspected terrorists. They have also challenged the misuse of terrorist legislation. For example, at the Labour Party annual conference in 2005, an 82-year-old party member was removed from the conference by security staff for heckling the then Foreign Secretary, Jack Straw, and refused re-entry under anti-terrorist legislation.

Academics and researchers have also protested against the potential implications of anti-terrorist legislation for civil liberties. They have resisted requests from the government to report any suspicious student activities on university campuses to security agencies. In 2006 numerous academics refused to participate in a joint ESRC and FCO research bid on radicalisation and security on the grounds that demands to provide information about suspect individuals and groups not only endangered PhD students and researchers studying the Middle East but also compromised the independence of academe. In 2008 a postgraduate student at Nottingham University was detained under the Terrorism Act for having downloaded materials on Al Qaeda for his thesis research, again raising issues around academic freedom.

The Muslim Council of Britain and the Islamic Human Rights Commission have reflected concerns regarding the stigmatisation of Muslim communities and Islamophobic incidents to the government. Local Muslim community leaders have protested against police targeting of Muslims in stop-and-search activities and the excessive use of force in apprehending suspect terrorists. Moreover, they have challenged the media use of language that associates Islam with terrorism and the failure to give publicity to the release of innocent suspects after raids. Muslim charities have led efforts to dispel ideas that terrorists divert funds through, or in other ways misuse, charities. Islamic Relief, for example, was instrumental in establishing the Humanitarian Forum, which has facilitated closer cooperation between Western humanitarian organisations and NGOs in Muslim-majority countries. A key part of its work was building the governance capacity of Muslim NGOs and promoting greater transparency and accountability in their operations.

Apart from Muslim organisations and human rights groups, British-based NGOs operating in conflict zones where terrorist groups are allegedly active have protested against the potential implications of new due diligence requirements under anti-terrorism and anti–money-laundering legislation for their operations. The British Overseas NGOs for Development established a Global Security and Development Network from 2003 to 2005 to examine the effects of and give recommendations on policies and measures that sought to combine development resources with security objectives. Other development NGOs, such as Christian Aid and Action Aid, have conducted their own investigations into the effects of the War on Terror on development policy and practice. Humanitarian organisations such as Médecins Sans Frontières (MSF) have voiced concern over the effects of increasing engagement by the military in development work in conflict areas on humanitarian groups.

However, it was only when the UK government widened its scrutiny of civil society to the voluntary sector in general with the launch of its review in February 2006 that mainstream civil society organisations began to voice concerns about the post-9/11 security regime. Up till then the effect of these measures had been felt most sharply amongst Muslim communities, refugees and asylum-seekers (Noxolo, 2006). Though anti–money-laundering regulations apply to all non-profit organisations, in general most voluntary sector organisations, pressure groups and social movements in the UK neither particularly felt the effects of the new counter-terrorist regime nor did they interpret the targeting of Muslim civil society organisations as a matter of concern for them. Indeed they failed to see the broader political implications of this targeting of Muslim organisations and communities for the independence and spaces of civil society.

In response to the Treasury/Home Office review of the links between charities and terrorism, the National Council for Voluntary Organisations (NCVO), the main umbrella body for voluntary and community organisations in the UK, organised a panel of advisors to prepare a shadow report entitled 'Security and Civil Society', which criticised the government for failing to consult with the sector on the counter-terrorist proposals. This failure to consult was particularly jarring set against the prevailing good relations that existed between the Labour government and voluntary organisations, as reflected in the Compact Agreements signed between the government and the sector (Quigley and Pratten, 2007, p. 7). The concerns of the sector were that legislation affecting charities was formulated by people who were unfamiliar with the sector and its broad benefits to society. They also questioned an approach that tended to target the sector as a whole, and thereby threatened to undermine public confidence in charities.

The European Union

Under pressure from the US the EU has adopted a range of hard and soft measures since September 11 to combat terrorism. In the climate of fear generated by politicians after the attacks the EU also succumbed to the idea of 'exceptionality'. This was despite its long and varied experience of terrorist activities that had already put in place diverse national counter-terrorist regimes. Within a few months the EU had drawn up its first-ever terrorist list, designating 29 individuals and 13 groups.[31] By December 2006 the list included over 50 groups and 50 individuals. Over the next few years the EU gradually built up its institutional and legislative armoury to demonstrate its commitment to fighting terrorism. In June 2002 the EU Council issued a Framework Decision on Combating Terrorism, which paved the way for the establishment of a committee of experts on terrorism (CODEXTER). In 2004 a new European

Anti-Terrorism Coordinator was appointed. Following the Madrid bombings in March 2004, the EU agreed an 'Action Plan on Combating Terrorism' and integrated security further into trade and development agendas. The following year the Council of Europe signed the Convention for the Prevention of Terrorism (CETS No. 196).

With the basic building blocks of a counter-terrorist response in place, the EU under the UK's presidency announced in December 2005 a new EU Counter-Terrorism Strategy. This has four key strands – namely prevent, protect, pursue and respond – a structure that is later reflected in the UK strategy. Cooperation on police and judicial matters within the EU has increased substantially since 2001. The EU strategy covers a range of counter-terrorism activities such as expanded data surveillance, inclusion of biometric information in identity and travel documents, anti-radicalisation programmes, border protection and security-related research.

This new EU-wide strategy set the scene for a series of counter-terrorist legislation, policies and measures, which directly and indirectly affected NGOs. As elsewhere, the linking of terrorism with non-profit organisations took place against a wider background of increasing concern amongst funders and political leaders about the transparency, legitimacy and accountability of NGOs. The launch of the War on Terror added a sense of urgency to the issue, casting suspicion over possible links between NGOs and terrorism and undermining a more rational evidence-based approach. The EU Counter-Terrorist Strategy had singled out the non-governmental sector as a priority in countering terrorist financing. Specifically, paragraph 29 of the EU Counter-Terrorist Strategy states, 'In addition, tackling the misuse of the non-profit sector remains a priority' (Council of the European Union, 14469/4/05 REV 4, 2005).

Key hard measures relevant to civil society groups were the July 2005 Commission Communication on the Prevention of and Fight Against Terrorist Financing Through Enhanced Level Coordination and Greater Transparency of the Non-Profit Sector (COM (2005) 620) and the Framework for the Code of Conduct for Non-Profit Organisations to Enhance Transparency and Accountability. In February 2006 the EU Council adopted the FATF Interpretative Note to SR VIII, which outlined the main elements of implementation. The goal of the Code was to protect non-profit organisations from the threat of being exploited for the financing of terrorism and other criminal abuse. What is ironic is that despite attempts by charities and foundations over the past two decades to introduce European Statutes for Associations and for Foundations (Breen, 2008), the introduction of counter-terrorist legislation that directly and indirectly affects civil society organisations has proceeded extraordinarily rapidly. Furthermore, as Breen warns, counter-terrorist policies could be used as a pretext by national member states to erect or maintain barriers to the free movement of civil society organisations in the EU and so further hinder the prospects of any such Europe-wide statutes. Nevertheless the speed at which agreement on the Code has proceeded has been considerably slower when compared to the UK and the US, not least because of the need to reach consensus amongst 27 member states. Following approval of the Code by the College of Commissioners in December 2005, the EU established a contact group in March 2006 made up of national experts and non-profit organisations to fine-tune the Code and to organise a consultative conference. However, approval of the contact group was delayed and as of the time of writing, it was still awaiting authorisation and the planned conference had not taken place. The European Commission (EC) Directorate-General for Justice, Freedom and Security commissioned Matrix Insight to assess the extent of abuse of non-profit organisations, including for terrorist purposes, and the European Centre for Not-For-Profit Law (ECNL) to examine the impact of FATF SRVIII on the non-profit sector. A key conclusion from the Matrix report was that the evidence base for non-profit abuse was poor, relying primarily on media reporting and anecdotal accounts leading, in their words, 'to a plethora of unwarranted inferences and inductions in the press' (Matrix Insight, 2008, pp. 8, 22, 67). The report thus recommended that the EC should be cautious in introducing any new forms of regulation and legislation and focus instead on developing existing forms but only after 'a proper impact evaluation' (Matrix, 2008, p. 69).

The response of member states to counter-terrorist measures has been varied, with agreement on some issues and controversy on others. Prior to 2004, only one country had laws against the glorification of terrorism, namely Spain; by 2006 all 25 European states had introduced this. Some member states have unilaterally entered into bilateral agreements with the US to provide data on passengers travelling to the US, despite efforts by the EU to negotiate a common position. There have also been reports of several EU member states partaking in processes of 'rendition' of suspect terrorists by allowing use of airfields and airspace. Similarly, there has been a varied response to the specific measures applying to NGOs. Whilst the Swedish government consulted non-profits on these issues, the French government did not alter its national legislation in line with the EU and FATF recommendations as the laws were deemed to be already adequate to purpose. The Dutch government passed the Act on

Terrorist Crimes in 2004 in line with the EU counter-terrorist framework and two years later issued further legislation proscribing organisations on the UN or EU watchdog lists, including charities (Sidel, 2008, p. 48). The UK government responded, as described earlier, by launching an enquiry into terrorism and the charitable sector in early 2006.

Apart from the anti-terrorist financing measures and the proposed EU Code of Conduct for NGOs, the EU Counter-Terrorist Strategy also engages civil society in other aspects of its work. A key strand of the strategy is to combat radicalisation through dialogue with moderate Muslims in Europe and elsewhere. As the document states, 'We need to empower moderate voices by engaging with Muslim organisations and faith groups that reject the distorted version of Islam put forward by Al-Qa'ida and others' (Council of the European Union, 14781/1/05, 2005, paragraph 11). The strand includes the training of foreign imams in European languages, changing perceptions of Western and European policies amongst Muslim communities, correcting inaccurate perceptions of Islam and Muslims and tackling radicalisation in prisons, in education and on the Internet. In July 2006 the Council of Europe approved guidelines to combat radicalisation and recruitment through media communication. Both the 6th and the 7th EU Research Framework Programmes have commissioned cross-border studies on radicalisation. The role of civil society is considered to be paramount to the success of the strategy, as seen in this statement: 'The key to our success will be the degree to which non-governmental groups – communities, religious authorities and other organisations – across Europe play an active part in countering the rhetoric of the extremists and highlighting their criminal acts' (Council of European Union, 14781/1/05, 2005). These various activities thus address a much wider range of civil society actors than just funded, welfare-focussed non-profit organisations, which had hitherto been the main interlocutors for civil society within the EU. However, the degree of attention given to these softer measures is likely to vary across states, depending on the perceived threat of Al Qaeda–related terrorism and state policies towards integration and migration.

The EU's external policies are also relevant to international humanitarian and development NGOs, especially those working in conflict zones. Counter-terrorism work is now mainstreamed into several of the EU's external agreements such as the 2005 Revised Cotonou Agreement,[32] the Euro-Mediterranean Code of Conduct Against Terrorism (2005) and the draft agreement on counter-terrorism and non-proliferation with Pakistan. The EU, like other bilateral and multilateral donors, also provides assistance for strengthening counter-terrorist capacity in aid-recipient countries such as Indonesia, Algeria and Morocco. It supports a range of counter-terrorism–related projects on border protection and anti-terrorist financing in several regions such as South-East Asia and the Balkans. The Stability Fund for 2007–2013 will increase resources available for such purposes. Since 2007 the EU has provided financial aid to the African Union's Center for Counter-Terrorism. Whilst these external policies on counter-terrorism may not directly target civil society organisations, they nevertheless alter the environment in which international and local civil society organisations operate and the perceptions of external assistance and strengthen the coercive capacities of states.

The responses of civil society actors to the post-9/11 counter-terrorism regime have been piecemeal and compartmentalised, the most robust challenges coming from human rights groups, lawyers and scholars and groups directly affected by the measures. For example, in December 2006 the European Court of First Instance ruled in favour of an appeal by the People's Mujahadeen of Iran, which had been placed on the EU's terrorist list and had its assets frozen. The Court ruled that the organisation had not received a fair hearing because it had not received a 'statement of reasons' for being placed on the list. Since then several designated groups have successfully appealed against their designation in the same Court.[33] The EU rulings have implications for the UN Security Council, which has yet to provide any reasons for designation and have very limited procedures for appeals to de-list.

The UK-based EU Statewatch is one of the only few organisations in Europe to monitor and critically analyse EU legislation from the perspective of civil liberties and human rights. It was a leading founding member of the European Civil Liberties Network that was set up by nine organisations in October 2005. Given the prior lack of any effective network linking human rights groups around counter-terrorist issues, its formation was significant. The network aims to share information and to respond jointly to the US, EU and UN anti-terrorist measures that affect NGOs. The network has argued that the procedures for removing innocent groups from the list are unclear and that there are no procedures for reconciling the UN, EU, US and member states' lists.

Up until 2005 when specific hard measures targeting civil society were announced, there was little co-ordinated debate across Europe about the implications of the new counter-terrorist regime for civil society and consequently few demands to be consulted by the relevant authorities on these issues. Nor was there substantial co-ordinated action around the implications of 'exceptional' laws and measures for civil societies and judicial oversight; nor indeed about the validity of the claim to 'exceptionality', which has proven to be a political and ideological device to re-define the boundaries between states and societies. There was also minimal Europe-wide civil society action on top–down anti-radicalisation initiatives, data surveillance or the increasing prominence given to security objectives in external agreements and foreign assistance. Some of this relates to the fact that apart from those in the UK, there are few civil liberties groups operating in Europe.[34] Furthermore, most mainstream civil society groups in Europe gave little attention to the effects of counter-terrorist measures on Muslim organisations, reflecting a more general attitude amongst the public and political society that such measures applied only to Muslims. This narrow and politically blinkered perspective hindered any serious political analysis of how the new counter-terrorist regime affected civil society across Europe.

However, there are two important European initiatives to counter the potential effects of the increasing suspicion cast over Muslim charities, namely the Humanitarian Forum and the Swiss Montreux Initiative. As discussed in the UK section, the Humanitarian Forum was established in June 2004 to foster closer co-operation between Western humanitarian organisations and NGOs in Muslim-majority countries. The Swiss Federal Department of Foreign Affairs set up the Montreux Initiative in 2005 to reduce the obstacles facing Islamic charities, to enhance their capacity and to increase confidence amongst Western donors and security agencies in the legitimacy and activities of such charities (Kroessin). One step in this direction has been the establishment of a 'white' list of Muslim NGOs.

Whilst large funded NGOs and EU umbrella groups had been largely silent on the effects of the post-9/11 counter-terrorist regime on Muslim groups in the EU, this changed when measures applying specifically to NGOs were announced in 2005, signalling that the sector as a whole was coming under scrutiny. It was then that organisations such as CON-CORD (the European NGO Confederation for Relief and Development) and Cordaid began to mobilise NGOs across the EU, focussing specifically on the issues of anti-terrorist financing measures and the proposed Code of Conduct for NGOs. A key concern they had was that because the interpretation of these measures would be left to member states, this could lead to a more restrictive regulatory environment for NGOs in countries where relations with governments were tense. In 2006, CONCORD organised numerous meetings with relevant EU officials and wrote letters expressing concern about the potential administrative burden that these measures would place on non-profit organisations, particularly small ones; the lack of evidence about links between NGOs and the financing of terrorism; and the non-proportionality of the code, given that such links were rare. Furthermore, it argued that the new EU counter-terrorist legislation passed the burden of liability on to civil society groups. This could create particular problems for humanitarian groups, which might find themselves inadvertently associated in an indirect way with a denounced organisation, and potentially risked the delivery of humanitarian aid in conflict areas. In 2008 Cordaid played a key role in organising a Europe-wide response to the study reports on the non-profit sector commissioned by the EC, involving organisations such as the European Foundation Centre, the Danish NGO Platform and Kvinna till Kvinna (personal communication, September 2008). It also liaised with coalition groups in the US about their experiences in advocacy work around counter-terrorist measures and their effects on charities.

There has also been some, but limited, exchange between Europe-wide civil society networks and the US. In early 2007, for example, the US groups Grantmakers without Borders, OMB Watch and Urgent Action Fund approached European NGOs to create a joint network to monitor the impact of counter-terrorist measures on civil society organisations in Europe and the US. Following an international conference held at the London School of Economics (LSE) in mid-2008, US and European civil society groups formally met and established an Internet network to exchange information. Other transatlantic initiatives include joint efforts by the European Foundation Centre and the US Council on Foundations to draft jointly Principles of Accountability for International Philanthropy.

Conclusion

Whilst the UK, the US and the EU have all introduced combinations of hard and soft measures to address the perceived international terrorist threat, there have also been significant differences in the emphasis given to these. The existence of a long-established independent charity regulator in the UK has meant that the government has relied on this as the first point of call for the implementation of measures to protect the sector from terrorist abuse. In contrast, the US has relied more on prosecutors than charity regulators to tackle allegations of terrorist financing in charities (Sidel, 2008, p. 7). As an interviewee described this, the US has adopted a 'sledgehammer' approach to civil society. The EU has fallen in line by introducing anti-terrorist financing measures relevant to NGOs and by proposing a framework for enhancing the transparency and governance of non-profits so as to safeguard against abuse by terrorist groups. However, with its burgeoning bureaucracy and convoluted processes necessary for consensus amongst 27 states, the processes have been much slower.

The effects of the emerging post-9/11 counter-terrorist regimes have been most acutely felt amongst migrant communities, asylum-seekers, Muslims and international NGOs (INGOs) working in conflict zones. The discourse of Islamic terrorism, media prominence given to raids on suspect terrorists in areas populated by Muslim communities and surveillance of Muslim charities, mosques and bookshops have cast a veil of suspicion over Muslims and Islam. The War on Terror regime has created a division between 'bad' and 'good' civil society and in doing so has rendered certain parts of civil society subject to intense scrutiny. It has been impossible to contain the labelling and scrutiny of 'bad' civil society to those isolated and rare groups that have proved to be engaged in terrorist activities. Moreover, it has been impossible to prevent the more generalised application of terrorist laws to citizen actions that have nothing to do with terrorism. Whether in the UK, Europe or the US, there is an almost Mc-Carthy-like atmosphere of 'you are guilty until proven innocent if you are Muslim or have any dealings with Muslim countries'. It is in this context that INGOs and local groups working in conflict areas where terrorists are alleged to operate have felt the brunt of the anti-financing regulations, especially if they receive US funds.

Civil society responses to the emerging post-9/11 counter-terrorist regimes have been disappointing. It has been primarily human rights groups, lawyers and scholars and Muslim leaders and organisations who have persistently challenged the implications of the War on Terror regime for civil liberties and human rights, and highlighted the way Muslims and Islam have been constructed as problematic and associated with terrorism. The silence of mainstream civil society in respect of the targeting of Muslim communities and the violation of civil liberties has been alarming. It is only when governments broadened their vista to NGOs or the voluntary sector that mainstream civil society paid serious attention to the emerging counter-terrorist regimes. Such silence raises key questions about the impact of government funding on the independence of NGOs and more generally about how funded organisations conceptualise practically civil society. The quiescence of mainstream civil society with the new counter-terrorist legislation, measures and practices reflects an understanding of civil society that not only is limited to funded, welfare organisations but also excludes other social organisations such as mosques, madrassas and Islamic community centres. It also reflects a disturbing depth of apoliticalness which fails to see the potential effects of restrictive legislation on the spaces of civil society.

In the next chapter we focus on the effects of the War on Terror regime on aid policy and practice, exploring the cases of the UK, the US, Australia, Sweden and the EU.

Notes

1. This quote was referred to in Quigley and Pratten, 2007, p. 27.
2. Here we draw on the work of Chris Sparks (2003), who suggests two types of governmental responses to the politics of fear, namely eradicating fear by 'hunt[ing] out and destroy[ing] agents of danger without and within' (p. 201) and managing fear.
3. Indeed the European Community and the 27 member states account for over half of all ODA recorded by the Development Assistance Committee (DAC) (2007, p. 1).
4. The FATF is the world's main anti–money-laundering body and has 31 member countries. In 2002 it agreed to try to make its new rules binding on all countries. These rules included freezing terrorists' assets and these rules were applied to not only banking but also money-service businesses such as the hawala system, charities and universities.
5. These include a good character test for registration as a British citizen and a lower threshold to permit deportation. See HM Government (2006, p. 19) for further details.
6. Senior researcher, Danish Institute for Strategic Studies, 28 November 2007.
7. Authors' interview with charity lawyer. Washington, DC. 24 April 2008.
8. *Ibid.*
9. *Ibid.*
10. Participants' contributions. 'Aid, Security and Civil Society in the Post-9/11 Context'. International Workshop Organised by the Centre for Civil Society, LSE. 28–29 June 2007. London.
11. 'Al Qaeda Masters Terrorism on the Cheap'. *Washington Post*. 24 August 2008.
12. Authors' telephone interview with civil liberties organisation officials. 13 May 2008.
13. Interview, USAID, April 2008.
14. 'USAID Tells NGOs It Will Proceed with Plan to Use Secret Watch List.' OMB Watch. 15 April 2008. Available at http://www.ombwatch.org/article/articleview/4228/1/{category_id}.
15. 'Foreign Aid Groups Face Terror Screens.' *Washington Post*. 23 August 2007.
16. 'USAID Announces that it Will Likely Proceed with Implementation of the Partner Vetting System.' Interaction. Press release. 11 April 2008.
17. Comments by Mark Sidel. International Society for Third Sector Research meeting. Barcelona. July 2008.

18. Authors' telephone interview with civil liberties organisation officials. 13 May 2008.
19. *Ibid.*
20. Authors' interview with charity lawyer. Washington, DC. 24 April 2008.
21. Authors' interview with human rights organisation official. Washington, DC. 25 April 2008.
22. Authors' telephone interview with civil liberties organisation officials. 13 May 2008.
23. Authors' interview with human rights organisation official. Washington, DC. 25 April 2008.
24. This is not to deny that the US had previous experiences of terrorism. The 1993 bombing of the World Trade Centre triggered legislation that proscribed terrorist organisations and barred 'material support' to such organisations. The International Emergency Economic Powers Act was enacted in 1977 and included terrorist financing through charities as an activity that was inimical to national security (Sidel, 2008, p. 11).
25. It was not until 1974, despite numerous bombing campaigns, that the Irish Republican Army (IRA) was banned because proscription was then considered a draconian measure (Gearty, 2007a, p. 356).
26. See Part 1, paragraph one (Encouragement of Terrorism), clause 3a, of 2006 Terrorist Act on Home Office website. As of August 2008 two groups have been proscribed under this offence, namely Al Gurabaa and the Saved Sect.
27. For Israel's and Islamic Relief's perspective on this see Israel Ministry of Foreign Affairs (2006) and Islamic Relief (2006), respectively.
28. The Charity Commission Operational Guidance, for example, states that 'the incidence of charitable involvement with terrorist organisations is very rare'.
29. Interview. Charity Commission. 29 July 2008.
30. In 2007 the Commission conducted 200 investigations on compliance, of which only 40 cases were formal statutory enquiries, and only one the Tamil Students Union, related to counter-terrorism, thus pointing to the rarity of links between counter-terrorism and charities.
31. The list appeared in December 2001.
32. The revised agreement provides for inclusion of a clause which confirms partners' international cooperation in the fight against terrorism.
33. For detailed information about these cases see the website of Statewatch.
34. Comment by human rights activists. LSE round-table. June 2006.

4
Civil Society, Security and Aid: Shifting Donor Perspectives

> We will direct every resource at our command – every means of diplomacy, every tool of intelligence, every instrument of law enforcement, every financial influence, and every necessary weapon of war – to the disruption and to the defeat of the global terror network. Our response involves far more than instant retaliation and isolated strikes. Americans should not expect one battle, but a lengthy campaign, unlike any other we have ever seen.
>
> George W. Bush, former US President, address to joint session of Congress, 20 September 2001[1]

Concerned about the perceived threat to global markets and global security, UN leaders, politicians in Europe and the US have articulated a discourse that links security more firmly with development. Kofi Annan, Tony Blair, Gordon Brown and George Bush have all rehearsed the refrain that poverty and terrorism are somehow interrelated. Though it has been increasingly acknowledged that the terrorists involved in the New York, London and Madrid attacks were not typically from impoverished backgrounds, illiterate or educated in madrassas, nevertheless the assumption of some connection between poverty, alienation, exclusion and radicalisation leading to terrorism continues to be made. Bilateral development agencies, international NGOs, some politicians in the South and development activists have in turn capitalised on this refrain to lobby for an increase in aid.

This chapter explores the proposition that the global War on Terror regime has contributed in diverse and complex ways towards the increasing securitisation of aid policy and practice. In this way the global War on Terror regime has highlighted the strategic relevance of aid to the pursuit of global and national security interests at a time when its ideological rationale in the post–Cold War era had almost disappeared. It is not the proposition here that the global War on Terror regime has singly subordinated development aid policy and institutions to the security agendas of the US or other advanced capitalist countries. Nor do we propose that the global War on Terror has had no impact on how development agendas are conceived, how aid policy is formulated or how aid institutions behave. Furthermore, we do not suggest that the War on Terror regime has wholly reframed the way donor agencies engage with non-governmental public actors. Rather we propose that the global War on Terror regime has accelerated and consolidated trends in development thinking and aid policy and practice that already were emerging during the 1990s. Specifically, we argue that the global War on Terror regime has built on these trends of the 1990s, leading to a more generalised securitisation of development and aid policy that is no longer just confined to conflict and post-conflict settings.

In this chapter we explore this proposition of an increasing securitisation of aid through the lens of selected bilateral donor agencies. We focus on those bilateral donor agencies that have moved furthest in linking development and security concerns, namely the US Agency for International Development (USAID), the AusAID and the DFID. However, we also bring out important differences in the way donors have realised these connections, be that in the presentation of these links in mission statements, in programming or in operational practices. We also include the contrastive case of SIDA, which has eschewed increasing links between aid policy, programming and practices and national security concerns in the post-9/11 context. The chapter identifies some emerging patterns across agencies and notes differences related to the security priorities of different governments, the bureaucratic architecture of aid and the historical backdrop to aid. The first section looks at how the global War on Terror regime galvanises the already existing trend towards the securitisation of aid. The subsequent sections look in turn at the various manifestations of these processes across USAID, DFID, AusAID and SIDA.

Out of the shadow into the limelight: The securitisation of aid

The securitisation of development and aid policy can be observed at a number of levels. First, at the macro-level, political leaders articulate a view that poverty, deprivation and terrorism are related, with the crudest versions claiming direct causality. The recruitment of development and aid policy into global security agendas is mirrored in the closer co-operation between global security, military and development agencies at the supranational level and the creation of new co-ordinating structures and positions; in the juxtaposition of security and development concerns in the speeches of UN leaders and the documentation of multilateral institutions; in the propagation of common approaches and conceptualisations such as 'whole-of-government approach' or 'fragile states'; and in the shift in focus away from globalisation and inequality to globalisation and security threats.

Second, at the meso-level, it can be observed in the closer interaction between aid, foreign policy and security agencies within national states. This is reflected, for example, in the creation of new co-ordinating structures, the establishment of liaison positions and the pooling of resources; in the direction of bilateral aid flows; in the grand mission statements and developmental plans of bilateral donors; in the percolation of common global discourses and approaches across bilateral development agencies such as fragile states or 'whole-of-government' approaches in the closer linkages made between foreign and domestic policies; and in the engagement with a wider range of donors. Third, it can be observed at the micro-level of programming and operations such as in increasing interaction between civil and military agencies, in counter-terrorist assistance, in support of curriculum reform in madrassas and in support to civil society.

The increasing securitisation of aid has to be understood against a background of several emerging trends in development thinking and aid policy. First, throughout the 1990s there has been growing recognition of the need for global responses to global issues such as climate change, child-trafficking and international crime, and with it the creation of new horizontal funds to support action on specific issues of international concern. Second, national donors were increasingly recognising the need for greater co-ordination in the delivery of aid, though attempts to co-ordinate at the operational level often withered due to a lack of institutional commitment or poor strategy. Third, the rise of the 'good governance' agenda in the wake of the Cold War drew systematic attention to the potential of civil society as an agent of development. As donors discovered the virtues of civil society, they began to systematically engage with non-governmental public actors through civil society–strengthening programmes. However, as donors gained more experience in working through and with civil society, they also began to have doubts about this engagement. Areas of concern included the accountability, legitimacy and transparency of NGOs; the transaction costs of working with a myriad of small, non-governmental development agencies; the balance between supporting civil society and funding government; and the most cost-effective and appropriate strategy for working with civil society. Beginning in the late 1990s, donors began to take stock of their relations with civil society. The heyday of civil society was about to take a new turn. Fourth, as discussed in Chapter 2, the increasing convergence of development and security agendas was already in evidence during the 1990s. This had led to the emergence of new conflict structures in development agencies, increasing co-operation between military and civilian actors and the seeping of conflict into development discourse, strategy and analysis.

The launch of the War on Terror gave added impetus to these trends, accelerating their progress and justifying their direction. First, concerns about global insecurity called for, amongst other things, responses from the development community. The perceived threat of global terrorism accompanied other 'global issues' that demanded global responses. Second, as development became co-opted into the global War on Terror regime, the need for a global response to issues of poverty and alienation added force to the emerging trend towards greater donor co-ordination. This trend found its most vivid expression in the Paris Declaration of 2005, which achieved consensus on the need for harmonisation and co-ordination of aid. Third, the global War on Terror regime added impetus to the process of donors reassessing their relations with civil society. The separate threads of caution and doubt that were already emerging from the late 1990s had formed a loosely woven cloth on which the events of 9/11 were to stamp their own motifs of suspicion and concern. Aware in theory that civil society constituted more than just developmental NGOs or community groups, the gaze of the War on Terror regime on Muslim communities opened donors' eyes to a previously little noticed part of civil society. At the same time global concerns about terrorist threats cast a shadow over donor perceptions' of NGO actors as untainted by extremism or radicalism. Now it was suggested that charities were vulnerable to manipulation by terrorist groups for money-laundering purposes and, even worse, that some charities might be mere fronts for terrorists groups. Fourth, the War on Terror had the effect of generalising the convergence of development and security interests beyond the confines of the 'New Wars'. Security concerns now became mainstreamed into development agendas and discourses, whilst development in turn became co-opted into global and national security agendas.

National games: Bringing security into the development mainstream and the co-optation of development into security

In this section we explore the securitisation of aid through the lens of four countries, namely Australia, the US, the UK and Sweden. In each case we trace the changes in development thinking, aid policy and practice since 2001. We draw attention to how security concerns percolate into development agendas, influencing the purposes of aid and the direction of aid flows. We examine the closer interaction between foreign policy, defence and development departments and the creation of new structures to better coordinate work across the three 'D's' – development, diplomacy and defence. We look at the way security issues become routinised through programme design, through on-the-ground relations between military, security and development personnel and through the re-shaping of relations with civil society. We examine each bilateral relation in turn and draw together the common patterns and the areas of difference in the concluding section.

Australia

The increasing convergence of security and development in Australian aid has to be set against the background of the bombing of a nightclub frequented by many Australian tourists in Bali in October 2002 and the shifting global politics arising out of the September 11 attacks in New York.[2] Australia has been an important ally of the US in the so-called War on Terror and has provided troops in Iraq and Afghanistan. The securitisation of aid in the Australian context can be observed in several respects: first, the statements by politicians and government leaders concerning the links between insecurity, development and fragile states and the subsequent policy documentation; second, the increasing interaction between security and development parts of government in addressing security issues; third, increases in aid transfers to front-line War on Terror states such as Iraq and Afghanistan; fourth, the increasing emphasis given to security objectives by aid agencies as seen in mission statements and departmental reports justifying policy; fifth, the establishment of specific aid programmes aimed at enhancing security on the basis that security and development are linked.

The shift in approach of the Australian government to the linkages between security and development post-9/11 and post-Bali are reflected in the statements of politicians and departmental leaders and in policy documentation. Within a year of the Bali bombings the government had issued a report entitled 'Counter-Terrorism and Australian Aid'. This report depicts terrorism as a key challenge to the aid programme's objective of 'advancing the national interest by reducing poverty and promoting sustainable development' (Australian Government/AusAID, 2003). It establishes a clear link between poverty and terrorism as seen in the report: 'While poverty provides no justification for acts of terror, entrenched poverty can create an environment in which terrorist networks may be fostered' (Australian Government/AusAID, 2003, p. 4). Aid can then be levered in two ways to contribute to counter-terrorism efforts: first, by building the capacity of partner countries to deal with terrorist threats; and second, by promoting environments that foster economic growth and poverty reduction, thereby minimising the opportunities for terrorist networks to emerge (Australian Government/AusAID, 2003, p. 5).

In a speech at the Australian Strategic Policy Institute in 2005, the Director General of AusAID, Bruce Davis, set out clearly in his introduction how development and security agendas had become increasingly aligned in the millennium:

> Indeed, it is a measure of the holistic manner in which strategic issues are now understood in Australia that an AusAID representative would be invited to address a "Defence and Security" forum on a topic of this kind. It was not too long ago that aid and development lay firmly on the periphery of serious considerations of Australia's security and strategic interests. Aid was often regarded as a somewhat ill-defined process of "doing-good", a process which had little tangible impact on the strategic environment faced by Australia and its policy makers. These times are now over. Today I would like to talk briefly to you about the alignment of the development and security agendas in recent years. ... And I will conclude by outlining the future directions of the Australian aid program, and the important role it will continue to play in building a strategic environment that favours Australia's interests.

Here he refers not only to the increasing coordination of government departments such as the AusAID, the Australian Federal Police and the Australian Defence Force around security issues but also to the gradual alignment of development and security objectives, a trend that he sees as continuing. Aid has now become, as Davis states in his conclusion, 'one part of an integrated Australian approach to the complex security challenges of our region'. With AusAID effectively downgraded from a department to part of the foreign policy portfolio within the Department of Foreign Affairs and Trade under the current government (O'Connor *et al.*, 2006, p. 176), it has been administratively and politically easier for the government to ensure that development goals resonate with Australia's commercial and security interests.

These shifts in the Australian development agenda are reflected in the increasing prominence given to fragile states. Australia is portrayed as an island surrounded by a sea of fragile states that potentially threaten its security for fragile states 'have proven capable of incubating and sometimes exporting problems as diverse as disease,...drugs smuggling...and potentially terrorism'. Moreover, Davis rehearses the theme that poverty and insecurity are inextricably linked. In his words,

> This is because security is a pre-requisite for development. ...Conflict and instability are powerful reversers of development gains and a primary cause of poverty. It is also recognised that underdevelopment is itself a security threat.... The development challenges of our region are thus – to a significant extent – also challenges to our own security.
>
> (Davis, 2005)

It is significant therefore that in the context of Australia's role as ally in the War on Terror and its self-portrayal as a developed country under threat from underdevelopment that providing aid to fragile states has moved to the forefront of AusAID's agenda.

The increasing securitisation of aid in Australia is reflected in a rise in aid flows to fragile states, including Afghanistan and Iraq. Indicative of this new emphasis of fragile states is the Australian government's policy paper in 2002 on 'Peace, Conflict and Development Policy' and the 2003 Department of Foreign Affairs and Trade Policy White Paper 'Advancing the National Interest', which laid out the rationale for this emphasis. With regard to fragile states, the percentage of funding allocated to the Pacific has risen from 30 per cent in 1995/1996 to 40 per cent in 2005/2006, the focus being on the 'fragile states' of the Solomon Islands and Papua New Guinea (Reality of Aid, 2006, p. 2). It is also noteworthy that Iraq figures ninth amongst AusAID's top ten recipients of gross ODA, with an allocation of AUD21 million, the rest all being Pacific-Asian countries.[3] Since 1999 the volume of ODA going to the Middle East has increased, primarily to support humanitarian and reconstruction efforts in Iraq and Afghanistan. Though assistance to the Middle East is not a substantial part of Australia's ODA, it is significant that this has increased since 1999 given the shift in global politics post-2001.

The concern over security has increased the interaction between government departments and promoted a 'whole-of-government approach' to aid and development policy. Aid and development are no longer issues of significance only to AusAID but now engage a range of ministries, including the Prime Minister's Department. The most prominent example of the 'whole-of-government' approach to aid is the Regional Assistance Mission to Solomon Islands (RAMSI), the budget of which was increased from 2003 to 2004 from AUD37.4 million to AUD168.5 million.[4] Almost half of this amount, that is AUD79 million, was contributed as ODA by other government departments such as the Attorney General's, AusAID, Department of Finance and Administration and the Australian Federal Police (Parliamentary Library, 2004). Of the AUD201.6 million budget for RAMSI in 2004/2005, almost half was allocated to the Australian Federal Police to build the capacity of the Royal Solomon Islands Police to maintain law and order (Parliamentary Library, 2004, p. 1).[5]

In terms of programming the growing convergence between development and security agendas has led to greater focus on governance, counter-terrorism assistance, checks on civil society partners, and closer civil–military relations. Since 2001 the percentage of funding allocated to governance compared to other sectors has more than doubled. Whilst in 1999/2000 15 per cent of aid was devoted to governance, by 2005/2006 this had more than doubled to 36 per cent.[6] Most of this allocation has gone to law and justice (47 per cent), compared to 21 per cent for public sector effectiveness and 13 per cent for civil society and human rights (O'Connor, 2006, p. 177). This investment in governance reflects the growing awareness by the government that certain Pacific nations increasingly resemble fragile states that for reasons of national security can no longer be overlooked (Parliamentary Library, 2004, p. 1). However, the 2005 OECD Peer Review expressed concern that the attention given to the law and order aspect of governance, as compared with say civil society and democracy or public sector effectiveness, could undermine the stated poverty reduction focus of Australian aid (OECD, 2005b, p. 39).

Over the last seven years the Australian government has established specific aid programmes to address issues of security and terrorism. Aid to counter-terrorism falls under the governance portfolio. According to the policy document of 2003, 'Counter-Terrorism and Australian Aid', the aim has been twofold: first, to strengthen local capacity to manage terrorist threats; and second, to promote an environment conducive to poverty reduction and economic growth so as to reduce the potential for terrorist networks to develop (Australian Government/AusAID, 2003).[7] The contribution of aid to counter-terrorism has focussed on developing capacity in countering terrorist financing and money laundering, and strengthening the counter-terrorist aspects of policing and border security (Australian Government/AusAID, 2003, p. 5). For example, in 2004 AusAID started a AUD10 million programme to strengthen counter-terrorist capacity in Indonesia. Plans were also afoot to roll out an educational programme to improve educational standards in Islamic schools. Similarly, in 2003 Prime Minister Howard launched a three-year AUD5 million package of counter-terrorist assistance to the Philippines, including border control, policing and port security (Australian Government/AusAID, 2003, pp. 5–7). The government also committed AUD500,000 to strengthening port security in the Pacific Islands.

In addition to these programmes AusAID also issued in July 2004 'Guidelines for Strengthening Counter-Terrorism Measures in the Australian Aid Program', which gave advice on how to avoid funding terrorist organisations in line with UN Security Resolution 1373 (2001). As of 19 February 2004, 16 organisations were listed as 'terrorist organisations' under Australia's Criminal Code (1995, part 5.3). AusAID agreements and contracts with recipient organisations now include a clause requiring aid recipients to ensure that neither they nor their funded partners are funding any terrorist organisations.

Finally, Australia's humanitarian assistance has more than doubled between 2000 and 2003, centred mainly on the Asia-Pacific region. As with other donor countries, the involvement of the military in humanitarian assistance has undermined the claims of civilian actors to be acting neutrally. It is noteworthy that a key recommendation of the 2005 OECD Peer Review of Australian aid was that 'Australia should affirm the primary position of civilian organisations in delivering humanitarian action' (OECD, 2005, p. 21). It also highlighted the risk that Australia's security interests and its regional focus could compromise a needs-based approach and the principles of neutrality and impartiality (OECD, 2005, p. 20).

These growing concerns over security and the sectoral shifts in funding towards governance have overshadowed the poverty focus of development policy in Australia. The 2005 OECD Peer Review of Australian aid, as well as NGOs, has expressed concern that the broad approach to governance had led to elements of counter-terrorism and illegal migration being included as ODA (OECD, 2005, p. 12). Moreover, it recommended that the government make clearer the links between governance and poverty reduction in its programming, policy statements and country operations (OECD, 2005, p. 12). It also warned that counter-terrorism, though crucial, should not 'override the development agenda' (OECD, 2005, p. 51) and that short-term national interests should not overshadow those of its partner countries (OECD, 2005, p. 24).

The United States

Since 2001 there has been a strategic realignment of USAID in line with a doctrinal emphasis in US national security policy on the contribution of development to counter-terrorism. This realignment is encompassed within a wide-ranging reorientation of statecraft to counter-terrorism objectives and new security imperatives. The US National Security Strategy of 2002 marked the encapsulation of the field of development into the War on Terror regime. It listed development alongside diplomacy and defence as the three central components of national security strategy, a tripartite approach designated as the 'three D's'. In line with this strategic approach, development became aligned with foreign policy priorities, key among which was the War on Terror. The doctrinal emphasis on the 'three D's' was re-emphasised in the US National Strategy for Combating Terrorism (2003), which defined the role of development as diminishing the underlying conditions that terrorists seek to exploit.

The newly important role attributed to development assistance in the US War on Terror regime was reinforced through institutional restructuring of US foreign aid in 2006. The changes were the execution of a vision of 'transformational diplomacy' pushed by former US Secretary of State Condoleezza Rice. Outlining the broad contours of the new diplomatic focus in testimony to the Senate Foreign Relations Committee, Rice maintained, 'It is impossible to draw neat, clear lines between our security interests, our development goals, and our democratic ideals in today's world. Our diplomacy must integrate and advance all of these goals together.'[8] The restructuring of the diplomatic corps resulted in the creation of the new post of Director of Foreign Assistance at the level of Deputy Secretary in the State Department, the foreign affairs docket in the US government. The Deputy Secretary concurrently serves as the USAID administrator.[9] The organisational change in US foreign assistance related to worries that rising levels of overseas assistance dating back to the middle 1990s had resulted in a fragmentation of foreign aid administration and programming. NGO critics warned that the restructuring implied a greater politicisation of US foreign assistance and the subordination of long-term development to diplomatic and military objectives. Observers noted that in the years immediately after 9/11, foreign assistance programmes earned the support of conservative Republican members of the US congress if they were packaged and presented as anti-terrorist programmes.[10] Programming and interventions by a spectrum of agencies have been rationalised according to their contribution to national security as a device to attain political support and thereby secure budgetary allocations.

The encapsulation of development into US foreign policy and security strategy has resulted in significant changes in orientation and emphasis of US development assistance. In 2004, for the first time, the State Department and USAID jointly issued a strategic plan that outlined their core values and shared mission, positing a role for development that mirrors that stated in the National Security Strategy. The most recent US Foreign Aid White Paper (2004) and USAID Bilateral Aid Policy Framework (2006) also focus on the contribution of development to counter-terrorism and protecting US national security. As emphasised in comments by the previous USAID administrator Andrew Natsios, 'Americans now understand that security in their homeland greatly depends on security, freedom, and opportunity beyond the country's borders. Development is now as essential to US national security as are diplomacy and defense' (United States, 2004). Proposals for a new international development strategy are to enshrine the national security emphasis of US development aid and entrench counter-terrorism as its core objective.[11]

Since 2001 the security juggernaut has come to determine the targeting of increasing amounts of US bilateral aid. There has been a surge in funding since the mid-1990s. A significant proportion of new assistance has been allocated to fragile states, which feature to a far greater extent in the operational emphasis and central objectives of USAID. For example, in 2003 nearly a third of USAID's resources were spent in unstable or fragile areas, excluding Iraq (USAID, 2005). In 2006, six of the top ten recipients of gross US ODA (US$ million) were unstable or fragile states, including Iraq (8,005), Afghanistan (1,361), Sudan (749), Colombia (588), Democratic Republic of Congo (491) and Pakistan (410).[12] Strengthening fragile states is one of five core operational goals of US foreign assistance. In 2005 USAID published a Fragile States Strategy, which establishes orientations for programming in states defined as 'vulnerable' or in 'crisis'. Programming in vulnerable states emphasises developing civilian control of the military, establishing capable police forces and strengthening courts. In crisis states, security efforts focus on security sector reform including deactivation, demobilisation and reintegration of fighters, establishing civilian oversight of the military and community level policing.

The contribution of US development assistance to security and counter-terrorism objectives is also evident in enhanced civil–military co-operation. USAID has sought to develop improved planning and liaison structures with the Department of Defense and as part of these efforts it created a Military Policy Board in 2005. It also established an Office of Military Affairs (OMA) within the Bureau of Democracy, Conflict and Humanitarian assistance. The OMA co-ordinates humanitarian efforts, planning and doctrine with the Departments of State and Defense and is headed by a senior military advisor (Ploch, 2007). It co-ordinates the posting of USAID liaison officers to the five geographic unified Combatant Commands to assist military professionals in assessing development needs and priorities. Already, USAID has been involved in military initiatives in Africa. It has contributed to the Trans-Sahara Counter-terrorism Initiative, which aims to disrupt the cycle of terrorist recruitment activities in a region likened to 'Afghanistan without drugs'.[13] USAID has initiated programmes on job training and youth, reintegration of combatants, water development, training of judicial and local officials in public service and starting a radio service.[14] USAID has also co-operated with military personnel from the Combined Joint Task Force (CJTF) – Horn of Africa – stationed in Djibouti, who are engaged in counter-terrorism against armed groups with purported ties to Al Qaeda. USAID has stationed a liaison officer with CJTF and has coordinated development inputs, such as supplying texts to schools built by the CJTF. USAID has assigned personnel to liaise with the new Africa Command (AFRICOM), which includes a 'soft power' mandate aimed at pre-emptive conflict prevention and incorporates a larger civilian component than traditional combatant commands (Ploch, 2007). Civil society is a particular focus of evolving Defense Department strategy and cross-agency planning on Civil-Military Co-ordination (CIMIC). A Defense Department official explained, 'We want to help develop a stable environment in which civil society can be built and that the quality of life for the citizenry can be improved' (quoted in Ploch, 2007, p. 5). Within CIMIC structures, the OMA has sought to expand co-operation between NGOs and the US military.

There has been internal dissent and debate within USAID regarding its expanding and deepening levels of co-operation with the military, revealing fundamental unease among civilian development personnel over what is perceived as military encroachment on development. There have been tensions around the balance of power in

CIMIC structures, with USAID personnel concerned that they are subservient in an unequal relationship driven by military objectives and strategy. Other disagreements have concerned mandates and competition for resources allocated to counter-insurgency operations. State Department and USAID personnel have voiced concern that the military may overestimate its capabilities as well as its diplomatic role in Africa, or pursue activities outside its mandate (Ploch, 2007).

New security imperatives in the aftermath of the 9/11 attacks have also factored in the 'freedom agenda', referring to the prioritisation of democracy promotion efforts in US foreign policy under the administration of President Bush. The opening sentence of the National Security Strategy of 2006 states, '[i]t is the policy of the United States to seek and support democratic movements and institutions in every nation and culture, with the ultimate goal of ending tyranny in our world'. US democracy promotion policies under the Bush administration became inextricably linked to the War on Terror. Emphasising the developmental contribution to fighting international terrorism, promoting democracy abroad has been seen to undermine the conditions that terrorist organisations seek to exploit (Dalacoura, 2005). Funding for democracy promotion is drawn from a range of State Department and development funds. Significant sources include the National Endowment for Democracy and USAID. Taken together, US democracy assistance amounted to $1.7 billion in 2006.[15] Among bilateral donors, USAID claims to be the largest 'democracy donor' (USAID, 2005). Counter-terrorism has become an important rationale and focus for USAID's own democracy initiatives. For example, USAID Democracy and Governance Offices have played a central role in the agency's assistance to states to pass counter-terrorism laws.[16] Through the Office of Transition Initiatives (OTI) in USAID, democracy assistance has been channelled to civil society groups seeking political change in states and areas of high strategic importance in the War on Terror including Iraq, Afghanistan, the West Bank and Sudan. OTI has been labelled the 'special forces of development assistance' and is explicitly tied to US foreign policy goals.[17]

However, Bush's democracy agenda proved divisive, even within the Republican Party. The triumph of Hamas in the Palestinian parliamentary elections in January 2006 was grist to the mill of 'realists' in the party who have doubted the ability of the US to foster democratic movements in states with weak civil institutions.[18] Critics outside the party argued that the administration's commitment to promoting democracy is inconsistent and has clashed with geopolitical realities and priorities in the context of the War on Terror.[19] There are inherent

contradictions between the professed commitment of the US to promote democracy movements and its prosecution of the War on Terror,
which has depended on nurturing ties with authoritarian regimes in
certain contexts.

These contradictions have been evident in US policy towards civil
society. While non-governmental public actors are crucial to US democracy promotion efforts, suspicion of civil society is registered at the
highest levels of US policy and strategy. In 2006 the State Department
published ten guiding NGO principles regarding the treatment of NGOs
by governments.[20] These emphasise the need for governments to show
regard for the rights of groups to organise outside the state and the
need for governments to protect this space. However, in the National
Strategy for Combating Terrorism, special mention is made of the risk
that charitable organisations and NGOs can be used wittingly or unwittingly for terrorist financing and recruitment. It called for government
co-operation with non-governmental actors to achieve the goal of
denying terrorists further sponsorship, support and sanctuary. New
checks and requirements for due diligence by governmental and non-
governmental grant-makers have been required on the basis that the
actors and spaces of civil society are at risk of being co-opted into
terrorist organising. The US Department of Treasury has issued voluntary guidelines for private grant-makers and charitable organisations to
prevent their funds from being used to finance terrorism.[21] Although
the guidelines are voluntary, in practice many organisations adapted
to the more stringent regulatory context and pressures to co-operate in
counter-terrorism (Sidel, 2007). USAID requires its grantees to sign ATCs.
Private grant-makers have introduced similar checks such as requiring
their grantees to know the backgrounds and physical addresses of their
trustees.

The United Kingdom

As a major ally in the War on Terror, it is particularly relevant to analyse the shifts in UK aid policy and its effects on aid programming,
aid flows, and civil society. The UK government had already begun to
weave the themes of conflict and security into aid policy since the early
1990s with particular reference to the so-called 'New Wars' in Africa and
the Balkans. As will be detailed further on, calls for more co-ordinated
approaches to conflict reduction were already expressed in New Labour's
first White Paper on Development published in 1997 and have led gradually to the formation of cross-departmental institutions. However, with

the launch of the War on Terror, this tendency towards convergence has become generalised throughout aid policy.

In the immediate months following the attacks on the Twin Towers UK politicians were already beginning to make connections between poverty, deprivation and terrorism. In an interview for an ITV documentary in November 2004, then UK Chancellor of the Exchequer Gordon Brown, for example, spoke of poverty as a 'breeding ground for discontent'. Similarly, then UK Prime Minister Tony Blair made a speech to the US Congress on 17 July 2003, where he juxtaposed poverty, lack of freedom and terrorism:

> The threat comes because, in another part of the globe, there is shadow and darkness where not all the world is free... where a third of our planet lives in poverty... and where a fanatical strain of religious extremism has arisen... and because in the combination of these afflictions, a new and deadly virus has emerged. That virus is terrorism.
>
> (Blair, 2003)

With aid as a potential soft tool for maintaining global economic stability whilst also counterbalancing the belligerent thrust of foreign policy, politicians such as Gordon Brown and Tony Blair have canvassed leaders of wealthy countries at key events such as the Monterrey Conference in 2002, the G7 meeting and the G8 summit in 2005 for an increase in aid budgets and a commitment to meet the UN target of 0.7 per cent of GDP devoted to aid. In this regard they have won support from aid officials, NGOs and campaigning groups who have opportunistically endorsed these ideational linkages to push the case for an increase in development aid.

This laid the ideological ground for a gradual shift in UK aid policy that wove together more firmly the threads of protecting national and global security interests and the delivery of aid and development. These shifts in policy can be observed in the changing language of policy documentation and the growing preoccupation, as in Australia, with fragile states. In 2005 DFID issued a document entitled 'Fighting poverty to build a safer world. A strategy for security and development', the very title stating boldly the causal links between poverty and security. In his foreword the then Secretary of State for International Development, Rt Hon Hilary Benn, stated, 'In recent years, DFID has begun to bring security into the heart of its thinking and practice. But we need to do more. As the Prime Minister said in his speech to the World Economic

Forum this year, "it is absurd to choose between an agenda focusing on terrorism and one on global poverty" ' (DFID, 2005a, p. 3). Importantly, the document acknowledges that increasing state security does not necessarily imply improved security for poor people but it does assume that conflict and development are negatively interrelated,[22] a position that Cramer in his book on civil wars strongly contests. Though the paper highlights the fact that casualties from international terrorism in Africa and Asia between 1998 and 2004 were almost six times the number in North America and Europe, it is noteworthy nevertheless that the strong drive towards linking security and development closely has come in the wake of the 9/11 attacks in North America. Had these and later attacks in London and Madrid not taken place, it is questionable whether there would have been such a strong and rapid thrust in this direction. The 2005 paper asserts resolutely that aid policy and practice should not be subordinated to global security objectives. Nevertheless, it underlines the need to make development and security goals 'mutually reinforcing' (p. 13), a desire which has fed into policy formulation, institutional arrangements and programming.

As well as these shifts in discourse reflected in policy documentation since 2001 there has been a deliberate move towards greater cross-departmental interaction to deal with the perceived terrorist threat. This in turn reflects the 'whole-of-government' approach adopted by other governments such as Australia, Canada, Germany, Sweden and the US (Patrick and Brown, 2007) and has to be located against a broader context of increasing co-ordination between donors as reflected in the Paris Declaration (as discussed earlier). As stated in the DFID 2005 document 'Fighting poverty to build a safer world' (p. 6), 'we need better collaboration between development, defence and diplomatic communities to achieve our respective and complementary aims'. The seeds of a 'joined-up' approach to governing conflict had already been sown by the late 1990s with growing official concern for the impact of 'New Wars'. The need for a co-ordinated approach to conflict policy-making found expression in both the 1997 and 2000 White Papers on International Development. The 1997 Paper called in paragraph 3.50 for the coherent deployment of 'diplomatic, development assistance and military instruments' to address conflict issues[23] (DFID, 1997). By 2000 the government was urging greater commitment to inter-departmental coherence for effective conflict prevention through the notion of 'a more joined-up approach to policy-making' (DFID, 2000, p. 30, paragraph 81). This called for the creation of conflict prevention pools, which drew together the resources and expertise of the Foreign and Commonwealth Office

(FCO), DFID and the Ministry of Defence and were supported by the Treasury and the Cabinet Office. The Global and African Conflict and Prevention Pools[24] came into operation in 2001. These focussed on supporting policing in Sierra Leone and disarmament, de-mobilisation and reintegration programmes, and providing £12 million in assistance to the African Union peace support operations in Darfur.

Also illustrative of the 'joined-up' or 'whole-of-government' approach is the formation of the Post-Conflict Reconstruction Unit in 2004. This is a cross-Whitehall department, involving the DFID, FCO and the Ministry of Defence, with DFID being the prime funder. Emerging out of the Iraq experience, the Unit was originally designed to manage the civilian component of immediate post-conflict intervention before other government departments took over longer-term development work. Recognising that there were unlikely to be any large-scale person deployments and that the concept of a post-conflict phase was problematic, the unit gradually shifted towards providing assessment and planning and operational expertise for stabilisation operations. Reflecting these changes, the unit was renamed in September 2007 as the Stabilisation Unit. At the operational level the government has fostered closer civil–military co-operation in development and humanitarian assistance through the creation of Provincial Reconstruction Teams (PRTs), an idea which was pioneered in Afghanistan and Iraq.

Recognising the inevitability in some circumstances of humanitarian and development actors working alongside military forces, as in the recent tsunami or the Kashmir earthquake in 2005, the DFID has supported the formation of a UK NGO–Military Contact Group to provide a forum for dialogue between UK NGOs and the UK military (DFID, 2005a, p. 20). The Contact Group was established in 2000 before the events of 9/11. It reflected the growing operational convergence between civil and military actors in humanitarian and development work and the need for dialogue around strategic policy and thematic issues. It is currently chaired by the British Red Cross[25] and its participants include nine NGOs, DFID and three sections of the Ministry of Defence.

Thus the various initiatives towards joined-up government such as the PRTs, the Global Conflict Pools, the Stabilisation Unit and the Counter-Narcotics Pool in Afghanistan have emerged out of the UK's experiences in Afghanistan and Iraq. Their effect has been to bring development policy and practice more closely into contact with the agendas of foreign policy and defence departments. Whilst the attempts at joined-up government may not always be as effective as intended (Stewart and Brown, 2007), the development of new cross-departmental institutions nevertheless points to the increasing securitisation of aid policy and practice.

The UK's close alliance with the US and its military involvement in both Iraq and Afghanistan have in turn led to a substantial increase in the volume of aid to those countries. Iraq became the top recipient of UK bilateral aid in 2003/2004, receiving £209 million, thereby usurping India from its leading position the year before. In 2005/2006 Iraq was the second top recipient of gross ODA, receiving £725 million, with Afghanistan close behind in fourth position with £110 million (OECD-DAC, accessed on website at www.dfid.gov.uk/Documents/Publications/sid/2006/tables, www.oecd. org/dataoecd/42/53/40039127.gif).[26] Though Iraq's position declined subsequently, it has remained within the top 10 recipients of UK aid and within the top 20 of DFID bilateral assistance (DFID, 2007a, p. 28).[27] This has been achieved in part through a diversion of existing aid budgets away from middle-income countries in Latin America. In 2006/7 Afghanistan ranked amongst the top three recipients of UK bilateral aid, receiving £134 million, and has remained within the top ten of DFID bilateral aid recipients since 2004.[28] It is significant that both Afghanistan and Iraq feature in the UK's top 20 recipients of net bilateral ODA and DFID bilateral aid in the years between 2004 and 2007 as this was not the case prior to 2002. Iraq, for example, did not receive any bilateral aid prior to 2002.[29] Prior to 2001 Afghanistan was not a major recipient of UK aid. The catapulting of Afghanistan and Iraq to the league of UK aid recipients reflects the linkages between development, security and foreign policy both nationally and internationally.

The growing concern of politicians and heads of development institutions with security issues has in turn fed into programming. This is reflected in the expansion and regularisation of programmes concerned with security sector reforms; the re-focussing of governance work on the security of the poor; greater attention to conflict reduction work, prevention and analysis; the emergence of fragile states as a category for intervention; the shift in aid flows; support to civil society; greater support for educational reform in countries with Muslim populations, focussing particularly on madrassas; and consultation with a broader range of donors and countries. These are examined in turn below.

First, DFID has expanded the number of countries where it supports security sector reform and safety, security and access to justice initiatives. The goal is to make these issues a standard part of programme design (DFID, 2005a, p. 24). This is significant because it involves greater interaction between development, diplomatic and defence professionals, contributing thereby to the 'whole-of-government' approach. It also contrasts with the approach outlined in the 2000 White Paper, where the call for increased support for security sector reform is aimed primarily at countries in conflict (DFID, 2000, p. 30, paragraph 82).

Second, greater attention to security has led to a re-focussing of governance work to include more direct support for the security of the poor. The intention here, as outlined in DFID's 2005 paper on 'Fighting poverty to build a safer world', is to promote stability and reduce conflict through, amongst other things, support for basic service provision, defined as not only health and education but also security and justice, and support for accountable government and transparent financial management. It is noteworthy, however, that the concept of 'human security' appears only once in DFID's paper on 'Fighting poverty to build a safer world', the report otherwise using the more ambivalent term 'security', which embraces both the more narrow and traditional meaning of national security and potentially the broader sense of human security. In the 2006 White Paper 'Eliminating World Poverty. Making Governance Work for the Poor' it does not occur once; instead the term 'security' is used throughout, often in conjunction with 'peace'. This is within a policy context where DFID has committed to devote half of all its direct support for developing countries to public services for the poor. Elements of a narrow and a broad interpretation of security permeate the White Paper.

Third, DFID has committed to integrating elements of conflict reduction such as support for disarmament, demobilisation and reintegration, and for work on small arms, more firmly into its programmes. This has required strengthening its expertise in conflict-related areas and applying a conflict analysis approach more systematically across programmes (DFID, 2005a, p. 25).

Fourth, and relatedly, there has been a growing emphasis on fragile states, part of the justification for which has been the assessment that 'They [fragile states] are more likely to become unstable ... and to be bases for terrorists. Afghanistan and Sudan are recent examples' (DFID, 2005b, p. 5).[30] Echoing the UN High Level Panel's report on 'Threats, Challenges and Change' issued in 2004, the DFID endorses the view that conflict, terrorism, state failure, poverty, disease and environmental degradation are all interrelated. In this way it justifies the need for increased attention and aid resources to be directed towards fragile states and reverses the trend of the 1990s, where fragile states were neglected as donors directed their aid towards relatively effective governments. In the context of fragile states, NGOs play the role of exemplifying approaches to service delivery which governments could later adopt, with little mention made of their role in facilitating key elements of 'good governance' such as accountability and citizen voice.

Bound up in the argument for greater emphasis on fragile states is the need for enhanced co-operation between development, foreign and defence ministries as epitomised by the Conflict Prevention Pools. DFID's concern over fragile states dovetails with increasing US attention and resources devoted to fragile states, which it justifies in terms of 'an investment in our own security' (Weinstein *et al.*, 2004, p. 3). Whilst DFID makes its case for greater support for fragile states in terms of the links between lack of development, instability and terrorism, its language is more moderated in terms of the benefit of development for UK national security and values, reflecting the different approaches between US and UK aid policies.

Fifth, DFID has broadened its operational approach to civil society. Though DFID uses a wide definition of civil society which acknowledges that this concept includes much more than international or domestic NGOs, in practice it has operated mainly with or through NGOs, and to a lesser degree business associations and trades unions. The discursive (and erroneous) identification of terrorism with Islam has been one of the reasons for a surge in interest in madrassas, Islamic NGOs and Muslim organisations. More generally, the religious convictions of both Bush and Blair have driven an agenda in the UK and US governments to raise the profile of faith-based organisations in service delivery, in community affairs and in international development. Indicative of this is the establishment in 2005 of a specialised Religions and Development Research Programme Consortium funded by DFID. As laid out in its 2005 paper on 'Fighting poverty to build a safer world', DFID views support to education reform and religious schools as a way of reducing the risk of poor countries to terrorism (DFID, 2005a, p. 12). In November 2006, for example, the UK government signed a ten-year Development Partnership Arrangement with Pakistan, which included, inter alia, support for strengthening the provision of, the oversight over and the quality of education, including madrassas (DFIDc).

Sixth, DFID has given greater support for educational reform in countries with Muslim populations, focussing particularly on madrassas. This growing interest in aid for educational reform complements parallel initiatives in the FCO to engage more strategically with the Middle East and with Muslim populations.

Seventh, DFID has begun to consult with a wider range of donor countries and agencies, and specifically with donors that support low-income countries with large Muslim populations, such as the Islamic Development Bank, Saudi Arabia and India (DFID, 2005a, p. 25).

Sweden

Since the Second World War, neutrality has been the guiding principle of Swedish foreign policy and the basis of its independent stance in international affairs. Sweden became a member of the EU in 1995. Although not a NATO member, it does maintain broad co-operation with NATO within an institutional framework known as the Partnership for Peace. The global War on Terror has tested Sweden's foreign policy principles as well as its societal values of openness and tolerance. Sweden was part of the Nordic bloc of countries that opposed the military invasion and occupation of Iraq. Former Swedish Prime Minister Goran Persson not only criticised the US- and British-led war in Iraq as a violation of international law but also committed Sweden to contribute to reconstruction and humanitarian assistance. The former Social Democrat–led government also challenged the US on various aspects of the War on Terror regime. A notable case concerned three Somali-born Swedish citizens whom the US put on the UN list of terrorists, one of whom was a candidate for the Social Democratic Party in the fall 2002 Swedish elections (Zagaris, 2002). A public debate ensued concerning the inability of the government to review the evidence and appeal. Against US objections, the Swedish government insisted on reviewing the cases of the suspects and requested the means to ascertain their guilt. Following the diplomatic row, Sweden became the first country to demand changes to the UN sanctions list, including a process and procedures to provide for de-listing and removal of contested names (Norrell, 2005).

The Swedish government has co-operated in other ways in the global War on Terror, including the introduction of a new terrorism law and formulating a comprehensive government policy on counter-terrorism. In December 2001, Sweden was involved in the CIA transfer of two Egyptian citizens suspected of terror links from Sweden to Egypt. The suspects were transferred in violation of Swedish and international human rights law that prohibits extradition of suspects to countries with the death penalty although the Swedish government sought assurances that the suspects would not be tortured in Egyptian custody or be sentenced under provisions for capital punishment in Egyptian law. It later emerged that at least one of the suspects was tortured. The UN investigated the incident and ruled that Sweden had violated the global torture ban.[31]

Sweden is one of the countries to lead a PRT in Afghanistan under the mandate of the NATO International Security Assistance Force (ISAF). Afghanistan was the eighth largest recipient of Swedish ODA in 2005 (US$45 million)[32] and Sweden was the eighth largest bilateral donor. Sweden's commitment to security and reconstruction assistance in Afghanistan was unaffected by the change in government following the Swedish elections in the autumn of 2006. The new centre–right government led by Fredrik Reinfeldt of the Moderates Party introduced a Bill in 2007 to extend the Swedish participation in ISAF until May 2009, which was approved by parliament.

Sweden's development co-operation is guided by the Policy for Global Development (PGD), an all-encompassing foreign policy that was introduced in 2003 by the previous Social Democrat–led government and endorsed by parliament. It specifies the overall orientation for Sweden's international assistance, key bilateral partners and budget frameworks. Within this framework, the Ministry of Foreign Affairs sets out the overall priorities and decides on the bilateral co-operation programmes in partner countries while SIDA works independently. The PGD mandated an integrated policy for global development encompassing all policy areas of government around a central theme of contributing to equitable and sustainable global development. Compared with other major bilateral donors, the priorities and geographic allocation of Sweden's development co-operation are more clearly guided by poverty reduction criteria. Least developed and other low-income countries are the target of an estimated 75 per cent of Sweden's allocable bilateral aid (OECD, 2005). In 2005–2006, Tanzania, Mozambique, Uganda and Ethiopia ranked in the top five recipients of gross Swedish ODA.[33]

New security threats that have influenced significant change in bilateral policy and practice in other countries are less important in understanding Swedish aid trends. Conflict management and security is one of eight central elements of the PGD and in many ways continues an emphasis in Swedish development co-operation since the 1990s on conflict prevention as part of human security. In 2005, SIDA developed a new policy on peace and security that replaced an earlier 'Strategy on Conflict Management and Peacebuilding' (1999) and, further, has established a Division for Peace and Security in Development Cooperation. Violent conflict, insecurity and human security are the focus of the new policy, which outlines approaches for development co-operation in conflict situations. These include attention to the threat of violence undermining development, conflict sensitivity in development action, and promotion of peace and security (SIDA, 2005). Under the latter, the sorts of interventions referred to include agricultural programmes to address land rights disputes and good governance and democracy initiatives to provide protection and security for minorities and marginalised groups.

Another significant feature of Swedish development co-operation is its reliance on NGOs (OECD, 2005a). The PGD calls for increased collaboration with Swedish organisations, religious organisations and popular movements both to implement programmes and to influence Swedish public opinion on development. The perspective on poverty adopted in the PGD also implies that specific efforts be undertaken to strengthen civil society in partner countries: 'poverty ... relates to a lack of power, security and the ability to make life choices'. An internal statement on SIDA's policy direction says, '[g]eneral budget aid for poverty reduction requires greater support for civil society, free debate and independent research so that the poor have opportunities to make themselves heard and so that the State is examined' (SIDA, 2006). Operationally, SIDA has a Civil Society Team, formerly its Division for Cooperation with NGOs, which oversees the development co-operation activities of 16 Swedish NGOs that have signed framework agreements with SIDA.[34]

The changing political context in Sweden has so far not affected the unambiguous focus on poverty reduction in its development co-operation. In 2007, the new conservative government completed a review of Sweden's bilateral aid portfolio with the intention of focussing assistance on fewer countries as a foundation of a new development co-operation policy. The broad rationale for the most recent incarnation of Sweden's development policy tied into the Paris Declaration and the bureaucratic pressures accompanying increasing levels of ODA:

> [a] smaller share of the total aid, increased concentration, greater programme aid and donor coordination mean that Sweden and SIDA have to make more and deeper strategic choices. We cannot expect SIDA's administrative resources to grow at the same pace as the aid. We therefore want Sweden to concentrate on fewer countries and fewer sectors.
>
> (SIDA, 2006, p. 11)

The outcomes of the 'country focus process' included a stronger focus on Africa and Europe as well as issues of peace, security, democracy and human rights. Following the policy review, the Swedish government is seeking to develop co-operation with a majority of states that are in conflict or post-conflict situations. Specific countries include Iraq, Afghanistan, the Occupied Palestinian Territories, Burundi, Somalia, Sudan, the Democratic Republic of Congo, Guatemala and Colombia.[35] Already, SIDA estimates that 75 per cent of its partner countries are affected by violent conflict (SIDA, 2005).

In the case of Sweden, an outstanding impact of the War on Terror has been an influx of refugees from Iraq since 2003. Nearly half of all Iraqis that fled to Europe in 2006 came to Sweden,[36] where a large diaspora community had formed during the regime of Saddam Hussein. The 8,951 Iraqi refugees that Sweden took in 2006 compared with only 200 for the US in the same year and 466 in total for the entire war up to the end of 2006.[37] However, a decision in 2007 by Swedish Superior Court of Migration signalled a policy change. It ruled that Iraq is not a 'conflict zone' and that Iraqis must prove they are in personal danger of persecution before being granted asylum, igniting opposition from advocacy groups and human rights campaigners.[38] Seen in a broader context, the decision reflects the anti-immigrant stance of the ruling conservative coalition government, which has expressed unease with aspects of the multicultural model that has been the basis of Sweden's immigration policy.

In comparing these four cases, we can observe both common patterns across the four countries as well as important distinctions. With its long adherence to a principle of neutrality in matters of foreign policy, Sweden stands out in its more measured position in relation to the War on Terror and the modifications of its development agenda in relation to shifting global security concerns. However, in other respects it has co-operated in global counter-terrorism efforts in ways that affect its engagement with populations in the South. Like most other countries it has introduced a new terrorism law and formulated a comprehensive national policy on counter-terrorism. It has assisted with the extradition of terrorist suspects and sent troops to Afghanistan, where it has led a PRT under the command of the NATO-led ISAF mission. Yet it has maintained an unambiguous focus on poverty reduction in its development policy. Like the other countries examined here it has focussed its aid more strategically on countries 'in conflict' or 'post-conflict', though, unlike Australia, the UK and the US, it has not used the language of 'fragile states' to describe this.

The UK and Australia have been close allies to the US in the prosecution of the War on Terror. Leaders in all three countries have drawn causal links between poverty, under-development and terrorism, which have brought development more firmly into line with foreign policy and national security objectives. The formation of joint defence, diplomacy and development coordination structures and the expanding involvement of governmental development departments in military affairs have progressed furthest in the US. DFID has maintained its focus on poverty reduction, though its policy pronouncements nonetheless conform to received wisdom regarding the links between poverty, insecurity and terrorism. The institutional architecture for security and development has influenced the extent and degree of interweaving between development, defence and foreign policy agency agendas. DFID was separated from the FCO in 1997 and has since then consolidated and strengthened its position as an independent government department, succeeding in regularly increasing its budgetary allocation. By comparison, USAID has been brought more directly under the administrative guidance and policy direction of the US State Department.

As well as sharing a common 'whole-of-government approach' to addressing terrorism, Australia, the UK and the US have prioritised the so-called 'fragile states' in their development co-operation and have increased their resources to these countries in tandem. All four countries including Sweden have increased their aid flows to both Iraq and Afghanistan. The whole-of-government approach has at the operational level led to closer civil–military relations in all four countries. Whilst Australia and the US have introduced counter-terrorist projects in their bilateral development assistance portfolios, the UK has expanded its support to security sector reform. Though not immediately intended for purposes of counter-terrorism, the UK government's support of security sector reform is linked clearly to the broader aim of enhancing security to reduce the perceived vulnerability of poor populations to terrorist recruitment. However, there is a greater emphasis on the security of the poor in UK development co-operation compared with the US, though, again, this is premised on the thinking that poverty and terrorism are intrinsically related.

Since 2001 donor relations with civil society have become increasingly contradictory and complex. This is illustrated most vividly in how the US government relates with non-governmental public actors. On the one hand, the US needs to recruit civil society actors into its agenda of democracy promotion, which in turn has been mobilised in the 'fight against terrorism'. On the other hand, there is growing suspicion of civil society, which has prompted the introduction of new oversight measures such as the inclusion of NGOs in new anti-money laundering regulations and the new requirement that USAID partners sign an ATC. In the UK, a greater scope of civil society actors has come into the view of

DFID. Specifically it has sought to engage Muslim groups and networks, with a particular interest in reaching out to groups that work with Muslim youth. This parallels expanding efforts of the FCO in Muslim countries as well as programming by the FCO and Home Office in the UK aimed at preventing the radicalisation of Muslim youth. Australia does not have a long history of working systematically or extensively with CSOs. Nevertheless, like the US, it has introduced clauses in its aid agreements requiring partners to declare they have no connections with terrorist groups.

Conclusion

This chapter shows how the War on Terror regime has shaped the various forms of engagement between donor agencies and non-governmental actors both in the North and in the South. The 'securitisation of development and aid policy' refers to the process whereby global and national security objectives and interests have merged into the framing, structuring and implementation of development and aid. We do not propose that the War on Terror regime has singly subordinated aid policy and institutions to the security agendas of the US or other advanced capitalist countries. Nor do we propose that the War on Terror has had no impact on how development agendas are conceived, how aid policy is formulated or how aid institutions behave. Nor do we suggest that the War on Terror regime has wholly reframed the way donor agencies engage with non-governmental public actors. Rather, we argue that the effects varied according to the specific bilateral or multilateral donors and the contexts in which they operated.

The chapter explored four cases to show the changing contours of development thinking, aid policy and practice, namely USAID, DFID, AusAID and SIDA. Three important findings emerge from these cases. First, the effects of the War on Terror regime on development thinking and aid policy and practice are country-specific. The extent to which bilateral development agencies absorb the mantras, rationale and policies associated with the War on Terror regime depends on the degree of independence of those agencies within government hierarchies, bilateral relations of certain countries with the US and, in particular, responses to military interventions in pursuit of the War on Terror and domestic perceptions of threats to national security. Second, in spite of country-specific manifestations, there are clear trends stretching across different donor agencies that suggest how far and wide security objectives and interests have merged with aid structures and processes, and this has been justified by the War on Terror regime. Third, the War on

Terror regime has cast suspicion on civil society in general and on specific interest groups within civil society such as Muslim communities and organisations. This has had contradictory effects. On the one hand, it has fuelled a trend towards tightening up and exerting greater regulatory control over charitable institutions, NGOs and especially Muslim organisations. On the other hand, it has brought Muslim organisations and groups into the policy gaze of development agencies, creating opportunities for dialogue, funding and implementation of development agendas. This latter point is important because it is all too easy to dwell on the repressive, negative aspects of the dominant, ideological machinery of the War on Terror regime.

These findings in turn have a number of implications for development actors. The absorption of security narratives into development policy and the concomitant recruitment of development into national security strategies underline the importance for non-governmental actors of maintaining organisational independence. Civil society has come to be perceived both as part of the terrorist threat and as indispensable to the ideological and political prosecution of the War on Terror. These tensions have led donors to reconfigure their relations with civil society actors to comply with new due diligence requirements as well as seek the contribution of non-governmental public actors to meeting new security imperatives. These shifting governance relations highlight the importance of independence to nurture the spaces for civil society to organise on a development agenda focussed on poverty reduction and defending the interests of marginalised groups including 'suspect' communities. In particular, more development-oriented civil society actors need to re-examine their own positioning in aid processes and to reflect more deeply and critically on how they relate to political and military interests at global and national levels. This is because in many contexts they have been reticent in speaking out against human rights infringements and anti-terrorism crackdowns on groups defending the interests of 'suspect' individuals and groups.

Notes

1. Excerpt from address by the former US President George W. Bush before a joint session of Congress. 20 September 2001. http://www.britannica.com/presidents/article-9398253. Accessed 22 February 2009.
2. Other factors also added to a growing concern about national security in Australia, such as instability in Fiji, the Solomon Islands and Timor-Leste, and influenced the overall context of aid and development policy. See OECD, 2005, p. 22.

3. In 2003, 47 per cent of total bilateral Australian ODA went to Papua New Guinea and the Pacific Islands and 42 per cent to Asia.
4. A similar project is the Enhanced Cooperation Programme directed at Papua New Guinea. For a detailed critical discussion of this see O'Connor, 2006, pp. 180–184.
5. The RAMSI is also interesting in that whilst the initial purpose was to restore peace and strengthen the police, within a year the Department of Foreign Affairs and Trade had released a report entitled 'Solomon Islands: Rebuilding an Island Economy', which pronounced a shift from peace-keeping to business promotion. This report was funded by the BHP-Billiton, an Australian mining company, which clearly had an interest in one of the key recommendations, namely to register landholdings, a procedure which would pave the way to the commercialisation of land. This demonstrates the subtle interweaving of security, development and commercial objectives. However, the OECD Peer Review of Australian ODA expressed concern that this increasing engagement of different government ministries in development could lead to a 'law and order agenda' dominating the development programme rather than an approach that fostered capacity-building, sustainability and local ownership (OECD, 2005, p. 16).
6. In contrast, the percentage of aid devoted to infrastructure over the same period fell from 15 per cent in 1999/2000 to 7 per cent in 2005/2006 (O'Connor, 1976, p. 177) and for education from 27 per cent to 14 per cent (Parliamentary Library, Department of Parliamentary Services, 2004, p. 1). Note that O'Connor puts the 1999/2002 figure for education at 18 per cent.
7. This document was a statement of principle, and more detailed guidelines were introduced in July 2004 in the AusAID document 'Strengthening Counter-Terrorism Measures'.
8. 'Realizing the Goals of Transformational Diplomacy'. Secretary Condoleezza Rice. Testimony to the Senate Foreign Relations Committee. 15 February 2006. http://www.state.gov/secretary/rm/2006/61209.htm.
9. 'Diplomats Will Be Shifted to Hot Spots.' *Washington Post.* 19 January 2006.
10. 'Transforming U.S. Foreign Aid'. Council on Foreign Relations. 17 March 2006. www.cfr.org/publication/10176/transforming_us_foreign_aid.html.
11. 'Foreign Aid and the War on Terrorism'. 2005 USAID Summer Seminar Series. www.usaid.gov/policy/cdie/session8-9.html.
12. Organisation for Economic Cooperation and Development. Development Assistance Committee. United States Donor Aid Charts. http://www.oecd.org/dataoecd/42/30/40039096.gif.
13. 'Foreign Aid and the War on Terrorism'. 2005. USAID.
14. Ibid.
15. 'Democracy Push by Bush Attracts Doubters in Party.' *New York Times.* 17 March 2006.
16. 'Foreign Aid and the War on Terrorism'. 2005. USAID.
17. 'Democracy's "Special Forces" Face Heat.' *Christian Science Monitor.* 6 February 2006.
18. 'Democracy Push by Bush Attracts Doubters in Party.' *New York Times.* 17 March 2006.
19. 'The Realities of Exporting Democracy'. *Washington Post.* 25 January 2006.

20. 'Guiding Principles on Non-governmental Organisations'. US Department of State. Bureau of Democracy, Human Rights and Labor. 14 December 2006. http://www.state.gov/g/drl/rls/77771.htm.
21. US Treasury, Anti-Terrorist Financing Guidelines: Voluntary Best Practices for US-based Charities, December, 2005.
22. As the 2005 DFID report (p. 5) states, 'insecurity, lawlessness, crime and violent conflict are among the biggest obstacles to achievement of the Millennium Development Goals; they also destroy development'.
23. It also urged 'better linkage of foreign, security and development co-operation policies' within the EU (paragraph 3.52, White Paper 1997).
24. The Global Pool is chaired by the Foreign Secretary and the Africa Pool by the Secretary of State for International Development.
25. It was originally chaired by the JDCC.
26. Nigeria ranked top with US$2,697 million, but this figure captures the one-off payment of debt relief to Nigeria and so distorts the picture given by the aid figures.
27. Iraq occupied fourth position in terms of UK net bilateral ODA at £150 million in 2004, second in 2005 at £725 million and with double the amount of aid to India, and eighth position in 2006 at £110 million (DFID, 2007a, p. 28). Iraq occupied tenth, eighth and then eighteenth positions as DFID aid recipient in the years 2004, 2005 and 2006, receiving £49 million, £87 million and £50 million respectively.
28. Afghanistan rose from fourth position in 2005 at £121 million and seventh position in 2004 at £122 million. In terms of DFID bilateral aid Afghanistan held fifth position in the years 2004/5 and 2005/6 and sixth in 2006/2007, receiving £80 million, £98 million and £99 million respectively.
29. Recorded flows to Iraq before 2003/2004 were for humanitarian assistance provided through UN agencies and CSOs for Iraqi citizens (DFID, 2007a, footnote 4, table 14.3).
30. This refrain is repeated again on page 10: "Fragile states are more likely to become unstable and fall prey to criminal and terrorist networks."
31. 'Sweden Violated Torture Treaty'. *BBC News Online.* 21 May 2005. http://news.bbc.co.uk/1/hi/world/europe/4568041.stm. Accessed 23 February 2009.
32. Sweden. Aid Statistics and Donor Aid Charts'. Development Co-operation Directorate. Organisation for Economic Cooperation and Development. Available at www.oecd.org/countrylist/0,3349,en_2649_34447_1783495_1_1_1_1,00.html#S
33. 'Sweden. Gross Bilateral ODA, 2005–2006'. OECD-DAC tables. www.oecd.org/dataoecd/42/51/40039148.gif.
34. 'Division for Cooperation with NGOs'. SIDA. http://www.sida.se/ngo. Accessed 23 February 2009.
35. 'Focused Bilateral Development Cooperation'. Ministry for Foreign Affairs. 27 August 2007. http://www.sweden.gov.se/sb/d/9382/a/86595;jsessionid=a58J02FBzBqg.
36. 'Sweden Tightens Rules on Iraqi Asylum Seekers.' *Reuters.* 9 July 2007.
37. 'The Tragically High Price of Helping Americans'. *Spiegel Online.* 23 May 2007. www.spiegel.de/international/europe/0,01518,484047,00.html.
38. 'Iraqi Afghan Refugees Face Explusion from Scandinavia.' *Oneworld News.* 8 August 2007. http://us.oneworld.net/article/view/152096/1/

5
Civil Society, Security and Aid Post-9/11: Afghanistan

Civil Society With Guns Is Not Civil Society
Civil society programme officer in
bilateral aid agency, August 2006

Accused of harbouring Osama Bin Laden, the Taliban regime in Afghanistan was to become the first target of President Bush's War on Terror. Within a few months, the Taliban had fallen under the weight of the US military and political war machine. By December 2001 the Bonn Agreement had been signed and agreement reached for the gradual installation of an elected government. The subsequent processes of political stabilisation, reconstruction and development have proceeded hand in hand with the relentless pursuit of the War on Terror, and in particular the dogged hunt for Osama Bin Laden and Al Qaeda supporters.[1] The US pursuit of its geopolitical interests through force and the soft touch of democracy and markets has accelerated and intensified the convergence of aid, security and foreign policy goals, operations and institutions. Afghanistan was the first battleground after 9/11 in which the seemingly contradictory goals of the War on Terror and the promotion of liberal democracy and freedom were played out to their full.

It is in Afghanistan, and in other War on Terror front-line states such as Iraq, that the effects of the increasing convergence of security and development objectives are most pronounced. Western governments have adopted a dual-pronged strategy comprised of militaristic and developmental elements to stabilise and reconstruct Afghanistan and to undermine support for the Taliban and anti-government forces. Through Operation Enduring Freedom (OEF) US forces have pursued Bin Laden and Al Qaeda elements still thought to be holed up in the mountainous borders between Afghanistan and Pakistan. Simultaneously, the NATO-led ISAF was deployed to protect the newly installed, democratically elected government of President Hamid Karzai, to stabilise the country and to win support for the government through 'hearts and minds' work. Afghanistan's economy is heavily dependent on foreign aid;[2] its government in turn relies crucially on external military and political support for its survival. Hence, we would expect there to be little political debate on counter-terrorism measures or pressure from domestic non-governmental groups – both modern, bureaucratised organisations as well as informal structures – on security strategies and practices in the country.

This chapter traces the effects of the increasing securitisation of aid and development in Afghanistan on aid policy and civil society. It begins by outlining the key changes in aid policy in Afghanistan since 2001, highlighting the gradual shift from humanitarian intervention to development activity, the increasing focus on state-building and the key elements of military intervention in development. It then sketches the trajectory of an emerging civil society up until 2001. This provides a backdrop against which to analyse, in the next section, the effects of aid policy on civil society since 2001. We also consider the longer-term implications for civil society of state-building strategies and their positioning of civil society within these. Finally we examine the short-term impact of security policies and objectives on civil society in Afghanistan, looking in particular at issues of humanitarianism and independence raised through military intervention in development.[3]

Development and aid policy in Afghanistan post-2001

Historically, bilateral and multilateral aid to Afghanistan was inextricably linked to foreign policy objectives in the region. External forces with diverse geopolitical interests in Afghanistan – notably Britain and Russia from the nineteenth century onwards, and the US, Pakistan, Iran and India from the 1950s onwards – have pursued their objectives by channelling military aid, development assistance, resources and advisors to incumbent rulers or their opponents. This has generated a fragmented, weak, rentier state that is substantially dependent on foreign rather than domestic resources (Rubin, 2002, p. 65; Saikal, 2006, pp. 117–132).[4] In the 1950s Afghanistan was not of major interest to US and other Western foreign policy-makers, though Cold War imperatives kept it within the orbit of political strategists. Following the invasion of Afghanistan by the Soviet Union in December 1979,

Western governments took a more focussed interest in Afghanistan, providing military funding to the mujahedin resistance and supporting development through international and local NGOs based in Pakistan.

US foreign policy interest in Afghanistan waned and aid commitments to the country declined following the withdrawal of Soviet forces in February 1989 (Rashid, 2008, pp. xliv–xlv). As mujahedin commanders battled for power, INGOs backed by Western donors continued with humanitarian interventions, gaining access where they could negotiate agreements with local warlords. In 1996 the Taliban took hold of Kabul, gradually reinstating some order. It was during this period that Bin Laden sought refuge in Afghanistan, having been forced to leave Sudan in 1996.[5] Though aid was severely limited during this period, both because of Taliban objections to the liberal values embodied in Western aid and because of Western disapproval of the illiberal nature of the Taliban regime, some INGOs continued to provide humanitarian aid in limited urban and rural areas.

It was following the overthrow of the Taliban regime in 2001 that Western aid commitments to Afghanistan increased. The signing of the Bonn Agreement in 2001 paved the way for the installation of a temporary government under President Karzai, and for presidential and parliamentary elections in 2004 and 2005 respectively.[6] At the Tokyo conference in January 2002 multilateral and bilateral donors pledged US$4.5 billion initially in aid for the reconstruction and development of Afghanistan. The US has been the largest donor to Afghanistan, contributing over one-third of all aid since 2001, with the UK, the EU, Japan, Germany, Canada and Scandinavian countries also providing significant amounts.[7]

However, these pledges took time to be realised and diminished as Western governments shifted their attention to the US invasion of Iraq in 2003. Once again the gaze of Western foreign policy-makers diverted from Afghanistan, with consequences not only for the realisation of aid pledges but also for the security of the country. Foreign assistance to Afghanistan has paled in comparison to other post-conflict contexts. According to Dobbins *et al.* (2005, p. 28), Afghanistan received US$57 per capita in international development assistance in the first two years compared to US$679 for Bosnia and US$526 for Kosovo. The Taliban and other anti-government forces used this opportunity to regroup and launch an insurgency against the Karzai government and occupying foreign forces. In January 2006 Western powers agreed the Afghan Compact, reasserting their commitment to Afghanistan through renewed pledges of aid. However, the ongoing war in Iraq continued to divert attention from Afghanistan and the aid pledges remained unfulfilled. Between 2002 and 2008 only US$15 billion of the US$25 billion pledged aid had been expended. The US had disbursed only half of its US$10.4 billion commitment. Moreover, aid critics lamented the wasteful and ineffective use of aid, not least because of the high profits, allowances and salaries granted to private sub-contractors.[8] According to the OECD (2006), the costs of technical assistance to Afghanistan amounted to 25 per cent of total development assistance, the bulk of this being uncoordinated with government. Mounting insecurity, the weak absorptive capacity of Afghan state institutions and corruption at high levels have further compromised the ability of the government and donors to deliver aid.

Though recent economic and development assistance flows to Afghanistan are substantial, they pale in comparison to military assistance, underlining the prioritisation of political and military objectives. According to Waldman (2008, p. 2), since 2001 international donors have provided US$7 million per day in aid. In comparison, US military expenditure in Afghanistan is approximately US$100 million per day. Also, since 2002 donors have spent around US$25 billion on security-related assistance, mainly for Afghan security forces, compared to only US$15 billion on civilian reconstruction and development (Waldman, 2008, p. 7). The geographic distribution of aid has also reflected the political and military objectives of donors, with some donors focussing their aid on the southern provinces where insurgency is most rife (Waldman, 2008, pp. 2–3). One-fifth of DFID's budget is allocated to one province, Helmand, which is also the focus of the UK's military involvement (Waldman, 2008, p. 12). By 2008 the perceived success of the surge strategy in Iraq, coupled with rising concern amongst Western governments about the deterioration of security in Afghanistan, led foreign donors to pledge greater assistance to Afghanistan. With the change in administration in the US in January 2009 the Obama administration has increased its military and development commitments in Afghanistan. Counter-terrorism objectives continue to top US priorities in the country (Cooper and Shanker, 2009).

After the demise of the Taliban, aid strategy focussed initially on humanitarian intervention and reconstruction. Decades of conflict had seriously eroded state capacities, with most educated and professional Afghans having fled the country. In the absence of a well-functioning state and resistant initially to the idea of state-building (Ghani and Lockhart, 2008, p. 12), donors had initially channelled their aid through the UN and NGOs. Once elections installed a democratic government, some donors, with the exception of the US, pledged to channel most of their aid through the Afghan government. By making the state budget the central policy instrument, donors committed to enhancing local ownership, building state capacity and harmonising and better coordinating their aid in line with the Paris Declaration principles. In this way the model of development policy in Afghanistan now came into line with that of other major aid-recipients across the world. In practice, however, the lack of a single stream of aid financing coupled with the fact that much aid bypasses the government has meant that the Afghan government still struggles to coordinate aid flows (Ghani and Lockhart, 2008, p. 109). According to the Afghan Ministry of Finance, only US$5 billion of the US$15 billion in aid disbursed in Afghanistan since 2001 had actually been provided to the government (Waldman, 2008, p. 16). In this model NGOs became sub-contractors of government, with reduced direct access to donor funds. This brings in obvious constraints on funding for NGOs not involved in aid delivery and which might also challenge the state, as has happened in Kenya.

The first post-Taliban development strategy for Afghanistan was set out in the National Development Framework of 2002. Other key documents are Securing Afghanistan's Future (2004), the Interim Afghanistan National Development Strategy of 2006 and the Afghanistan National Development Strategy of 2008. The vision of the state embodied in these documents is profoundly neo-liberal. The ideal role of the state is to create an enabling environment for market forces to flourish. Though the state guarantees universal access to health and education, it plays a minimal role in delivering social welfare. Rather, the role of the state is to manage at arm's length an array of sub-contracted private and non-profit agencies. The implications of this for the role of service-delivery NGOs and, more broadly, civil society are profound and are explored later.

There is an important democratic thread implicit in the model of state-building being pursued in Afghanistan. As stated in the National Development Framework (2002, p. 6), 'Sustainable development requires citizen participation and adopting of methods of governance that enable the people to take decisions on issues that affect them and their immediate surroundings.' The Afghan government has introduced a series of national programmes to enhance citizen trust in the government (Ghani and Lockhart, 2008, pp. 198–220). The most important of these is the National Solidarity Programme (NSP), which has sought to channel resources to communities and enable local people to determine their own development plans.

Establishing this citizen trust had become increasingly important with the passage of time. From the beginning the apportioning of offices to members of the interim administration in the Bonn Agreement had led to these being treated as rewards for political loyalty, with little attention paid to building public trust (Maley, 2006, p. 38). The failure of the government to govern effectively beyond Kabul jeopardised donor-funded government programmes that were crucial to securing public support. Ironically, donors' objectives to strengthen the legitimacy of the Afghan state through development initiatives such as the NSP stood in stark contrast to Western government policies of tolerating the inclusion of criminal and warlord elements in parliament. This was deemed necessary to ensure their cooperation in Western counter-terrorism objectives and reflected the prioritisation of security interests over reconstruction objectives (Goodhand and Sedra, 2007). Still, the NSP was innovative because it attempted to empower the general public to engage in the reconstruction process.

The NSP introduced two key changes in the way that civil society actors were conceptualised in the development process. First, it entailed the creation of new rural structures, namely Community Development Councils (CDCs). These are distinct from pre-existing village structures in three ways. First, the leaders of the Council are elected. Second, the mandate of CDCs covers development issues. However, unlike pre-existing village structures in some areas, these are not involved in resolving local-level disputes. Third, CDCs are required to involve women in decision-making positions, either through the formation of separate female and male sub-committees or through joint male–female Councils. The CDCs added to the new non-governmental terrain in the post-Taliban context, and the values and purposes that it espoused. However, the construction of CDCs presumed that customary local institutions were destroyed during civil war. Existing local structures were bypassed and thought to be inappropriate since they were not wholly inclusive.

The second change was the role assigned to Northern development NGOs, which now had to apply for donor funds through the NSP and so effectively seek government approval for their activities. Under the NSP Northern NGOs and local Afghan NGOs were to facilitate local communities in prioritising their needs and drawing up community development plans. Donors and government officials in Kabul regard the NSP as a flagship programme for delivering development and, in turn, strengthening the competencies of the state. This is despite the fact that the NSP has encountered several problems of implementation, including ensuring the participation of women in decision-making processes, relating the new structures to pre-existing village leadership structures, resolving conflicts that arise over CDC priorities and plans,[9] negotiating local-level power relations and ensuring the timely disbursement of funds to CDCs.[10] This latter issue has contributed to local suspicion of both the government and the Northern NGOs. As will be discussed below, the vision of state–civil society relations embodied in state capacity-building initiatives had implications for the future trajectory of civil society.

Foreign militaries have played an important role in delivering development in Afghanistan. The main mode for the military's involvement is PRTs, the primary model for civil–military cooperation in Afghanistan. The first PRTs were established by the US in 2002. By 2007 there were 25 PRTs under NATO-led ISAF, varying considerably in their size, activities and effectiveness, and in the balance of military and civilian staff.[11] The prime mission of these civilian–military units as described in the ISAF PRT Handbook is to 'assist the Islamic Republic of Afghanistan to extend its authority, in order to facilitate the development of a stable and secure environment in the identified area of operations, and enable security sector reform and reconstruction efforts'.

Increasingly aware that military action could not alone win the War on Terror, US coalition forces and the Afghan government in 2006 adopted an 'ink-blot' approach, which focussed on combining military manoeuvres with winning the hearts and minds of the local population.[12] This approach was piloted in Helmand province and drew upon a similar approach adopted by the British Army in Malaysia during the Second World War. The idea was that once the military had secured an area, aid projects with civilian development workers could be set up, thus creating Afghan Development Zones. Whilst villagers in the secure areas would have access to medical care, education and other welfare services, those in insecure areas would, it was argued, eventually realise there were peace dividends to be had.

Since 2007, this specific approach was superseded in areas of intense fighting as coalition forces were unable to hold territory sufficiently long enough to start development projects[13]. Nevertheless, military strategy continues to comprise both the hard element of force as well as the soft element of PRTs and 'hearts and minds' activities. Such a strategy explicitly links and subordinates development strategy to military objectives. Inevitably this poses strategic and moral dilemmas for NGOs, which wish to prioritise human security and claim neutrality and impartiality in their operations. However, the involvement of the military in the same sorts of activities that NGOs routinely undertake makes them appear complicit in a grander scheme of occupation, as will be discussed later.

Having outlined the key contours of aid, in the following sections we examine how aid policy has affected the development of civil society in Afghanistan. First, we consider the trajectory of civil society in Afghanistan before and after 9/11.

Civil society in Afghanistan

Whether conceptualised sociologically as an arena of voluntary association or politically as a sphere of deliberation around political affairs,[14] the empirical manifestations of civil society in Afghanistan are weak. The predominance of tribal, kin and clan identities, a primarily rural socio-economy, the ongoing conflict and the weak authority of the state all potentially militate against the emergence of a vibrant civil society.[15] However, over the past half century elements of a 'modern', proto-civil society have emerged at key moments in Afghanistan. These include clubs, professional and trades associations, women's organisations, trades unions, discussions forums, developmental NGOs and cooperatives. Domestic politics, external engagement and the exposure of Afghan refugees to civil societies in other contexts have together nurtured these seeds. These have emerged alongside and often fused with the so-called 'traditional associations' such as jirgas and shuras, which function mainly to make collective decisions and to resolve disputes over land, property and honour within and amongst families, tribes and clans. The shape and significance of such traditional associations is peculiar to particular tribes and regions, the jirga being a primarily Pashtun form of association for example. They are also not static structures and have been subject to manipulation during different periods of rule in Afghanistan.[16]

The emergence of a proto-civil society is inextricably linked to the historical processes of state formation in Afghanistan. The tribal nature of parts of Afghan society within a social context of regional, linguistic and ethnic diversity has proved an enduring constraint on building a centralised, nation state with the capacity to provide security, raise revenues and steer a developmental agenda. This has simultaneously inhibited the emergence of an associational realm that reaches beyond clan or tribal identities to concern itself with broader public affairs nationwide. The fragmented, rentier state created by decades of external interference has not only incubated political elites from the rest of society but also removed any imperative for the state to develop regular, intermediary institutions of dialogue and negotiation. Rulers have sought to maintain control over society through varied combinations of repression, encapsulation[17] and the manipulation of social segmentation. Elements of a proto-civil society have emerged either during periods of political liberalisation and/or as a result of external influences. The politico-economic forces which have made Afghanistan a rentier state have in turn generated at certain historical moments a rentier civil society, the Soviet and post-Taliban periods being cases in point. Parallel to this, people have also come together routinely on their own accord to cope and survive in conditions of conflict and uncertainty, independent of externally provided aid. The historical path of civil society formation thus closely shadows the ebb and flow of state formation processes in Afghanistan.

There are six key phases in the elemental development of a civil society since the late 1940s, each of which gave rise to different organisational forms, ideologies and values of varying durability. Each of these phases bears the footprints of different external forces and interests in the developmental trajectory of Afghanistan. At each stage we see the different engagement of civil society actors from outside. The first and second phases are, respectively, the period of the 'Liberal Parliament' from 1949 to 1952 under Shah Mahmud and the longer period of the New Democracy from 1963 to 1973 under Zahir Shah. It was during these periods of relative political liberalisation that the first familiar signs of liberal civil society such as clubs, women's groups[18] and informal student discussion groups at Kabul University emerged (Rubin, 2002, p. 58; Saikal, 2006, p. 159). The expansion of foreign aid for secondary and university education from the mid-1950s onwards, particularly from the US, played an important role in cultivating a stratum of urban, educated youth, who were exposed to new ideas and values. Whilst Daoud relied on the Soviets for the equipping and training of Afghanistan's military cadre in the 1950s and 1960s,[19] educational exchanges were also part of Soviet Cold War tactics to nurture alliances with a future generation of leaders. This newly educated elite, whose ties with tribes and regions were loosened through their sojourn in urban boarding schools, provided the intellectual seeds not only for a modernising state but also for an incipient civil society.

During the Soviet Occupation from 1978 to 1986 three strands competed for hegemony, representing socialist, liberal and Islamist imaginations of state–society relations. The first strand introduced into Afghanistan Soviet, modern forms of state socialist associational life. The occupying Soviet forces constructed Leninist-style mass organisations such as the Democratic Youth Organisation of Afghanistan, trade unions and craft unions. In this way they tried not only to bridge the gap between the political elite in Kabul and society through intermediary structures reaching out to women, youth, workers and professions, but also to modernise associational life away from 'traditional' organising principles such as tribe, clan and region to 'modern' organising principles of class. However, they were confined to the cities because of the limited reach of the state into rural areas. In this process the proto-elements of liberal civil society that had emerged under New Democracy were crushed.

The second strand relates to the increasing involvement of international European and American NGOs in the refugee camps in Pakistan and in cross-border humanitarian work.[20] In this way educated Afghan refugees became involved in NGO work, which familiarised them with liberal discourses and provided them with knowledge of international institutions, policies and networks that they could apply on their return to Afghanistan.[21] The involvement of INGOs at this point has to be set against the context of the Cold War. The Swedish Committee for Afghanistan, for example, was set up in 1980 to support the national independence of Afghanistan and the withdrawal of Soviet troops. Indeed, humanitarian assistance of the US was deliberately aimed at supporting the Islamist resistance to organise base areas of control (Rubin, 2002, pp. 224–225), a strategy that echoes 'hearts and minds' policies in Helmand province over 20 years later.

These INGOs also established humanitarian operations in the mujahedin-held areas of Afghanistan, particularly from the mid-1980s onwards, often channelling their aid directly to commanders. For example, Ahmad Shah Massoud, one of the three commanders of Jamiat-i-Islami, who had developed an extensive proto-state in the area he occupied, had strong working relations with the Swedish Committee for Afghanistan, Afghan Aid as well as USAID, and reportedly received substantial sums of aid for schools, health facilities and engineering projects (Rubin, 2002, p. 220). Afghan and international NGOs were often perceived as being linked to particular commanders and political parties. For example, an Afghan employee of an international NGO explained that many CARE staff were associated with Hekmatyar's Hezb-i-Islami, whilst Afghan Technical Consultants, a de-mining agency, was perceived as being close to Masood's Jamiat-i-Islami.[22] Similarly, the Co-operation Centre for Afghanistan, an Afghan NGO established initially in Pakistan in 1990, is allegedly linked to Mustasafin, an Islamic Shia political party.[23] Though INGOs may have forged these links for expediency, the perception of them as being associated with particular parties implicitly undermined their claims of being impartial and independent. The mujahedin commanders used shuras, where these functioned at all, to consolidate their control over rural areas.

The third related strand is the encounter of Afghan refugees with Middle Eastern humanitarian and development NGOs, mainly in Pakistan and to a limited extent in mujahedin-controlled areas. The use of Saudi aid to support madrassas and mosques not only served to spread Wahhabi Islamism but also implicitly challenged both Soviet and liberal secular notions of the state and civil society. Indeed it was from the radical madrassas in Pakistan that the first generation of Taliban fighters emerged (Burke, 2004, pp. 91–96).

The fourth phase covers the warlord period from approximately 1992 to 1996, when the Taliban captured Kabul. With the withdrawal of Soviet troops, the mass organisations they had built also crumbled. Foreign aid and international NGO operations increased in the immediate years after the Soviet withdrawal. However, the ensuing chaotic warlord struggles for power heightened insecurity and impeded the access of humanitarian workers to many of the rural areas. INGOs negotiated safe routes with individual commanders where possible.[24] Apart from this they were not subject to any central government controls over their operations, and providing they had the agreement of powerful warlords, they could operate with minimal restrictions.

As the Taliban extended their power across Afghanistan and restored some degree of security, INGOs such as the Save the Children Fund, MSF and Danish Committee for Aid to Afghan Refugees (DACAAR) extended their humanitarian projects, heralding the fifth phase in the development of a proto-civil society in Afghanistan. Many INGOs clashed with the new government over gender and rights issues and its attempt to control their activities (Rashid, 2000, pp. 64–66, 114). Within a year of gaining control of Kabul the Taliban had already begun to introduce controls on NGO activities. In May 1997 all aid projects were to be cleared not only by the relevant ministry but also by the police, the ministries of Public Health and Interior and the Department of the Promotion of Virtue and Prevention of Vice (Rashid, 2000, p. 114).

In 2000 the Taliban regime introduced Regulations for the Activities of National and International NGOs, the first such regulations governing NGOs in Afghanistan's history. The only other related law was the Law on Social Organisations, issued in line with the 1964 Constitution, which applied to 'communities and associations' engaged in cultural, educational, legal, artistic and vocational activities. In practice, however, the regulations did not unduly hinder the operations of NGOs, which had more latitude to operate during the Taliban period than Western media reports liked to project (Johnson and Leslie, 2004, pp. 67–68). There were also reportedly around 16 Islamic charities from Kuwait and Saudi Arabia operating in Afghanistan during the Taliban period. Though these were formally engaged mainly in welfare and relief work, some such as the Al Rashid Trust allegedly operated training camps for Islamic militants, exploiting their charitable status as a front to raise money.[25] Despite the Taliban strictures on girls' schooling and women's employment, some women managed to organise home study groups, sewing centres and community development councils underground, which after the Taliban's demise were then able to formally register.[26]

The Taliban were also to put their mark on local institutions such as shuras. Whilst NGOs used shuras as implementing vehicles for projects, the Taliban in some areas used these for tax collection. They also Islamicised the shuras by making village religious leaders heads, thereby sidelining khans and secular sources of authority.[27] However, the Taliban were not able or necessarily willing to exert total control over civil society. Neighbourhood groups and trade shuras were largely left alone to organise so long as they did not promote ideas and values or engage in activities that offended the ideals of Taliban rulers.[28] They were thus not vulnerable to arbitrary administrative interference or intimidation as they had been in other periods.

The sixth phase in the post-Independence history of civil society in Afghanistan dates from the overthrow of the Taliban regime in December 2001. It is during this phase that international aid agencies expanded their relief and development efforts. The collapse of the Taliban heralded renewed discussion about the idea of civil society and new donor support for building civil society. These trends are examined in greater detail in the following section.

The changing landscape of civil society post-911: Aid and civil society

The landscape of civil society changed substantially after 2001 as external forces imported their own visions of the ideal-type state and role for civil society. External developmental intervention has created a new layer of civil society consisting of funded NGOs, which donors and the Afghan state view instrumentally as service deliverers rather than actors promoting democratic spaces. Aid dependency of NGOs in turn has contributed to negative public perceptions of NGOs. This is in spite of NGO efforts to enhance their accountability through various self-regulation measures. Furthermore, the image of civil society promoted in state-building efforts in Afghanistan has overlooked the potential role of religious and 'traditional' institutions in promoting social welfare, peace and recovery.

Since the collapse of the Taliban regime in 2001, the complex genealogy of civil society in Afghanistan has acquired another layer of organisational forms, values and purposes. Foreign NGOs poured into Kabul on the heels of Western troops and Afghan fighters allied with the Northern Alliance. Those NGOs already operating in Afghanistan expanded their programmes, often under pressure from headquarters back home (Johnson and Leslie, 2004, p. 206). The numbers of INGOs spiralled, increasing from 46 registered INGOs in 1999 to over 350 in November 2002 (Johnson and Leslie, 2004, pp. 206–207). By 2003 this figure had leapt to an estimated 2,000 or more, including both international and Afghan NGOs and private sector agencies that were mainly involved in construction.[29]

With a vacuum in political leadership and a weakened state administration in the early post-Taliban years, donors relied mainly on NGOs to deliver relief aid. Given the paucity of pre-existing Afghan developmental NGOs, aid was also used to create and consolidate a layer of local NGOs and community organisations. For example, USAID supported neighbourhood associations in Kabul to collect waste and clean streets.[30] UN agencies supported Wassa, a prominent women's organisation in Herat, to work on women's hygiene and shelter.[31] The hope was that local organisations like these would over time become equipped to implement aid projects, thereby strengthening ownership over the development process and enhancing its legitimacy. Aid agencies' need to deliver services and relief assistance through local partners nurtured a climate within which local NGOs organising around women's issues, human rights, health and education could emerge and flourish.

The overthrow of the Taliban regime and the prospects for an elected government ushered in a period of relative political liberalisation. Professional associations such as the Afghan Lawyers' Association and trades associations re-emerged from the crevices, often bolstered by the inputs of Afghan returnees. Study groups and intellectual associations began to mushroom, such as the Freedom of Expression Association.[32] New women's organisations were set up; others were able to extend their activities; and some of these have linked up with international networks such as Women Living under Muslim Laws.[33] In Herat a professional shura was established in 2001 to discuss social issues, democracy and human rights and to strengthen the position of professionals.[34] Islamic study circles and associations such as the Afghan Society for Social Reform and Development also flourished in the liberalised environment.[35] The emergence of independent media outlets, such as Tolo TV, bolstered these new spaces of freedom. On various occasions these played a vital role in holding government leaders to account, exposing privilege and corruption and, most importantly, creating a public sphere of critical discussion.[36]

The first formal civil society consultation with donors took place in Bad Honnef in November 2001 parallel to the Bonn Agreement process. The consultation was an afterthought, reflecting the fact that civil society actors were treated as marginal players in the reconstruction and state-building processes in Afghanistan. This led to the formation of the Afghan Civil Society Forum, with the support of Swisspeace, to provide a space for civil society to discuss Afghan development issues and to increase their influence.[37] This experience led to a similar consultation at the London Conference on the Afghan Compact, Afghanistan's new five-year development plan in January 2006. Though this marked an attempt to widen the social spaces of politics and public life, civil society still remained marginal to these political processes.

This sudden influx of INGOs and the concomitant mushrooming of Afghan NGOs inscribed the associational landscape of Afghanistan with new contours, meanings and values. Propped up by aid flows, this new tide of NGOs began to assume a salience in reconstruction efforts. They overshadowed the potential contribution of pre-existing institutions such as shuras, jirgas, khans, maliks, ulema, village elders and mosques and newly emerging organisations such as professional and trades associations. In the early post-Taliban years aid agencies bypassed these other institutions of local decision-making, which were seen to embody illiberal values. It was also in part because donors have a 'bureaucratic understanding' of civil society, preferring to operate with formal, registered organisations through which aid funds can be easily disbursed.

As in other aid-recipient contexts NGOs came to embody the very essence of civil society[38] (Howell and Pearce, 2001). This contrasted with the efforts by militaries and foreign governments to engage with traditional institutions in political dialogue. This reflected the division of labour between militaries that focussed on security and governance and aid agencies that focussed on service-delivery. Yet donor support for local service-delivery organisations meant these were effectively excluded from debates and activities relating to security, reconciliation or peace-building. Aid support to NGOs legitimised their role as players in reconstruction and development, thereby endowing them with power, authority and resources but not necessarily legitimacy. Though donors funded local NGOs such as the Afghan Civil Society Forum to conduct civic education in the run-up to the parliamentary elections in 2005, donors focussed primarily on supporting NGOs to provide services. As will be seen later, this top-down approach to civil society led to confusion surrounding the concept of civil society and resentment towards NGOs.

Donors supported the new government's attempt to reconfigure power relations in rural areas by establishing new institutions. In particular, the CDCs set up under the NSP overlaid pre-existing structures and authorities in rural areas. However, CDCs were unique in having a singular focus on delivering development at the local level rather than becoming involved in social affairs generally. Though they formed part of a grander scheme of state-building, there was some ambiguity as to whether CDCs were NGOs or a first step in building local government structures.[39] They were not, however, about developing Afghan civil society as such. Rather, they were intended to implement development projects in a more participatory and equitable way through elections and requirements for women's participation. An Afghan employee of an international NGO commented, 'CDCs are not real civil society since they have been created from the top-down, and partially for political purposes. There has been no awareness-raising or capacity-building. CDCs do not consider themselves to be civil society but instead a mechanism for the delivery of aid – implementers of development projects. They could evolve into civil society ... If government or donors pull out of the NSP, there is a concern that the shuras [CDCs] will collapse.'[40]

The strategies of donor agencies drew on a language that was new in Afghanistan in order to conceptualise relations between citizens and the state; that is, the concept of civil society. The arrival of a civil society discourse in Afghanistan provided a focus for reflecting on some of the tensions that were already beginning to emerge around the rapid proliferation of international and local NGOs and their relation to the state and society. These tensions revolved around divisions between Afghan and international NGOs and whether the latter were part of Afghan civil society;[41] fissures amongst Afghans along organisational, ethnic, returnee and political lines in a context where groups vied for legitimacy, resources and space; growing resentment amongst political leaders concerning the resources, power and authority that NGOs seemed to command; and public unease with the lifestyles and behaviour of NGO workers, their elitism, the importance given to NGOs and a perception that they were stooges for foreign interests.

Along with key civil society players, such as the ACBAR, donors and government leaders supportive of civil society sought to regularise and legitimise the position of NGOs through the introduction of a new NGO law. Debate on the new NGO law revealed the unease felt by some Afghan ministers and bureaucrats towards NGOs and triggered a sharp critique of the genuineness and probity of NGOs. Though donors have channelled increasing amounts of aid to government, there is still residual resentment amongst government officials towards NGOs. Some Afghan ministers had a background working in NGOs and thus approached proposed regulation sensibly. However, others vehemently resisted the consolidation and legitimisation of NGOs' position in the development process that the new legislation would bring. Ramazan Bashar Dost, Minister of Planning in 2004, reportedly went as far as to condone the killing of five MSF workers in 2004 and had even compared NGOs to warlords (Saeed, 2004). The large disparity in the salaries paid to NGO local staff and civil servant salaries, often more than 20-fold, has fuelled this resentment.[42]

The passing of the NGO Act in June 2005 not only brought some order to the non-governmental realm and helped to define NGOs as non-profit agencies but also provided the possibility for the state to exert considerable control over NGOs. For example, Article 23 requires NGOs to submit their project documents to the Ministry for verification before starting work. The number of national and international NGOs registered with the Ministry of Economy fell from 2,400 under the 2002 NGO law to around 1,100 as of February 2007 (USIG, 2007).[43] In addition, there were approximately 700 social organisations registered with the Ministry of Social Justice. As in other countries, the NGO Act merged elements of counter-terrorism into charitable regulation. So, for example, article 8:5 warns organisations not to engage 'in terrorist activities or support, encouragement or financing of terrorism'.

Political attacks on NGOs fed into negative public attitudes towards the lifestyles of expatriate NGO staff and discontent over wage disparities between foreign and local NGO workers. A woman parliamentarian and activist explained the unease felt towards NGOs and, by extension, donors: 'They do flagship projects, meaning they put up a big sign saying "gift of the American people" but there is nothing else. The money goes back to the donors' countries. A large portion of funds goes to foreign experts. The money is spent on bodyguards, chauffeurs, holidays. When they come here, they demand per diems, holidays, high fees and they don't pay tax.'[44] Similarly, an Afghan worker in an international NGO in Herat commented, 'People supported and trusted NGOs during the Taliban time. This was the best image of NGOs but the number of NGOs was few. I was proud then to work for an NGO. Now it is 100 per cent opposite. People are now negative. Now I'll never tell anyone that I work for an NGO.' To some extent NGOs are a scapegoat for a more general frustration with the development industry, the worsening security situation, persistent corruption, and the complicity of foreign governments in allowing criminal elements to take senior government posts. An advisor to the EC remarked, 'NGOs are the whipping boy for government and blamed for corruption.'[45]

These frustrations reached a climax in May 2006 when US forces shot into a crowd protesting at the killing of civilians in a car accident involving US troops in Kabul. The protest quickly spiralled as hundreds of people rampaged through the streets. NGO offices were attacked and burned. Staff sought refuge in neighbouring buildings whilst some street residents tried to divert the rioters. The offices of CARE International were burned down whilst others such as Oxfam saw their offices pillaged. The attacks prompted two key responses. First, most development agencies, including NGOs, tightened their security arrangements. The types of measures adopted included removing signboards outside offices, increasing the number of security guards, appointing security coordinators, formulating anti-kidnapping policies and training, moving offices to less conspicuous locations, restricting the movement of staff around Kabul and strengthening physical barriers around office premises. Second, NGOs promoted a Code of Conduct for NGOs that was launched by ACBAR before the riots in May 2004. In this way, NGOs tried to alter their public image as being predatory and corrupt.

By August 2006 approximately 115 NGOs were deemed compliant with the Code of Conduct, thereby strengthening the institutional base of NGOs. In addition, officials with ACBAR met with President Karzai on at least three occasions to lobby on behalf of NGOs for a more even-handed approach to NGO regulation and to present the Code of Conduct as evidence of their efforts at self-regulation and encouraging transparency. However, NGOs were caught in a dilemma because security precautions made them even more distant from the communities they served, allowing for suspicions to arise and less opportunity for building relations of trust. An Afghan worker for an international

NGO in Herat commented, 'NGOs keep themselves separated from communities, such as driving big cars, hiring people from the outside, drinking mineral water and soda when out in the field. ...They need to be accountable to communities...They should involve them and share the budget and be transparent. That includes mosques and shuras...They should give a report to the beneficiaries, not just to donors.'[46] The issues around the probity and legitimacy of NGOs have endured and continue to be a refrain in political debates on NGOs in Afghanistan.

As previously discussed, the shift towards channelling resources directly to the Afghan government embodied a particular vision of civil society in the future Afghanistan. The primary role of civil society was to be a service-delivery agent, implementing government and donor-funded development projects. Such a vision underplays other critical roles of civil society such as acting as a watchdog on the state, holding officials to account, demanding transparency or advising in policy formulation. This is unsurprising in that these other varied roles would unmask the hypocrisy of the liberal-democratic ideal being promoted by the US and allies, which dance in tune to the accommodation of war criminals in the Afghan government as a presumably necessary measure to win their cooperation in counter-insurgency.[47] Moreover, it is in line with the general tendency since the Bonn process to sideline civil society actors as marginal players in the development process. In this way the prioritisation of stabilisation and security over peace and reconciliation has shaped this instrumental approach to civil society, giving priority to the service-delivery role of civil society over its potential contribution to peace-building and reconciliation. In effect, donors and the Afghan government have sought to emasculate civil society by emphasising its contribution to delivering development. This is depoliticising in two respects. First, this ideal overlooks the political role of civil society as a sphere of citizen engagement and deliberation in public affairs. Second, it glosses over the inherently politicised and contested nature of the terrain of civil society, which comprises a multiplicity of actors with divergent interests, values and ideologies and purposes.

The organised part of civil society that depends on external aid has quietly acquiesced to its depoliticised role. There has been little debate about the implications for civil society of the state-building processes envisaged in the Afghan National Development Strategy. There has been no discussion about how such sub-contractual relations might jeopardise the assumed independence of civil society; or of how taking on these state functions relates to any citizen discussion of the appropriate responsibilities of the state; or of the role of external agencies in refashioning state–civil society relations in this way; or of how the creation of CDCs is part of a dual process of implementing development projects and enhancing the legitimacy of the state.

Donors have been reluctant to stimulate a more critical debate on the roles of civil society, as well. Instead, most donors are complacent with the position being carved out for civil society in delivering aid-funded projects. This in turn relates to the lack of conditionalities placed upon aid in the rush to sign the Bonn Agreement (Goodhand and Sedra, 2007), with security objectives being prioritised over peace. This prioritisation of foreign security objectives has required that civil society contributes to donor-defined state-building strategy, rather than promoting a genuinely independent realm that promotes political deliberation and demands accountability. The dependency of most of these organisations on external funding has led to the creation of a 'rentier civil society' in Afghanistan that struggles to maintain its autonomy or define its own priorities, goals and roles.

In recent years, some donors have initiated programmes aimed at strengthening civil society in Afghanistan. The largest of these is the US$15 million programme of Counterpart International, which was established in 2006 and is funded by USAID. As of 2006 USAID was the largest donor of civil society in Afghanistan, with implications for how 'modern', organised civil society will be shaped over the coming years. Counterpart International is essentially promoting a liberal democratic image of civil society in the Tocquevillian tradition, where people voluntarily form associations to address their diverse needs. Its plan for Afghanistan draws particularly upon the programme it developed in Kazakhstan[48] with some later modifications to account for religion. Such an image plays little heed to the power relations and tensions within civil society or the ongoing conflict within Afghanistan. The use of blueprints for strengthening civil society which are inadequately contextualised to the situation in Afghanistan and the rotation of expatriate development personnel have ensured that a particular notion of civil society is spread through the structures of aid. The other key initiative is led by the Swedish Committee for Afghanistan (SCA). It organised a major workshop in 2006 on the future role of civil society in Afghanistan with a view to guiding its future strategy towards civil society. The SCA image of civil society emphasises more the idea of civil society as a realm for public participation within a social democratic framework that assumes greater responsibility by the state for providing welfare. However, its level of support pales in comparison to that of USAID, which is likely to dominate the development of formally organised civil society in the country through the sheer volume of resources.

These initiatives are not merely about defining the functional roles of civil society. They also have a broader ideological purpose to create modern institutions that are deemed appropriate to building a neo-liberal state. However, they are also deeply contradictory as the Bonn Process had prioritised security and stabilisation over peace and reconciliation. Since then the promotion of a public realm where ideas could be contested and groups engaged in public affairs could organise has been undermined. The diplomatic and aid establishment could have more effectively leveraged their resources to ensure that President Karzai fostered these democratic spaces. However, this would have undermined diplomatic and strategic objectives in the War on Terror.

Thus, manufactured civil society in Afghanistan is depoliticised and this fact cannot be disconnected from the ongoing War on Terror that is being waged by foreign militaries in the country. The following section examines more closely the unsettling alliances and relations between militaries, development and civil society actors against the backdrop of counter-insurgency and worsening security in Afghanistan.

Civil society, the military and the War on Terror

The battle for the ideological terrain in Afghanistan has been highly contradictory. Policy and practice on civil society is going forth without taking heed of the continuing conflict, power relations and the prioritisation of stabilisation goals over fostering democratic spaces. For example, Counterpart International, which is USAID-funded, has a grant scheme on truth and justice. However, USAID refused to have its logo used on informational literature for the scheme as they considered this would risk adding pressure on the US government to draw a line under the issue of warlords in the Afghan government. In general, there is reluctance amongst donors to deal with the contradictions and complexities pervading a situation of multiple conflicts, which in turn shape how people view the state, donors and non-governmental actors. These contradictions and complexities have been most acute with respect to the involvement of foreign militaries in development. Debates have ensued around the risks posed to humanitarian and development NGOs, and in particular the effects of such military-led developmental intervention on the presumed neutrality and independence of humanitarian agencies. This, in turn, has impinged on the development of civil society in Afghanistan.

The War on Terror has greatly complicated and undermined development agencies' attempts to strengthen liberal civil society for several reasons. First, and most obviously, because of the ongoing insurgency an increasing area of Afghanistan has become virtually inaccessible to NGOs. By the end of 2006 the insurgency had already spread across most provinces in the country with attacks increasing on Kabul itself (Giustozzi, 2007). The dynamics of the insurgency tie into the War on Terror strategy and the failure of Coalition forces to prioritise security for the civilian population. It also relates to the reluctance of foreign powers in Afghanistan to engage in any peace-building or reconciliation efforts out of fear that this would undermine stabilisation of the country. NGOs still send local staff to visit project sites but at considerable risk to their personal safety. Local workers for national and international NGOs use local transport and do not take with them any project documentation that would identify them as working for an aid agency.

Second, and most importantly, military strategy for addressing the ongoing insurgency has included a developmental dimension, which has infringed upon the work of developmental NGOs. This has generated a heated debate amongst NGOs as to whether or not to cooperate with the military and compromised their claims to be independent and neutral. Although these debates are symptomatic of tensions more generally after the Cold War between civilian and military actors in conflict settings, what is different in Afghanistan is a much more concerted effort to promote the military's involvement in development and encourage close civilian–military cooperation in stabilisation and reconstruction. Most INGOs we interviewed stated that they did not and would not work with the PRTs.[49] Beyond this principled stance, INGOs varied as to how much contact with the military they would entertain in the field, ranging from having no contact to providing advice or maintaining limited dialogue and coordination.[50] US NGOs have come under considerable pressure from military powers in Washington to work with militaries and some have found ways around this by funding local organisations, which in turn work with PRTs.[51]

There are also different perspectives and perceptions amongst Afghan NGOs. In Herat, the PRT was invited to the monthly meeting of an umbrella NGO but stopped coming when their representatives were asked not to come with guns.[52] The engagement of PRTs in activities commonly undertaken by NGOs has heightened divisions and distrust amongst NGOs, with each accusing the other of working with the military.[53] In some areas PRTs are viewed positively, partly because they focus on hard infrastructural projects, for which local leaders can claim credit. They also provide short-term opportunities for acquiring wealth and status that longer-term NGO activity cannot so easily provide.

The key issue for NGOs concerns humanitarian principles of independence, impartiality and neutrality. By engaging with the military, NGOs fear that local people will see them as being aligned with the military and in so doing put them at risk of attack. Development workers argue that by using vehicles similar to those of NGOs, and without any military insignia on them, the local population is unable to distinguish between military and NGOs. In the words of an Afghan employee in an international NGO, 'Military personnel providing relief blurs the lines since communities are not able to differentiate between military and aid agency actors. Some day military actors are in fatigues, other days in civilian clothes. Sometimes they are in military vehicles, other days in white Land-cruisers that NGOs also use. It puts us at risk.'[54] There is already considerable confusion amongst local people about the distinctions between different international actors providing aid on the ground, as an Afghan NGO director pointed out: '.... To [Afghan] people, anyone who helps them is an NGO. They think PRTs are NGOs, that the UN is an NGO, that private sectors are NGOs. People don't have bad perceptions of the PRTs. They don't know who PRTs are and don't realise the differences between different militaries and different PRTs...'[55]

The increasing number of attacks on aid workers since 2003 has made this debate especially vigorous and poignant. For example, the number of attacks on NGOs attributed to armed opposition groups doubled from 8 in the first quarter of 2007 to 16 in the same period in 2008 (Afghan NGO Security Office (ANSO) report 2008). NGO representatives have argued that attacks on aid workers stem from the blurring lines between the military's aid and civilian assistance. For example, between January and November 2006 at least 30 aid workers, including NGOs, the UN and humanitarian contractors, had been killed, more than double the figure in 2003 (IRIN, 2006, 2007).[56] NGOs also stress that military engagement in development also endangers local communities. As the director of a UK NGO remarked, this also endangers the inhabitants of local communities: 'We are concerned as NGOs because as soon as it is clear that this is linked to the military, the communities will be targets of armed conflict and it will be unsafe for NGOs to work there.'[57]

Military players have countered and won this argument by claiming that there is no evidence that NGO workers have been attacked because they are aid workers. Rather, they argue, aid workers are soft targets and such attacks are random, criminal acts. However, it can also be argued that there is no evidence to suggest that they have not been attacked because of perceived links to the military. Indeed the so-called 'night letters' warning people not to cooperate with NGOs have been delivered to clinics, schools and the homes of individual aid workers. In some places mosque leaders have warned people not to work in NGOs.[58] All this lends credibility to NGO critiques that they are being deliberately attacked because of their perceived links to the Afghan government and foreign militaries. Clearly insurgents do target aid workers as part of their strategy to rid Afghanistan of foreign forces. Nevertheless they are also not entirely opposed to NGOs, seeking rather to negotiate the terms under which NGOs can operate in some situations. Further, it is telling that there were reportedly no deliberate attacks on aid workers during the Taliban period.

The NGO critics also argue that quick impact projects are often ill-thought through, unsustainable and of limited developmental value. NGO workers related instances where the military hastily constructed school buildings but without first ensuring new teachers had been recruited. The thinking underlying quick-impact projects – that development works can buy the trust of local communities, who in turn will provide valuable intelligence – is seriously misguided. However, quick impact projects by the military also provide greater opportunity for patronage as local leaders can claim credit for the construction of new schools, clinics and roads. In contrast, longer-term development projects undertaken by NGOs might offer fewer direct opportunities for patronage and, in general, require greater commitment and scrutiny of funds (Gordon, 2006, p. 49).

Umbrella organisations like ACBAR have played a key role in scrutinising the military's role in development. In the summer of 2006 ACBAR led a process for developing a strong civil society position towards civil–military relations in order to ensure greater harmonisation amongst the PRTs and greater clarity about their mandates. They have called for the military to focus on improving security and stability and to leave development work to civilians. An ACBAR press release in December 2006 stated, 'Official development assistance (ODA) should not be used to fund PRTs or military objectives such as force protection, intelligence-gathering or hearts and minds operations.'[59] They have also maintained a sharp critique of civilian casualties of military attacks on insurgents. ACBAR stated in an August 2008 press release, 'Searches conducted by Afghan and international forces have on some occasions involved excessive use of force, extra-judicial killings, destruction of property and/or mistreatment of suspects.'[60]

The strategic engagement of the military in development highlights the challenges for NGOs to maintain a façade of neutrality. NGOs are part of the political fabric and political actors in their own right. It is not surprising that many local people do see NGOs, whether foreign or local, as part of a government–West alliance.[61] There is a startling contradiction amongst NGOs in wanting to adhere to the idea of neutrality without recognising how their own actions jeopardise such a stance. Just as NGOs served as fronts for Western governments' Cold War policies during the Soviet Occupation (Johnson and Leslie, 2004, p. 148), so developmental NGOs post-2001 are also implicitly supporting the Afghan government and Western policy in Afghanistan. The Chair of an Afghan cultural foundation observed, 'Maybe NGOs have to work with government to meet people's needs. So they should stop talking about being neutral. We're not neutral in supporting a democratically elected government put in place by force...'[62] The reluctance of NGOs to recognise their inherently political nature has no doubt contributed to their failure to mount a robust counter-argument to the position of donors and militaries, which have insisted that increasing attacks on aid workers have nothing to do with greater civil–military cooperation.

Moreover, the idea that a peaceful civil society can flourish or be strengthened in a context of armed conflict and where military interventions in development are accompanied by weapons of coercion is paradoxical. Such a proposition is to turn Hobbes on his head and argue that the 'state of nature' is a kind of civil society. As highlighted at the start of the chapter, an international aid worker in Kabul poignantly stated, 'Civil society with guns is not civil society.'[63]

Linked to this is the subtle sidelining of any non-governmental or governmental efforts at national reconciliation or peace-building. Given the long history of conflict in Afghanistan, it is extraordinary that there are so few initiatives to promote peace-building or reconciliation amongst communities or counselling for civilians traumatised by war. Underlying this is a persistent refrain amongst external actors that Afghans are particularly resilient in the face of civil war, fundamentalist rule and warlord violence. Yet by the end of 2006 there were only three such initiatives in the whole of Afghanistan, namely the Cooperation for Peace and Unity (CPAU), the Sanayee Development Organisation and the Afghan Women's Education Centre. Apart from these, some individuals are members of international networks working on conflict such as Action Asia.[64] The promulgation of the Amnesty Bill in 2007 put a lid on any further attempts by civil society to hold former warlords and political leaders to account for their roles in Afghanistan's long history of conflict. Indeed it points to the priority given to the goals of the US-led War on Terror over the long-term reconstruction and stabilisation of Afghanistan. It also reflects the failure of the Bonn Agreement to promote serious peace-building because of broader geo-strategic and military interests and the urgency of installing an elected government.[65]

In the last two years, some donors have widened their gaze to the so-called 'traditional' and religious institutions, commissioning studies on these institutions and their potential role in peace-building (Borchgrevink and Strand, 2007; CPAU, 2007) This shows a growing realisation among donors that they have overemphasised NGOs in their strategies and programming at the expense of understanding the much broader and varied associational landscape in Afghanistan, a problem that is seen in other aid contexts as well.

In brief, following the invasion of Afghanistan in early 2002 the landscape of civil society has become increasingly complex and contested. The influx of international humanitarian and development agencies, the mushrooming of Afghan developmental NGOs and the more recent establishment of CDCs in rural areas have led to new flows of resources, new nodes of power and authority and new vehicles of patronage. This top-down approach has culminated in the establishment of a rentier civil society consisting of donor-funded NGOs whose purpose is conceived narrowly as delivering services rather than necessarily representing the interests of the people they claim to speak for. Organisations have been formed to draw on aid largesse rather than to address public interests, and, unsurprisingly, many of these recently formed groups represent parochial interests to gain access to resources rather than a desire to contribute to a greater collective good. In the end this has been deleterious to the development of non-governmental actors who genuinely work for accountability in governance. The rise of these new civil society organisations is thus intimately related to the development priorities of donor institutions that in turn are embedded in the complex geopolitics of the War on Terror.

Conclusion

The interlinking of civil society, security and aid in Afghanistan since the overthrow of the Taliban regime demonstrates vividly the prominence of Western security objectives in guiding development in the country and external engagement with civil society. Although aid policy has not been wholly subordinated to security objectives, the allocation of a disproportionate amount of aid to southern parts of Afghanistan where the insurgency is rife suggests that poverty reduction is not the primary criteria being used to target aid. As seen throughout Afghanistan's recent history, foreign aid has been used to leverage external security interests, which since 2001 have centred on fighting elements of Al Qaeda as well as a resurgent Taliban. Though the coupling of development with security is more pronounced in Afghanistan as a key battleground in the War on Terror, these trends are observed in development aid policy more generally (Howell and Lind, 2009).

The convergence of military and development objectives, and the partial subordination of the latter to the former, has in turn had consequences for aid policy and civil society. In constructing a neo-liberal state in Afghanistan Western governments have channelled increasing volumes of aid through Afghan government–controlled programmes that necessitate the involvement of non-governmental groups in their implementation. The number of NGOs in Afghanistan has mushroomed since 2001, feeding off the opportunities made available by foreign aid. This has resulted in the creation of a rentier civil society consisting of bureaucratically amenable NGOs that deliver aid. These organisations are instrumental agents that function to act as sub-contractors to the Afghan government and foreign donors. They are not sowing the seeds for the establishment of a deliberative, more politically engaged civil society. Their purpose is not to contribute to building democracy but rather to contribute to the stabilisation objectives of foreign powers through enhancing the legitimacy of the state.

Ironically, the co-option of civil society into state-building strategies in Afghanistan as a way of strengthening the state has actually undermined the legitimacy of civil society and contributed to negative popular attitudes of NGOs. Foreign assistance approaches to civil society in Afghanistan, geared as they are to service delivery, have also entailed a singular focus on NGOs. As in post-conflict settings elsewhere, donors assume that social breakdown has happened and thus there is a lack of local decision-making structures with sufficient authority to guide and deliver development. Since political debate is not being encouraged, and arguably is actively discouraged by foreign donors, 'customary' structures, religious groups and organisations working on peace-building and reconciliation have been largely ignored. Promoting the growth of spaces for political debate and deliberation is regarded as risking the overall priority to stabilise the country and prevent terrorists or anti-government elements from organising.

The other aspect of foreign aid strategy impinging on the actors and spaces of civil society in Afghanistan concerns the increasing involvement of foreign militaries in delivering certain types of aid. Many NGOs in Afghanistan have refused to cooperate with foreign militaries, which have nonetheless expanded their involvement in development work. This has created political and moral dilemmas for NGOs acting on a humanitarian mandate as to how to act impartially, independently and neutrally and, moreover, be perceived by the general public as doing so. NGOs have struggled to make their case in a situation of deteriorating security and increasing risks to the safety of aid workers. Many parts of Afghanistan have become too insecure for most NGOs to operate and those that do have had to modify their practices to promote the safety of their employees. What makes these operational difficulties more challenging is that many NGOs have been reluctant to critically evaluate their own principled stance and recognise the political contradictions of their own positions in a deeply politicised and shifting political context.

Civil society will continue to occupy a prominent place on the political battlefield in Afghanistan, regardless of NGO claims to the contrary. Robert Gates, Defense Secretary under former US President Bush and now in the same position in the Obama administration, has called upon European allies 'to be more responsible for building civil society institutions in Afghanistan', underlining again the instrumentalisation of civil society in politico-military strategy in the country. Foreign-funded civil society groups should be alert to the politics, framing their own position and roles in stabilisation and state-building efforts. However, the past unwillingness of NGOs to recognise that they too are actors in a deeply politicised drama points to the dangers for NGOs in trying to maintain a guise of neutrality.

Notes

1. For a highly informative account of Al Qaeda see Burke (2004).
2. Over 90 per cent of Afghanistan's public expenditure comes from developmental assistance. Net official development assistance in 2005 was US$2.3 billion, accounting for 38 per cent of gross national income (OECD, 2006, pp. 7–20).
3. This chapter draws upon the fieldwork carried out in Afghanistan in the summer of 2006, interviews with key informants in NGOs and government in the UK between 2005 and 2008, and secondary sources. Over 58 semi-structured qualitative interviews and a round-table were conducted in Afghanistan with key informants in local and international civil society organisations, bilateral and multilateral development agencies, government officials and ISAF.

4. Rubin (2002, pp. 65, 311) notes that a rentier or allocation state is one where the state derives more than 40 per cent of its revenue from oil or foreign sources. In the case of Afghanistan the significant sources are foreign aid and the sale of natural gas (at least up till 1989).
5. On Bin Laden's sojourn in Sudan and the politics behind his departure see Burke (2004, pp. 143–157).
6. It is beyond the scope of this book to cover in depth the politics of these political processes. For a flavour of these issues see Maley (2006), Leader and Atmar (2004), Johnson and Leslie (2004), Saikal (2006), Starr (2006), Thier (2004) and Rubin (2004).
7. The UK government committed £500 million to Afghanistan from 2002 to 2007, though additional funds are also channelled through other mechanisms such as the Global Conflict Prevention Pool (see Cosgrave and Andersen, 2004). However, establishing precise promised and actual aid flow figures for different donors is hampered by the lack of available data for the early years, the different categories and reporting mechanisms used by donors and the flows of funds to support the UN and other international institutions.
8. See 'Afghanistan, Inc.: A Corpwatch Investigative Report'. Fariba Nawa. April 2006.
9. For example, one interviewee from a peace-building NGO recounted a clash involving one death and nine injuries in a district in Kabul over who would benefit from an electricity system being introduced under the NSP. Authors' interview. CPAU. Kabul. 24 August 2006.
10. For a critique of NSP finances see Action Aid Afghanistan and ELBAG (2007).
11. For example, US PRTs are predominantly made up of military personnel, with a handful of civilians (3 out of 80), whilst German PRTs are larger, with over 300 personnel and a sharp division between the civilian component and the much smaller military unit (Perito, 2005, 2007).
12. Foreign Minister Rangin Dadfar Spanta lamented in an interview in 2006 that external powers and the government had paid too much attention to the military aspects of the War on Terror and pointed out that 'the anti-terrorism fight is not only a military task, it also involves development policies and social programmes' (Deutsche-Press Agentur, 6 September 2006). Development policy was thus a crucial 'soft means' to establishing a state presence in insurgent areas.
13. For further information on this see Gordon 2009.
14. See White (1994) for a discussion of different disciplinary interpretations of civil society.
15. It is important to stress that they potentially rather than absolutely militate. For example, Bangladesh has a vibrant civil society yet is primarily a rural economy. Actually existing civil society is much more complex than idealised notions of civil society suggest. Gellner eloquently argues how tribal and clan societies are counter-posed to modern, civil societies. However, in reality, social relations based on tribal and kin identities fuse with seemingly modern associational structures. In Afghanistan, too, the social fabric of life is criss-crossed with 'modern' associational structures, such as political parties, trade associations and NGOs.

16. For example, both Rubin (2002, p. 52) and Johnson and Leslie (2004, p. 41) point out how rulers such as Abdul Rehman Khan (1889–1901), Daud in 1977, Najibullah in 1987 and others have used grand loya jirgas to legitimate decisions they have already made rather than to debate. They also point out how the term 'shura', meaning council, has been variously deployed by the Soviets as a means of social control, by the mujahedin, whose use of it signified the Islamicisation of political relations (Rubin, 2002, p. 229), and by aid agencies to facilitate the implementation of projects (Johnson and Leslie, 2004, p. 42).

17. Rubin (2002, p. 62) uses the term 'encapsulation' to describe the strategy of rulers to balance out potential opponents, such as khans or ulama, by giving them symbolic roles without real power and granting them autonomy over local issues.

18. LSE/ACBAR round-table. Kabul. 11 September 2006.

19. Saikal (2006, pp. 123–124) points out that the Americans refused Daoud's request for assistance.

20. Some such as CARE International had previously been based in Afghanistan (Authors' interview. CARE International. Kabul. 24 August 2006).

21. For example, the Afghan Women's Education Centre was established by Afghan refugees in Pakistan in 1991 and began its work in Afghanistan in 2001. Similarly, the Sanayee Development Foundation was founded in 1990 in Peshawar and entered Afghanistan in 2002.

22. Authors' interview. Christian Aid. Herat. 3 September 2006.

23. Authors' interview. UNAMA. Kabul. 7 September 2006. And with researcher, Kabul. 7 September 2006.

24. One interviewee from an international financial institution with experience of working in NGOs during the anti-Soviet mujahedin period claimed that movements of aid workers were less restrictive than in the post-Taliban era (Authors' interview. Local gender consultant. Asian Development Bank. 30 August 2006).

25. In September 2001 Al-Rashid Trust was put onto the US list of terrorist organisations. It was allegedly close to Al Qaeda and coordinated with Wafa Khairia, an Arab NGO formed by Osama bin Laden. It set up networks of Deobandi madrassas across Afghanistan and took over the bakeries that the UN World Food Programme abandoned after the 9/11 attacks (Escobar, 2001). Its funds come mainly from the Middle East and Pakistan and Osama Bin Laden was reportedly a recipient of the Trust's funds. Its activities were continued by the Al Akhtar Trust, which in turn was designated by the US as a terrorist organisation. In April 2007 Al-Rashid Welfare Trust was allowed to resume its activities (Latif, 2007). Similarly, the Afghan Support Committee was allegedly set up by Osama Bin Laden and affiliated with the Revival of Islamic Heritage Society.

26. Authors' interview. Female parliamentarian. Kabul. 27 August 2006. Authors' interview. Headmistress of primary school. Kabul. 28 August 2006.

27. Authors' interview. Local aid worker. Christian Aid. Herat. 4 September 2006.

28. Authors' interview. Head of trade shura. Kabul. 25 August 2006.

29. As the private sector was discouraged during the Taliban period, existing businesses sought legal shelter under the nomenclature of NGOs,

contributing to the layers of confusion around the terms NGO and later 'civil society'.

30. Authors' interview. USAID. Kabul. 31 August 2006.
31. Authors' interview. Wassa. Herat. 3 September 2006.
32. Authors' interview. Afghan Women's Education Centre. Herat. 31 August 2006.
33. Authors' interview. Afghan Women's Education Centre. Herat. 31 August 2006. And Wassa. Herat. 3 September 2006.
34. Authors' interview. Head of professional shura. Herat. 4 September 2006.
35. Authors' interview. Afghan Society for Reform and Development. Kabul. 9 September 2006.
36. For example, journalists from Tolo were detained for covering a protest by the poor in a Kabul neighbourhood against the landholder, who was a warlord from their region. The media have also exposed parliamentarians sleeping and fighting in parliament.
37. Authors' interview. Director. Afghan Civil Society Forum. 23 August 2006.
38. Authors' interview with a representative of Friedrich Ebert Stiftung. Kabul. 10 September 2006. And with a local gender consultant. Asian Development Bank. 30 August 2006.
39. Authors' interview. CARE International. 24 August 2006. And also, according to one account the Ministry of Rural Rehabilitation and Development reportedly supports the idea of converting the CDCs into formal government structures, though on another occasion the opposite was claimed, namely that the Ministry wanted to keep CDCs as social organisations whilst the Ministry of the Interior wanted them to become government bodies (participants' comments at LSE/ACBAR round-table. Kabul. 9 September 2006).
40. Authors' interview. Christian Aid. Kabul. 21 August 2006.
41. As one interviewee bluntly put it, 'International NGOs are not part of Afghan civil society' (Authors' interview. Local aid worker. Kabul, 21 August 2006).
42. Authors' interview. Representative of Friedrich-Ebert Stiftung. 10 September 2006. And LSE/ACBAR round-table. Kabul. 11 September 2006.
43. Authors' interview. Head of civil society support programme. August 2006.
44. Authors' interview. Female parliamentarian. Kabul. 27 August 2006.
45. Authors' interview. Advisor to EC. Kabul. 7 September 2006.
46. Authors' interview. Local aid worker, Christian Aid. Herat. 3 September 2006.
47. For example, whilst Gulbuddin Hekmatyar, founder of Hezb-e-Islami and a notorious warlord, has been put on a US terrorist list, others such as General Abdul Rashid Dostum, once Chief of Staff of the Armed Forces, and Ismail Khan, once Minister of Energy, were also prominent and ruthless commanders, whose acts of violence could also be designated as war crimes.
48. Authors' interview. Head of Civil Society Initiative. Counterpart International. Kabul. 29 August 2006.
49. The Dutch Committee on Afghanistan was cited in an interview as one of the few that had coordinated with the local PRT on the distribution of aid (Authors' interview. Oxfam. Kabul. 23 August 2006).
50. Authors' interview. Policy and advocacy officer. Oxfam. Kabul. 23 August 2006. See also Perkins (2006).

51. For further reading on the controversy over PRTs, see Uesugi (2006), McNerney (2006), Hendrickson *et al.* (2005) and McHugh and Gostelow (2004).
52. Authors' interview. ACBAR representative. Herat. 5 September 2006.
53. Authors' interview. Afghan Civil Society Forum. Kabul. 23 September 2006. And Oxfam. Kabul. 23 September 2006. One interviewee gave the example of the Afghan NGO Coordination of Humanitarian Assistance.
54. Interview. Local aid worker in INGO. August 2006.
55. Interview. Head of local umbrella organisation. August 2006.
56. According to ANSO, 12 aid workers, including Afghan and international staff working for NGOs, the UN and development contractors, were killed in 2003; 24 in 2004; 31 in 2005; and 29 up to August 2006 (Authors' interview. ANSO. Kabul. August 2006).
57. Authors' interview. International aid worker. Save the Children Fund. Kabul. 27 August 2006.
58. Interview. INGO worker and local head of international foundation. Herat. September 2006.
59. Press release, December 2006, full statement available at www.baag.org.uk. This statement pointed out that 'There have been instances of military actors in Afghanistan behaving in ways that are confusing to local populations and compounding the security risks facing aid actors. Examples include: dressing in civilian clothing, driving white vehicles that resemble aid agency transport, and using NGO resources, such as vehicles, office equipment and premises without permission.'
60. 'Civilians under threat'. ACBAR press statement. 3 August 2008. Available at: http://www.afgana.org/showart.php?id=351&rubrica=218. Accessed 16 February 2009.
61. See Perkins (2006) for an in-depth exploration of the political dilemmas facing NGOs in Afghanistan.
62. Interview. Head of local cultural association. August 2006.
63. Interview. INGO worker. August 2006.
64. Interview. Local gender consultant. August 2006.
65. Interview. International UN worker. September 2006. For a robust critique of the Bonn Agreement and aid conditionality, see Goodhand and Sedra (2007).

6
Aid, Civil Society and the State in Kenya

> The US can put up fifty schools in Northeastern Province but this doesn't change local perceptions.
> Kenyan Muslim leader and NGO head, January 2007

The horrific bombings of the US embassies in Nairobi and Dar es Salaam thrust East Africa to the centre of world concern over the threat of terrorism and presaged the events of September 11 and the declaration of the global War on Terror. Images of crumbled office blocks and the twisted wreckage of buses and vehicles on the streets of central Nairobi gave rise to public consciousness of Osama Bin Laden and a new brand of international terrorism. Following the attacks, then US President Bill Clinton ordered an air strike on a pharmaceutical plant in Khartoum that US intelligence sources indicated was a disguised weapons-making facility (Wright, 2006). Sudan remains on the US list of state sponsors of terror and for a time in the 1990s was official host to Bin Laden. Kenya has since been the theatre for further attacks targeting Israeli tourists and commercial interests. When the Islamic Courts Union (ICU) briefly governed southern Somalia in 2006, the US perceived this as a radical group with ties to international terrorists and engineered the invasion of Somalia using proxy Ethiopian troops. This drew Kenya deeper into the prosecution of the War on Terror.

Some Western security analysts suggest that Kenya faces the greatest threat of terrorism in the Horn of Africa, an assessment that derives from Kenya's strategic value to the US and other Western security interests as well as its location in an unstable region. This explains the considerable security-oriented assistance directed to Kenya by foreign governments and diplomatic pressure on the Kenyan government to institute new counter-terrorism structures, especially since 2001. The

Kenyan government has been pressed to cooperate on the War on Terror at a time when the country is still undergoing a destabilising economic and political transition from former one-party rule. Its efforts on global counter-terrorism co-operation, in turn, have renewed concerns over the treatment of Muslims and Somalis and highlighted the fragility of civic space that was carved out during the democracy struggles of the 1990s. Yet, Kenya is seen as the strongest democracy in East Africa and also having the most effective and vocal civil society of any other country in the region. Thus, we would presume that civil society actors in Kenya would assert their views in political debates on counter-terrorism and pressure the government on aspects of its counter-terrorism responses.

The chapter begins by examining the establishment of new counter-terrorism structures. These have raised human rights concerns, especially for Muslims and Somalis, and threatened subtly the spaces for civil society to organise. In Kenya, aid has tended to support misconceptions embodied in the underlying logic of the global War on Terror. The changing role of aid in Kenya is assessed in the subsequent section, spanning the time of donor support for civil society during the democratisation struggles in the 1990s up to more recent efforts of donors to align with the development priorities of the state. Our analysis moves on to consider the politics of aid, civil society and the state in a deeper historical context. The chapter concludes by critically examining the differential responses of civil society to the state's counter-terrorism responses. In particular, it examines the failure of mainstream groups and the media to interrogate the pretext of counter-terrorism in Kenya or the methods and strategies employed under the guise of security.[1]

Division and distrust: Creating counter-terrorism structures in Kenya

With a background of previous terrorist attacks targeting US and Israeli interests and situated within an unstable yet strategically important region, Kenya is thought to have a high terrorist threat (Harmony Project, 2007). This risk assessment, originating as it does from external security and intelligence agencies, has led to international pressure on Kenyan authorities to introduce a raft of new counter-terrorism structures. These encompass measures to enhance intelligence-gathering and the policing and surveillance of suspect communities and legal provisions to prosecute terrorism suspects and their financiers. Unsurprisingly, foreign security assistance and training aid, especially from the US, were pivotal to the establishment of many post-9/11 counter-terrorism structures in Kenya. In spite of disagreement with the US over anti-terror legislation, as explained below, Kenya was one of eight countries globally to receive the largest proportional increase in US military assistance between 2000 and 2005 (Whitaker, 2007). Between 2002 and 2008, Kenya was the largest recipient in sub-Saharan Africa of US counter-terrorism funding.[2] In 2005, Kenya was one of only five states to receive special training through the US government's Anti-Terrorism Assistance Program, which included support for the establishment of the Kenyan National Security Intelligence Services (NSIS) (Harmony Project, 2007). The Kenyan government has established complementary security institutions, including a Joint Terrorism Task Force in 2003 and the National Security Advisory Committee in 2004 (Harmony Project, 2007, p. 57). Kenya also received support from the US to establish a National Counter Terrorism Centre that notionally sits within the NSIS but is rumoured to be under the direct operational guidance of Washington.[3]

Kenyan authorities have also stepped up anti-terror policing operations. The Anti-Terrorism Police Unit (ATPU), a special police branch established in the aftermath of the US embassy bombing in 1998, has led raids to round up suspected terrorists. However, it is mostly Muslim neighbourhoods and Muslim residential and business premises that have been targeted. This has created a perception of a state crackdown on Muslims. Police swoops in November 2002 on Muslim neighbourhoods in the aftermath of the Israeli-owned hotel bombing in Kikambala generated scrutiny and public debate on the involvement of foreign security agencies in the surveillance, arrest, torture and interrogation of terror suspects (Amnesty International, 2005; authors' interviews). After the US-backed Ethiopian invasion of Somalia, civilians and fighters fled to Kenya in early 2007. Some were arrested as terrorist suspects and interrogated by the FBI in Kenya. Some were sent to Somalia, illegally transferred to Ethiopia and then questioned by American intelligence agents.[4] One suspect was rendered to Guantanamo Bay.[5] Kenyan authorities thus failed in certain instances to comply with both international human rights law and standards and Kenyan law. Suspects reported being tortured and mistreated, and denied family visits, medical attention, legal counsel and consular access.[6] The rendition controversy caused a further breakdown in relations between the government and Muslims. As an official with the Open Society Institute in Nairobi explained, 'The trust of Muslim communities has been lost. They give information and cooperate with security agencies and the outcome is renditions.'[7] More robust policing has been matched by the closer scrutiny of individuals applying for identification papers and travel documents. These efforts, and other post-9/11 CTMs, tie into broader historical contexts concerning the identity, citizenship and political rights of Muslim communities along the coast and in North Eastern Province. Many Muslims, especially along the coast, feel neglected by Kenya's political establishment and controlled by 'upcountry' Kenyans (Barkan, 2004). A local official with an international grant-making agency commented, 'They (Muslims) feel like second-class citizens. They feel the state has gone along with the War on Terror and Islamicised it.'[8] As explained below, groups advocating for Muslim human rights and social justice allege that it is more difficult for Muslims to obtain identity cards that are required for employment and passports.

These anti-terror measures were introduced in a legal vacuum. In 2003 the Attorney General published the Suppression of Terrorism Bill (SOT), which received strong political backing from Western diplomats and the US in particular, albeit quietly.[9] Whitaker (2007) argues that US influence has been great in the transnational diffusion of public order norms, particularly those relating to anti-terror provisions in law. The SOT Bill was alleged to share many similarities to the US Patriot Act. A coalition of human rights activists and organisations through the Kenya Human Rights Network organised a concerted campaign against the bill, as described later in the chapter. They objected to the definition of 'terrorism' in the bill, which was felt to be vague and open to interpretation. Another concern was that the bill lowered fair trial standards by requiring the prosecution in terror cases to show only 'reasonable suspicion' rather than prove their case beyond reasonable doubt. Another controversial provision in an early version of the SOT Bill was that it granted wide discretionary powers to authorities to stop and search suspects without warrant and to detain terror suspects without charge. Objections were also raised that the bill targeted Muslim communities. In this regard, a clause of considerable concern created an offence for people dressed in a way 'as to arouse reasonable suspicion that he is a member of a declared terrorist organisation' (Republic of Kenya, 2003). The bill also granted the minister responsible for national security the powers to make exclusion orders but only against individuals with dual citizenship. This was perceived as directly targeting Muslims, many of whom descend from immigrants from Somalia, the Arabian Peninsula and South Asia. In response to the bill, the Kenya National Commission on Human Rights, the governmental human rights watchdog, stated, '[l]aws or policies must not target or appear selective by community or group' (KNCHR, 2003, p. 8).

The government withdrew the bill following intense public opposition by the media, human rights organisations and Muslim groups. Another crucial opposition to the bill was from members of the parliamentary Departmental Committee on Administration of Justice and Legal Affairs, who were charged with reviewing and approving the bill before it was tabled for debate in parliament. The bill stirred considerable anti-populist sentiment that Kenya was being forced to do the bidding of the US in the region. Commenting in 2006 long after the SOT Bill was withdrawn, a Western diplomat explained, 'Generally, Kenyans do not feel that terrorism is their issue and believe that it is a Western agenda that is being unfairly imposed on the country. So far, cooperation has been poor with the Kenyan government.'[10] Paul Muite, who was chair of the Administration of Justice and Legal Affairs committee at the time, commented, 'the Departmental Committee formed the opinion that this essentially draconian legislation elevated terrorism above all other crimes. This has tended to distort the true reality of crime for most Kenyans who live in constant fear, not of terrorism, but of armed robberies, car hijackings, banditry, sexual attacks, violent muggings, beatings and mob violence.'[11] Civil society critics similarly emphasised that terrorism was not a concern to most Kenyans.

Foreign aid officials quibbled that the Kenyan government did not do enough to inform public opinion on the need for an anti-terror law. As a DFID official explained, 'There has been no real attempt in Kenya at initiating a civil and national debate on countering terror. The Kenyan public believes the SOT bill is a Western agenda that does not concern average Kenyans.'[12] Another official commented, 'Counter-terrorism is not the top priority for the Kenyan government. We would like them to give this more priority and we think there are things they did badly such as the anti-terror law (SOT). They have not done a political campaign to generate public support for the legislation. They are now in a situation where they cannot prosecute suspects. So they are exporting them to Somalia, which is causing them political problems.'[13] In 2005, the government initiated fresh discussions on anti-terror legislation and circulated an updated Anti-Terrorism Bill to government departments in 2006. Although this bill incorporated concerns that had been raised in public debate on the SOT Bill, it too was opposed. Since then, the government has tried to introduce anti-terror provisions into other proposed laws. In late 2007, it introduced the Proceeds of Organized Crime and Anti-Money Laundering Bill. However, an audit of the bill by the parliamentary House Business Committee revealed that 22 clauses in the SOT Bill had been lifted word for word and incorporated into the Proceeds of Crime Bill.[14] The government pushed for the House Business Committee to prioritise consideration of the bill for parliamentary debate before the 2007 election. However, Muslim parliamentarians refused to debate the bill and protested by walking out of parliament.[15]

Although politicians and civil society activists highlighted American support for anti-terror legislation, there were other important sources of pressure on the Kenyan government. For example, UN resolution 1373 (2001) linking money-laundering and terrorism was a key determinant in the government's efforts to pass anti–money-laundering legislation.[16] NGOs have been a specific focus of money-laundering suspicions in Kenya. A prominent human rights lawyer claimed that the Kenyan government has pressured banks to scrutinise and, in certain cases, obstruct the banking activity of human rights groups. The matter came to a head when an influential NGO working on governance issues was barred from setting up an account at Barclays. A former official with the organisation explained, 'When we enquired into this it came to our knowledge that the FBI had sent a circular two or three years previously to the Central Bank of Kenya [requesting] that they should track money transfers to accounts with Muslim names. I suspect there were other instructions that CSOs needed to be tracked as well. Informally, I heard that people in the government believed terror funding was going through NGOs.'[17]

In general, the Kenyan government has increased checks on NGOs as part of its counter-terrorism efforts. The closer inspection of NGOs goes back to the aftermath of the 1998 bombing of the US embassy, when several Muslim organisations that provided relief and welfare services to refugee communities in North Eastern Province were proscribed on suspicion that they supported terrorist groups (USIP, 2006). In the longer term, the clampdown cast suspicion over Islamic charities, including organisations with connections in the Middle East and mosques and madrassas. Security concerns have also crept into discussions around a proposed new regulatory framework for NGOs as signalled in the Sessional Paper Number One of 2006 that was agreed by the cabinet. At the time, various political leaders associated the activities of some organisations with terrorism. One official from a respected governance NGO stressed, 'the proposed NGO [framework] is about using global thinking on security for the government to pursue its own agenda'.[18] Officially, the political rationale for the new framework was to fight corruption in NGOs, which are widely thought to be misused for personal enrichment. However, some government officials stated their concern that NGOs were being used for terrorist fund-raising and money-laundering. This reflects the global circulation of concerns over the probity and transparency of NGOs, which has been manipulated by political leaders in some contexts to target opposition supporters and dissidents.

Aiding security? The politics of aid and counter-terrorism

Before the 9/11 attacks, security was comparatively insignificant as a guiding objective of aid to Kenya. Rather, poverty reduction and, in particular, good governance and democratisation were the central aims of most donors. However, since 2001 security concerns have crept into the development strategies of many donor agencies operating in Kenya, reflecting the increased emphasis on security in development more generally (see Chapter 2). As analysed in Chapter 4, the national security strategies of several leading donor countries now posit a role for development assistance as part of 'soft' security and counter-radicalisation strategies. Such 'soft' security approaches have been tried in Kenya and elsewhere in the Horn of Africa. As detailed below, they include civil affairs projects by US military personnel in the region as well as various types of outreach to Muslim groups and organisations. This section explores the ways in which security concerns have crept into development policy and practice in Kenya as well as the bilateral politics surrounding these changes in aid.

There is anecdotal evidence that counter-terrorism and security priorities have influenced shifts in the targeting of aid to different regions in Kenya and new support for security-oriented activities. USAID has supported projects within communities that are perceived as a security risk, including Somalis in eastern Kenya and Swahili Muslims in the Kenyan coastal belt who have historical linkages with Yemen and Oman. One example of this security-determined targeting is a new USAID initiative on pastoralist livelihoods and peace-building in the 'Mandera Triangle', a predominantly Somali-inhabited region in the extreme northeast corner of Kenya bordering Ethiopia and Somalia. The project derives from an assessment that development can help to change the conditions of underdevelopment and severe poverty in Mandera that terrorists might seek to exploit. However, while USAID has expanded its programming in the Kenya–Somalia borders region, at the same time it has scaled back its efforts on conflict reduction and peace-building in the 'Karamoja Cluster', the border region between Uganda, Kenya and Sudan. It is of certain less strategic value to regional counter-terrorism strategy. DFID has sponsored research into the causes of radicalisation in the Mandera Triangle as well.

USAID has also sought to develop curricula for madrassas under a new strategic objective on education that was added to the agency's programme portfolio for Kenya in 2003. This was ostensibly to support the new government's policy reform to provide universal free primary education.[19] However, many Kenyan Muslims interpreted specific efforts on madrassas as an attempt to influence teaching and support US policies inside madrassas. More recently, USAID has been involved in teacher development of madrassa *maalims* (teachers) in Coast Province as part of an initiative on 'Education for Marginalised Children in Kenya'.[20]

The greater interest, generally, in supporting initiatives in Muslim communities shows how Muslims have come into the gaze of donor agencies post-9/11. USAID support for madrassa reforms indicates that greater funding is available for organisations working within or on 'suspect' communities, such as Muslims and young men. A European diplomatic official in Nairobi commented, '[i]f you look at the engagement of donors with Muslim civil society, it is greater now than it was before and this is because of 9/11. You don't see us engaging to this extent with Hindu groups, or Buddhist groups, for instance. We wouldn't engage with Muslim groups as we are doing if there wasn't a problem of Islamic extremism.' The same official went on to say that 'there are some in Muslim communities who have a self-interest in perpetuating the message that Muslims are marginalised as a community. If you compare to 2001, you'd find that our engagement, both specifically and generally, with Muslims has increased.'[21] Another European diplomat confirmed this outlook: 'Why do we really want to engage with Muslim communities? It is because of the threat of terrorism.'[22]

The nature and objectives of this engagement, however, seem to be the issue for many leaders and activists within 'suspect' communities, who have taken issue with this new donor engagement. A representative with the Nairobi office of an international grant-making agency stated, 'Muslim groups are not comfortable with donors.'[23] Many Muslim civil society activists we met distrusted donor agency motives. This unease relates to global politics and the perception of a 'war on Islam'. It also ties into national politics in Kenya and the feeling among Muslims that they have been victimised by the government in its anti-terror operations (Barkan, 2004). It is also noteworthy that leaders and activists within Muslim communities indicated difficulty in gaining funds for work that could be construed as challenging Western security objectives in the region, such as human rights advocacy around issues of counter-terrorism.

Still, there are mixed and not entirely negative outcomes of donor efforts to engage with groups working within Muslim communities. One initiative that has generated significant interest among aid agencies in Nairobi is by the Danish development agency DANIDA. It provides small grants to several community organisations in Coast Province under the rubric of 'Peace, Development and Security', a euphemism for assistance directed at furthering counter-terrorism objectives. Groups supported under the initiative have undertaken a variety of outreach and advocacy activities that address problems of social justice and conflict. One group brought together church leaders and Islamic clerics for dialogue on issues such as the inclusion of *kadhi* courts for Muslim personal law into the draft constitution, an issue that had broken interfaith unity over broader constitutional change. The same interfaith group also mediated between the provincial security apparatus in Kwale, south of Mombasa, and the *Mlungunipa*, a group of mostly armed youth who had retreated to forests along the Kenya–Tanzania border to protest their socio-economic marginalisation.[24]

Other donor agencies have sought to involve civil society in discussions on security and the need to establish new counter-terrorism structures. UNDP and the Commonwealth Secretariat have both provided technical assistance to the Kenyan government to develop and implement counter-terrorism legislation. Internationally, UN efforts on counter-terrorism have been monitored by a Counter Terrorism Committee (CTC). The Danish chair of the CTC in 2005 took steps to enhance the technical assistance provided through the UN counter-terrorism programme and link it to expanded development assistance efforts.[25] In Kenya, these efforts have taken the form of capacity-building through UNDP, which includes a provision for working with civil society. UNDP officials in Nairobi have also sought to encourage dialogue around claims that Muslims have been targeted by the government's counter-terrorism operations.[26] The CTC has proposed supporting civil society to address the presumed causes of terrorism and radicalism as an alternative to hard security measures. Assisting civil society is seen instrumentally as helping to build broader public support for CTMs in Kenya. Work with Muslim groups, particularly, is thought to promote the co-operation of Kenyan Muslims in intelligence-gathering and surveillance. In these ways, civil society is thought to lend an aura of popular legitimacy to security strategies and activities while also representing the views of 'suspect' communities in dialogues with government agencies and foreign diplomatic and security personnel.

However, in spite of this interest in nurturing strategic links with certain civil society actors, donor attitudes towards civil society remain mixed. Some of the concerns surrounding 'bad' civil society have percolated down into donor engagement with Kenyan civil society actors. For example, as explained in Chapter 4, USAID requires its grantees to sign an ATC. However, a USAID official in Nairobi suggested the ATC was simply a bureaucratic necessity but had little, if any, real impact: 'if we have any doubts about an NGO in the sense they may support terrorism or violence, we would not support them anyway. The global War on Terror has not changed this.'[27] Still, there is counter-evidence to this that a fear factor has caused some donors to be more cautious in their dealings with partners and in the sorts of groups they will consider for funding. One civil society veteran observed, 'donors have become more conservative. In a world where we don't know who is who, we'll be more conservative and cautious. There is concern [among donors] of inadvertently supporting terrorism.'[28] Unsurprisingly, the chill factor has been more acute for Middle Eastern and Islamic charitable groups. Many have scaled back their giving, such as the Africa Muslim Agency and the Young Muslims Association, while others have ceased their operations altogether, such as the Crescent of Hope.[29] There have been alleged knock-on effects in the communities in which these groups previously worked.[30] A Gulf philanthropic group, for instance, was hesitant to fund a new Islamic university in Coast Province without US embassy assurance that this would not be seen as support for 'Islamic radicalism' (Harmony Project, 2007; footnote 89). However, at the same time, the climate of fear and suspicion surrounding Islamic charities has not prevented new advocacy efforts in Muslim communities from emerging, as described later. Philanthropic organisations with roots in the Muslim world continue to have an important presence in Kenya, the Aga Khan Foundation being a prime example.

The greater emphasis on security in aid to Kenya is also evident in the new involvement of military and security actors in development activities. Since 2002, personnel from the CJTF, a US counter-terrorism base in Djibouti, have carried out 'hearts and minds' projects in Coast and North Eastern Provinces. These activities include building schools, operating mobile veterinary clinics and providing immunisation for children. The CJTF is developing liaison positions and coordination mechanisms with civilian agencies and departments such as USAID to institutionalise its efforts on development. CJTF development projects have so far been implemented mostly independently of aid agencies, many which have a long presence in the region. Indeed, there are no regularised contacts or coordination meetings between CJTF and NGOs even though there is an NGO liaison position within CJTF.[31] Civilian personnel in the CJTF do consult with community groups in project implementation and these ties are seen as helping with intelligence-gathering. There is varying and contradictory evidence on public responses to military involvement in development in these communities. Infamously, a former US ambassador and CJTF personnel were stoned when they visited Garissa town in North Eastern Province to promote the military's efforts. Islamic clerics and tribal elders in North Eastern Province have condemned the involvement of US military personnel there in aid activities. However, there is anecdotal evidence that villagers in communities in and around Lamu in Coast Province welcomed the assistance of the US military.[32]

As explained before, foreign donors have sought the cooperation of the Kenyan government in counter-terrorism efforts in the Horn of Africa. However, foreign development aid to Kenya has not been tied to such cooperation. Nevertheless Kenyan authorities have been under intense pressure to pass an anti-terror bill. After the 1998 US embassy bombing, the US, the UK and Israel all strongly criticised Kenya for inadequately pursuing terror suspects. They attributed this to institutional weaknesses in the police forces and to inadequate criminal codes. However, it was only after 9/11 that intense diplomatic and aid pressure was put on Kenya to pass anti-terrorism legislation. Still, the Kenyan government's failure up to now to pass an anti-terror law has not affected US aid flows to Kenya. This tallies with key points made by Whitaker (2007) that it is unclear whether the US is financially rewarding countries that pass anti-terror laws, and that the US is not the only source of pressure on developing countries to pass such laws. What is certain is that Kenya has been treated as something of an exception by the US due to its strategic value to US counter-terrorism goals in the Horn of Africa. For example, Kenya lost an estimated $8 million in military financing and training aid after refusing to sign a Bilateral Immunity Agreement with the US that would have granted its nationals and non-national contractors immunity from the International Criminal Court (ICC) (Citizens for Global Solutions, 2006). The suspension of military aid to Kenya was thus required under the Nethercutt Provision in the Foreign Operations Appropriations Bill, which ties US foreign assistance to countries signing a bilateral immunity agreement. However, a special exemption was eventually agreed for Kenya, and the US resumed its security and military training aid to Kenya in the summer of 2006. The

US thus prioritised Kenya's co-operation on counter-terrorism over US opposition to the ICC.

Still, there is a popular perception in Kenya, including, amongst many, senior Kenyan politicians and government officials, that the US and the UK governments have sought to harm Kenya's tourism industry by issuing advisories against travel to Kenya as a punitive measure for not passing the SOT Bill. The issue topped the agenda of President Kibaki during his state visit to Washington in November 2003. However, the US and the UK refused to rescind their travel advisories.

Yet, in other ways the Kenyan government has used its diminishing dependence on aid to leverage its own interests in counter-terrorism co-operation. Elsewhere in Africa, it is observed that by targeting its aid to regions where the threat of terrorism is perceived to be high, the US has encouraged governments to exaggerate the threat and, in extreme cases, to instigate instability, which it then attributes to militants as a way of securing security assistance and military training aid (Keenan, 2006). The Kenyan government has played on the perception of a significant terrorist threat in the Horn of Africa for diplomatic advantages. Internally, it has reacted to populist sentiment against counter-terrorism measures and legislation backed by Anglo-American pressure. Senior politicians have criticised US counter-terrorism policies in the region and have pressured the Kibaki administration to wager its co-operation on the receipt of various security hardware.[33] Paul Muite, a respected former parliamentarian and chair of the Departmental Committee on Justice and Legal Affairs, commented, 'the Kenyan government ought to bargain harder for its interests where it contemplates supporting the foreign policies of other states.'[34]

The perception that there is American largesse to be tapped for working on security has also shaped civil society outlooks on aid. As one European diplomat spelled out, 'The Kenyan government prefers hard assistance rather than training. There is frustration between the Kenyan government and donors on this account.'[35] An NGO head and Muslim leader observed, 'fighting terror is big business. Probably I could get money as an NGO if I said I was going to fight terrorism. If I want to do this, I can go to the Americans tomorrow and get money for training in counter-terrorism and equipment. Counter-terrorism is used as an excuse for agencies and organisations to procure. Every government department wants to cash in on this to get training and equipment.'[36] A civil society activist with connections in the Anti-Terrorism Police Unit (ATPU) claimed that the police branch tries to frame ordinary criminal incidents as acts of terrorism: 'the ATPU stokes these rumours to get funding. They receive massive funding and need to build up a perception of a terrorist threat. I spoke to the Chief Inspector and he said that [its] existence is justified as long as [it has] detained and renditioned terror suspects.'[37]

These challenges reveal that Kenya's incentives in counter-terrorism are not fully aligned with those of donors since Nairobi can benefit materially from its co-operation. It has been suggested as a way of overcoming this dilemma that donors reorient their assistance to areas where there are fewer opportunities for patronage, such as increased police and governance training and anti-corruption efforts (Harmony Project, 2007, p. 71).

Democratic transition and civil society–state relations pre-9/11

A renewed emphasis on security in foreign aid to Kenya and debates within the country on the introduction of new counter-terrorism structures tie into various divisions and debates in Kenya on uneven development, inequality and marginalisation of certain communities and areas of the country. A deeper understanding of the positions different communities are staking in relation to global politics and counter-terrorism responses thus requires examining the broader social and political context of state–civil society relations.

The perception that Kenya is a linchpin of stability in East Africa and the Horn of Africa belies its history of armed conflict, social violence, subversive political struggle and the abuse of powers by successive political leaders. Armed conflict and violence were constitutive of the modern Kenyan nation state. Notable examples include the pacification campaigns against pastoralist populations in the north, the displacement of Maasai peoples from high potential agricultural areas[38] and the Mau Mau insurgency against British colonial rule in the 1950s. The provincial administration is a notable vestige of colonial governance and oppressive politico-administration (Branch and Cheeseman, 2006). The Kenya National Police is both feared and reviled by a general public that has grown accustomed to corruption and human rights abuses in policing practices.

State bureaucratic practices of control in turn are perceived to disadvantage certain marginalised communities, in particular pastoralists, the urban destitute and slum dwellers, and Muslims. The state has failed to provide social welfare for these groups and allocated only minimal resources for development in their areas. High levels of social violence and chronic low-intensity conflict in some parts of Kenya are thus unsurprising in this context of oppressive state machinery and unequal development. In response to substantial development challenges and widespread poverty, the post-independence regimes of Jomo Kenyatta and Daniel Arap Moi promoted a notion of self-help, known as *harambee*, as well as missionary activity such as providing health and education services to rural populations. Welfare-oriented community organisations such as women's and youth groups mushroomed under the state-promoted ideal of *harambee*. However, these were distinctly apolitical and mainly existed to address the manifestations of poverty while providing a clear channel for political patronage by political elites (Con Omore and Gachucha, 2003). This helped to create a precedent in Kenya in which charity is understood as gift-giving and not something that involves challenging power relations and the structures that uphold these.[39] Under Kenyatta, Kenya became a one-party state and there was a distinct intolerance for political organising outside of the ruling party machinery.

Kenyan civil society was shaped greatly by state-building processes that began with colonial rule and continued during industrialisation after independence in 1963. These processes led to the formation of modern forms of civil society such as trade unions, NGOs and professional societies, setting the stage for external engagement with civil society. A more politically conscious form of civil society rose to prominence with the advent of multi-party politics in the early 1990s and subsequently during the struggle to secure a genuine democratic space through electoral reforms.[40] As noted before, faith groups, including the Catholic Church and Protestant denominations, were instrumental in leveraging a politicised civil society in the late 1980s and early 1990s during the struggle for democratic reforms (Ndegwa, 1994). Civil society enjoyed public confidence and popular support throughout this period. Donors extended crucial financial and political support to human rights, democracy and governance, and law reform groups at the time. Kenya was regarded as a near pariah state under the regime of former President Moi. Several leading donors ceased to channel funding through government offices or state institutions, instead favouring to support civil society rights groups to pressure the government on political reforms.

Moi regarded civil society with undisclosed contempt and, not inaccurately, as a way for donors to channel support to political opposition. In 1990, just before the introduction of multi-party politics, the government passed an NGO law (Ndegwa, 1994). Before its inception, civil society lobbied the government to create an enabling legal and policy framework to co-ordinate the activities of the sector, which had expanded enormously since Kenya's independence in 1963. However, the NGO Act sought to restrict civil society by establishing a government NGO Bureau and a quasi-independent NGO Council stuffed with government appointees. Controversially, the law required re-registration of NGOs every five years, which NGOs viewed as a tactic of intimidation meant to limit their engagement in politics.[41] The Act became a focus of NGO protest and in 1993 the government entered into dialogue with civil society over the content of an NGO policy framework. Although a policy was never agreed, NGOs were successful in pressuring the government to agree several changes to the legal framework that resulted in greater independence of the sector and self-regulation through an NGO Council whose leaders would be elected by NGO representatives themselves.

Whither civil society? Aid and the shifting political landscape in Kenya

The victory in the December 2002 election of the National Rainbow Coalition (NARC), a motley grouping of political parties and former adversaries that campaigned on a political reform platform, was viewed as a triumph for civil society and its efforts to consolidate democratic space. NARC's parliamentary majority,[42] and the election of its coalition leader Mwai Kibaki as president, tied into its pledges on governance reforms and a new political dispensation to address corruption, predation, bureaucratic incompetence and routine abuses by the police. Several key positions in the new government were filled by veteran civil society activists and human rights campaigners, including the Minister for Justice and Constitutional Affairs and the chief of a new ethics division in the Office of the President, who was previously head of the Kenya Chapter of Transparency International. Indeed, civil society perceived the NARC government to be its own.[43] The struggle of a liberal, politically active civil society was about gaining access to decision-making and influencing government policy and bureaucratic practices. Civil society, blinded by its apparent triumph in helping to elect NARC, was slow to define its purpose in the post-2002 political context. Its growth before then was driven by popular democratic struggles and defined by its opposition to the former Moi regime.[44] The failure of civil society to adequately define and articulate its role after the 2002 election has cast doubt over its purpose in the new political dispensation.

Following the 2002 election, the NARC coalition divided over disagreements on proposed constitutional reforms. These centred on changing executive authority and dividing powers between the president and a new post of prime minister. The first draft of the constitution known as the Bomas Draft was prepared by a broad constitutional assembly but subsequently amended by elements close to the president. The amended draft, known as the Wako Draft, was voted on in a plebiscite in November 2005, which was won by the 'No' camp, which supported shifting power to an executive prime minister as proposed in the Bomas Draft.[45] This led to a split in the government and the resignation or firing of ministers aligned with the 'No' camp, leaving the cabinet composed of close allies of the president.[46] Divisions surrounding constitutional reforms carried over into the 2007 election. The Orange Democratic Movement (ODM) led by Raila Odinga, a charismatic veteran political leader from western Kenya, drew its support from opponents of the Wako draft. President Kibaki sought re-election under the Party of National Unity (PNU), which drew its main support from Kibaki's base in central Kenya and was associated with the 'Yes' campaign in support of the Wako draft (Barkan, 2008b).

In the lead-up to the election in 2007, debates on constitutional reforms and opposition to CTMs reinvigorated civil society to an extent. However, regional, ethnic and religious fractures were becoming increasingly apparent. Many in civil society were aligned with opponents of the Wako draft and became deeply involved in civic education on the constitution before the plebiscite. However, the leadership of the NGO Council, the government-recognised representative body for NGOs, supported the Wako draft. These differences contributed to acrimony within civil society and fed into a management crisis that engulfed the NGO Council. Hence, after the plebiscite, civil society could not agree who would speak for the sector nationally. This impeded what contribution it could make to political debates including those that directly affected the sector and had implications later for responding to counter-terrorism. In this changing political landscape, alternative ad-hoc civil society groupings have emerged to advocate on specific issues but these have not been able to coalesce around a common cause or position. Divisions within civil society were further laid bare during the post-election crisis in 2008. Civil society did not agree a common position on the contested presidential vote or with respect to the violence that quickly engulfed the country. There were notable exceptions, namely certain groups and networks which worked in various ways to promote truth, justice and reconciliation.[47] However, civil society generally showed itself to be an arena of competing regional, ethnic and religious tensions.

Alongside this fragmentation of civil society, there have been significant changes in aid policy and practice towards non-governmental groups since the 2002 election, which heralded a new trust and confidence in the state. This, in turn, dovetailed with shifts in donor aid approaches more widely to align with the development priorities of aid-recipient governments, and better co-ordinate and harmonise bilateral aid. Further, there is much in common between these approaches and post-9/11 state-building agendas that profess a need to redress institutional, bureaucratic and policing weaknesses as part of counterterrorism. Many bilateral agencies have increased their aid to the Kenyan government and shifted support to sector-wide programmes as opposed to providing project-based funds to individual NGOs. These changes are similar to donor approaches to governance in Afghanistan, where civil society is a mere afterthought in state-building strategies. Governance is equated with government and the emphasis on checks and balances fades away once a government that speaks the good governance language of donors comes to power.

These changes in aid approaches are acutely evident in the democracy and governance sector, where many leading bilaterals after the 2002 election supported a large reform programme on the Governance, Justice, Law and Order Sector (GJLOS), which incorporates a fund for supporting civil society.[48] The Kenyan government resisted the inclusion of civil society in GJLOS although it has welcomed its contribution in other sectors such as health and education.[49] Further, civil society actors have objected fundamentally to receiving support under a government-controlled programme. In recent years, many prominent democracy, governance and human rights NGOs experienced funding difficulties and NGO leaders explain this as symptomatic of donors' renewed emphasis on the state. Leading donors including USAID and DFID have maintained that their funding for Kenyan government programmes is drawn from new financial assistance.[50] Hence, aid has not been diverted from civil society. However, donors have tacitly recognised the difficulty that many NGOs have encountered in accessing donors' funds to work on democracy and governance issues. The EC established a funding facility for non-state actors outside of GJLOS, in part as a response to the funding problems facing democracy and governance groups.[51] But here, too, divisions emerged between civil society, which insists on greater representation in deciding the use of these funds, and donors who believe this could lead to partiality and disagreements.[52] Ultimately, the tensions point to a lack of trust between civil society and donors that has arisen in the post-2002 political landscape.

Another highly significant factor affecting donor engagement with civil society is fluctuating levels of funding for bilateral agencies and the concomitant shrinking of aid bureaucracies. Reductions in staffing levels have forced several donor agencies in Kenya to shift their approaches to working with civil society. These changes have involved greater outsourcing of key administrative and oversight functions to the private sector and large NGOs. An official with SIDA explained, 'in 2003 we found ourselves stuck with partnerships with 30 to 35 CSOs. It was impossible for us to handle that and to have dialogue with all of them. We didn't want to be a bank and that is the role we found ourselves [serving].'[53] In practice, donor agencies are giving larger grants to fewer, larger organisations with the administrative capacity and competence for large grant administration. These trends have disadvantaged smaller, local organisations that lack such administrative capacities.

The changing aid context in Kenya has highlighted the fragility of mostly urban-based NGOs in the democracy, governance and human rights sector. They have attributed their recent funding constraints to the renewed emphasis on the state in development strategies. However, by doing so, NGOs have deflected attention from issues that are more fundamental to their longer-term existence and position in Kenyan civil society. These include the dependence of most democracy, governance and human rights organisations on external aid and their disconnectedness from a domestic constituency that could guarantee such groups an element of independence.

Yet, the closer intertwining of aid and security in the post-9/11 context further complicates the situation of these groups. The greater emphasis on security in bilateral relations, and the expectation of leading donors that the Kenyan government will do its bidding on counter-terrorism in the region, implies that donors are less likely to prioritise governance and human rights concerns. Regardless of the strategic interests impinging on aid, the leverage of donors to influence the Kenyan government's policies and practices that affect civil society is declining due to Kenya's decreasing aid dependence. In recent years, the Kenyan government has relied on ODA to cover less than 10 per cent of its recurrent expenditure.[54] As noted before, this reduced dependency on foreign aid has enabled the Kenyan government to strike a populist chord in stalling anti-terrorism legislation that is widely perceived as an imposition of US priorities.

Aid officials claim their commitment to transparency, accountability and human rights as reasons for continuing support to civil society. The new mission statement of the Democracy and Governance office of USAID emphasises governance and the balance of powers between branches of government and between government and civil society.[55] However, these objectives seemingly contradict the US government's support for anti-terror legislation. Behind the official proclamations of support for civil society, many donors support moves by the Kenyan government to extend its regulatory control over civil society through a proposed new NGO policy framework and by way of anti–money-laundering legislation, as explained before. Thus, donor pronouncements on governance reforms would appear at odds with the macro-strategic considerations that determine aid flows in pursuit of co-operation on global counter-terrorism. These signify a return to a Cold War era politics of aid that demotes human rights and democracy matters to the disadvantage of civil society groups organising around these interests.

Counter-terrorism, the politics of fear and civil society responses

Kenya's counter-terrorism structures have been instituted contrary to widespread opposition among domestic political constituencies. Human rights networks, legal groups and Muslim organisations have been galvanised to organise against proposed anti-terrorism legislation through the formation of new ad-hoc networks and groups such as the Muslim Human Rights Forum and the Coast Anti-Terror Network. A subcommittee of the Kenya Human Rights Network organised civil society opposition to the SOT Bill. They argued that fundamental human rights must be protected, mechanisms to fight terrorism must safeguard human rights and counter-terrorism should be a partnership between the state and society and not one against the other. In 2007, several human rights and Muslim groups formed the 'Tetea Initiative' to work on issues of counter-terrorism and human rights. Crucially, they have tried to move away from Islamicisation of the government's anti-terror responses by linking these to broader concerns of accountability and transparency in public institutions and security agencies.

The thinking of groups opposed to the SOT Bill was informed by the struggle for democratic spaces during the 1990s. Provisions in the SOT Bill threatened to circumscribe these nascent democratic spaces. Section 9 of the bill conferred on the minister responsible for national security the powers to proscribe any organisation they suspected of supporting terrorism. Yet, it did not set out the norms to be used in determining suspicion. Further complicating the picture was that the definition of 'terrorism' in the bill was broad and unclear. There is no consensus definition of terrorism even within multilateral institutions such as the UN, which has complicated crafting anti-terror laws in Kenya and elsewhere since there is no internationally agreed legal definition. Northern governments, in passing their own anti-terror legislation, have tended to define the terrorist threat as qualitatively new and different, requiring extraordinary legislation.[56] Kenyan scholar Professor Ali Mazrui noted that the 'bill is so wide-ranging that the police or the minister can decide which kind of public demonstration constituted support for terrorist forces abroad' (2003, p. 5). The bill did not propose any appeal mechanism or independent adjudication authority in cases where an organisation wants to contest the minister's declaration. New offences were also proposed for persons who are members, supporters or fund-raisers of organisations declared to support terrorism. The vagueness of the language used in the SOT Bill made non-state actors vulnerable to accusations of terrorist links. As an official from a human rights NGO referred to the risks in a statement to the Kenyan media, '[t]his is a threat to civil society and activists. They can choose to declare the KHRC (Kenya Human Rights Commission, an NGO) a terrorist group for speaking out and demonstrating against detention. It even puts you [the journalist] at risk for the simple reason that you are writing about and against the anti-terrorism bill, making you a target and possible terrorist suspect' (*The Weekly Brief*, 2003, pp. 15–16).

A contributing factor to civil society opposition to the SOT Bill was the sentiment that Kenyans were being made to pay the price for a terrorist threat that was not theirs. One civil society activist explained it this way: 'the perception of most Kenyans is that the Kenyan victims of [terrorist] attacks are collateral damage and not targets themselves... Kenyans view themselves as caught up in the crossfire and [believe] that the conflict is not ours. It is Western targets that have brought terror to Kenya.'[57] Most Kenyans do not consider the threat of terrorism to be a domestic policy priority, or at least believe it should not be. Civil society critics of the bill have argued that other causes of insecurity should be prioritised, such as economic disparities and crime.[58]

However, views within Kenyan civil society on security and the need for anti-terrorist legislation are far from uniform. Justice and legal reform experts in civil society who opposed previous anti-terrorism bills have nonetheless argued that an anti-terrorism law be passed that incorporates human rights protections. A legal practitioner explained, 'We (in civil society) seem to think that the human rights framework is unresponsive to security. That is not the case. Security and human rights are not opposed. What we see for Kenya is that we leave the state to its own devices because it does not have a law. I think we need a counter-terrorism law... We cannot cry out for the state to protect victims of terrorism and not allow it (to acquire the) devices to pursue terrorists. We need to choose what view we hold.'[59] Human rights activists have rejected this, arguing that existing criminal codes are adequate and that the priority should be redressing abuses of power within the security, intelligence and policing agencies. The head of a human rights network commented, 'We think the penal code is adequate to address terrorism. Civil society should definitely work with the government to build up its enforcement capacities. Issues like corruption have an impact on the capacity of the government to fight terrorism. The infiltration of terrorists is not a problem of not having laws in place but the lack of police capacities to man borders.'[60]

There are also inherent risks for civil society in advocating around human rights aspects on counter-terrorism when its own credibility has come under fire. A commissioner at the Kenya National Commission on Human Rights explained, 'While human rights groups have largely been erratic and inconsistent in their response to terrorist violence, they have developed a significant capacity to challenge questionable CTMs. This dissonance has tended to feed the perception that they are concerned more about the rights of terrorism suspects and less about the victims of terrorist violence.'[61] Such negative popular perceptions of human rights advocates have caused critical debate and self-reflection within human rights networks on what strategies and approaches to adopt. A contributor at a round-table discussion in Nairobi on civil society and security maintained that 'Civil society needs to clarify whether it has to be right or popular... The popularity of civil society is currently low. Should the test of civil society relevance be popularity or what is right however that be defined? And what does this mean for civil society? Civil society need not apologise. It need not be popular. It should be right.'[62]

Invariably, outlooks on the failed SOT Bill vary. While rejection of the bill has been held up as a significant victory for civil society, government authorities and some Western diplomatic officials regarded it as a major setback. The view of a European diplomat at the round-table in Nairobi was that 'the failure of the SOT Bill... was a tactical victory (for civil society). But you can also see it as a defeat. Governments have a responsibility for security... If government lacks the legal means it is in an impossible position. It has to act illegally because it lacks the measures it requires to tackle the problem (of terrorism). Civil society needs to help encourage debate on counter-terrorism that is sensible and proportional. There is constantly a tension between the balance of security and human rights.'[63]

Although new restrictions on the spaces to organise outside of the state were an integral part of the SOT Bill, mainstream civil society was largely silent in its response, leaving human rights groups and organisations representing Muslim communities to organise against the bill. Church clergy have been silent on the treatment of Muslims in counter-terrorism operations. Though they had worked previously with Muslim religious scholars and leaders on constitutional reform issues in the lead-up to a 2005 plebiscite, disagreements then arose around the inclusion of *Kadhis* courts in the draft constitution for safeguarding Muslim personal law. The disagreement led to Muslim clerics withdrawing from the inter-faith Ufungamano Initiative that had lobbied for constitutional reform.[64] The media, as well, has tended to cover human rights violations of terror suspects from a security perspective without interrogating government actions in the name of security.[65] Public opinion in Kenya is that CTMs affect Muslims. Mainstream civil society is also blinkered in its view of what constitutes 'civil society', one that does not include Muslim organisations and civic groups, and thus does not seek common cause with organisations for whom counter-terrorism is a major concern. The leader of one Muslim organisation explained the divisions within civil society:

Civil society is split into three groups. One group, out of fear, has stayed out of the question (of counter-terrorism) altogether. They fear being implicated by association and fear that their funding from Western governments will be withdrawn. This is mostly Kenyan NGOs. But international NGOs have also not raised their voice on terrorism in Kenya, at least not locally. I can be clean as snow but if I am arrested on suspicion of terrorism, then everyone in the NGO community abandons me. There is a whole environment of fear. A second group take this as a *fait accompli*, that this is part of American power. The USA is the strongest power and you cannot do anything is their view. They will talk with us [Muslim organisations] and identify right and wrong in the Global War on Terror, and even sympathise with us, but they are resigned. Then there is a third group, consisting of a handful of organisations, that is challenging this directly...Almost all non-Muslim NGOs are in the first and second group. They are silent and not opening up much to us and we don't know why.[66]

A further factor that contributed to the lack of response by civil society in general is that since the NGO Council is moribund there is not a broader unified civil society voice speaking out on these issues. Human rights organisations and Muslim groups have tried to work around these constraints by coming together in ad-hoc coalitions and networks to oppose particular measures and laws but this way of working is no substitute for an umbrella body to give leverage to the advocacy issues of a smaller number of organisations and groups.

The production of suspicion and fear around the Muslim charitable network has undoubtedly influenced the reticence observed in civil society as a whole. Pressures and threats for civil society generated by new counter-terrorism structures have disproportionately had an impact on Muslim organisations and groups where a 'siege mentality' has begun to take hold. After the US embassy bombings in 1998 five Muslim NGOs were proscribed, usually at the behest of foreign governments, and other groups continued operating under a haze of suspicion and despite administrative interference.[67] A clampdown on Muslim NGOs has been matched by greater restrictions on the flow of funds originating from states in the Gulf and Middle East. Donorship from this region was relatively important for Muslim organisations working in North Eastern Province, where, again, the impacts have been felt disproportionately although precise evidence to quantify these claims is lacking.

In other ways, the spaces for Muslims to organise have been constrained by various counter-terrorism measures and practices. Madrassas and mosques have been constructed as sites for radicalisation and extremism and have come under greater scrutiny. Consultants for the Ministry of Education suggested assessing the content of madrassa curricula.[68] Other recent proposals have sought greater regulatory oversight of mosques through central registration and monitoring charity flows through mosque networks. Currently, there is no central registration or regulatory authority for mosques or madrassas. These proposals have not been pursued but they have had the effect of intimidating local people who would otherwise give donations to madrassas or mosque committees.[69]

There have been different responses within Muslim communities to these various pressures and threats. In regard to monitoring mosques, some Muslims proposed that mosques register with the government and keep a list of their members, which would then be made available to the state as is done in Turkey. Others within the community strongly resisted any attempts at government oversight.[70] Some Muslim leaders and groups have vocally opposed counter-terrorism measures, laws and practices, as seen in their efforts to organise against the SOT Bill. The Muslim Human Rights Forum, which was established in 2006, documented the culpability of the Kenyan government in the regional rendition programme in the Horn of Africa (Muslim Human Rights Forum, 2007). Groups such as the Council of Imams and Preachers of Kenya and the National Muslim Leaders Forum have publicly condemned ATPU raids on Muslim neighbourhoods and have met with politicians and government officials to voice their concerns. In other ways, Muslims are adapting to, rather than resisting, increased pressures but this typically involves restricting their own efforts and rights to organise. Many groups are not seeking to formally register because they are resigned to the possibility of being denied registration.[71] This self-censorship is also seen in organisations avoiding the use of Arabic names or the word 'Muslim'. Some groups have sought legal shelter by becoming a programme of a registered organisation, a tactic used in the 1990s by human rights organisations who encountered difficulties registering during the Moi regime.

Part of the difficulty for civil society organisations that want to work on these issues is the lack of donor support as well as the acute bureaucratic pressure on organisations that speak out against government counter-terrorism policies and practices. Human rights organisations have complained that the government uses the Kenya Revenue Authority to intimidate groups that speak out.[72] But democracy and governance civil society organisations can no longer rely on donors to pressure the government. This is because donor strategies have shifted and many now emphasise the importance of civil society working with the state, rather than opposing the state and pressuring it to reform. As previously explained, levels of aid dependency in Kenya have fallen and thus donor influence has diminished as well. Further, some civil society activists claim that mainstream NGOs risk losing donor support if they are seen to be helping Muslim organisations and human rights groups organising on these issues.[73] Muslim organisations and human rights groups that have organised on issues of counter-terrorism have done so in spite of little funding and also faced with administrative harassment and bureaucratic obstruction in gaining access to sensitive information on terrorism suspects and police raids. However, the effective efforts of the few organisations and groups that have taken up these challenges in documenting and exposing government practices as well as opposing the SOT Bill show there is scope for civil society to organise more determinedly and coherently around the ongoing establishment of new counter-terrorism structures.

Conclusion

The encapsulation of Kenya in the global War on terror has coincided
with democratic strides and a widening space for deliberative politics.
There have been significant shifts in the terrain for organising outside
of the state as well. Although in recent years new spaces have opened
for political debate, this has been matched by the fragmentation of civil
society around regional and ethnic divides, reflecting centrifugal forces
seen in society more widely. Whitaker (2007) suggests that the extent
of political liberalisation in a country is significant in determining the
degree of debate that occurred before passage of anti-terror laws. She
notes that there has been greater debate on such laws in young democracies like Kenya, South Africa and the Philippines than in countries where
political rights are restricted. Thus, she notes that fighting terrorism can
go hand in hand with spreading democracy. Proposed anti-terrorism
legislation has been galvanising in Kenya but for no more than a minority segment of civil society consisting of urban-based lawyers, human
rights organisations and networks, and groups representing Muslims
who are disproportionately affected by new counter-terrorism measures
and practices. Opposition in Kenya to specific anti-terror structures has
occurred in spite of a lack of institutional support and funding, intimidation by governmental regulatory bodies and the associated risk of
de-registration and blacklisting for groups organising on these issues, as
well as the possibility of losing donor funding for other activities on the
basis of being perceived as sympathising with terrorists.

The challenges for civil society in Kenya consist of persisting international pressure on the Kenyan government to co-operate in global
counter-terrorism efforts, the subtle introduction of CTMs outside of a
supportive legal framework, and internal divisions within civil society
that preclude a more coherent advocacy strategy and plan. The role of
development aid has been problematic by reifying certain misconceptions that Kenyan Muslims are radicalised and sympathise with foreign
terrorists. Despite this, there have been some positive impacts of some
security-oriented development assistance to grass-roots groups working
on issues of human rights, conflict management and community development. Unfortunately, the securitisation of development has on the
whole too often prompted a shift away from human security approaches
to complex political and governance problems. The efforts of some aid
donors to promote capacity-building of counter-terrorism institutions or
to encourage public awareness of the presumed need for new counter-
terrorism structures have alienated the few civil society groups that are

trying to domesticate the debate by conducting their own research, documentation and advocacy. The use of more overt political criteria in targeting some types of aid in Kenya has also minimised the potentially ameliorative impacts of development. Or, as the head of a Muslim NGO put it, 'the US can put up fifty schools in North Eastern Province but this does not change local perceptions'.[74]

Although the space for political debate and discourse is comparatively large in Kenya compared to other countries in the region, civil society has fragmented into disparate groups coalescing around discrete economic, ethnic and regional interests. The effects of fragmentation are magnified by the disintegration of the NGO Council as the representative body of NGOs. The failures of NGO representation at a national level have impeded greater levels of connectivity among different interest groups, which could leverage the interests and concerns of smaller groupings and thus inject civil society more forcefully into discussions around the War on Terror in Kenya and the region. The formation of ad-hoc coalitions and networks to advocate against specific counter-terrorism practices, measures and proposed laws is an adaptation to the post-2002 political landscape in which civil society engaged in democracy, governance and human rights issues has come under greater pressure to define and assert its role and purpose. This is especially urgent in view of aid trends towards supporting government programmes and state-defined development priorities. These trends have entailed a de-emphasis on civil society support as a component of better governance. The strong protestations of democracy and governance civil society in the face of these changes ultimately points to its aid dependence and the want for private donorship in Kenya in support of human rights.

In many ways, these difficulties speak of the divisions seen in wider society and the lack of political consciousness among many mainstream groups. Counter-terrorism issues such as police raids and the treatment of terror detainees are perceived to involve Muslims, which again ties into larger political discourses beyond Kenya that construct Muslim communities as suspicious. Thus, in mainstream public debate the significance of new counter-terrorism structures for the fundamental human rights of all, as well as for the actors and spaces of civil society, is lost. Many young Muslims in Kenya, in turn, feel targeted by counter-terrorism operations and believe their interests are sacrificed in discussions on 'security' that predominate policy in the global War on Terror. However, all this points to a continuing need for civil society to make its contribution to policy discussions and public debates on the War on Terror. The effective efforts of the few organisations and groups that have taken up these challenges in documenting and exposing government practices shows there is scope for civil society to organise more determinedly and coherently around new and emerging counter-terrorism measures, laws and security practices.

Notes

1. The chapter draws upon fieldwork in Kenya carried out on several trips between July 2006 and June 2007. The research is based on a review of primary and secondary sources including government and donor documentation and media reports as well as qualitative interviewing with aid and donor agency staff, government officials, democracy and governance NGOs, humanitarian organisations, human rights activists, Muslim community leaders and journalists. A total of 56 interviews were carried out in Nairobi and Mombasa. Further, a round-table was organised in Nairobi with donor agency officials, civil society activists and NGO representatives to scrutinise important themes arising from the interviews and to assess the wider context of donor–civil society relations in Kenya.
2. Muslim Human Rights Forum (MHRF). 2008. 'Civil Society Responses to Counterterrorism Measures in Kenya'. Special Brief. September 2008, p. 4.
3. LSE/Chatham House Roundtable on 'Human Rights in a Cross-Border Context: Kenya and Ethiopia'. Chatham House. 2 April 2007.
4. 'Ethiopia Holding 41 Suspects Who Fought with Somali Islamists, Officials Confirm.' *New York Times*. 11 April 2007.
5. 'Family Wants Suspect Returned from Guantanamo.' *The Daily Nation* (Nairobi). 29 March 2007.
6. MHRF, 2008, p. 5.
7. Authors' interview. Open Society Institute of East Africa. Nairobi. 5 June 2007.
8. Ibid.
9. Authors' interview. Kenya National Commission on Human Rights. Nairobi. 18 January 2007.
10. Authors' interview. European diplomatic mission. Nairobi. 19 July 2006.
11. MHRF, 2008, p. 8.
12. Authors' interview. DfID. Nairobi. 19 July 2006.
13. Authors' interview. European diplomat. Nairobi. 5 December 2007.
14. MHRF, 2008, p. 9.
15. Authors' interview. Muslim Human Rights Forum. Nairobi. 6 December 2007.
16. Authors' interview. International Commission of Jurists. Nairobi. 20 January 2007.
17. Authors' interview. Human rights lawyer. Nairobi. 5 June 2007.
18. Authors' interview. Head of governance NGO. Nairobi. 26 July 2007.
19. USAID Kenya. http://www.usaid.gov/ke/ke.progdevan/programs.html. Visited: 18 May 2007.

20. USAID, 2006. 'USAID/Education for Marginalised Children of Kenya (EMACK): Quarterly technical report'.
21. Authors' interview. European diplomatic mission. Nairobi. 1 February 2007.
22. Authors' interview. European diplomatic mission. Nairobi. 5 December 2007.
23. Authors' interview. International grant-making agency. Nairobi. 5 June 2007.
24. Authors' interview. Council of Imams and Preachers of Kenya. Mombasa. 25 January 2007.
25. Cortright (2005). 'A critical evaluation of the UN counter-terrorism program: accomplishments and challenges'.
26. Authors' interview. UNDP. Nairobi. 8 June 2007.
27. Authors' interview. USAID. Nairobi. 20 July 2006.
28. Authors' interview. International Commission of Jurists. Nairobi. 20 January 2007.
29. Authors' interview. Muslim Human Rights Forum. Nairobi. 31 January 2007.
30. Authors' interview. Institute for Security Studies. Nairobi. 22 January 2007.
31. Authors' interview. USAID and CJTF. Nairobi. 23 April 2007.
32. Personnel communication with Paul Goldsmith. 28 June 2007. London. See also Harmony Project, 2007, footnote 92.
33. 'Michuki Off to the US for Terror Talks'. *The Daily Nation* (Nairobi). 23 April 2007.
34. MHRF, 2008, p. 9.
35. Authors' interview. European diplomat. Nairobi. 5 December 2007.
36. Authors' interview. Muslim NGO head. Nairobi. 16 January 2007.
37. Authors' interview. Muslim civil society activist. Nairobi. 3 December 2007.
38. See Hughes (2004).
39. Authors' interview. Allavida. Nairobi. 20 July 2006.
40. Authors' interview. University of Nairobi lecturer. Nairobi. 23 April 2007.
41. Ibid.
42. See Anderson (2003) for a detailed analysis of the 2002 election results.
43. Authors' interview. Education Centre for Women in Democracy. Nairobi. 20 July 2006.
44. Authors' interview. University of Nairobi lecturer. Nairobi. 23 April 2007.
45. See *Africa Confidential* 2005.
46. Authors' interview. European Commission. Nairobi. 2 February 2007.
47. 'Special Brief: Civil Society Responses to the Kenyan Crisis'. February 2008. Kenya Human Rights Institute. http://www.equalinrights.org/fileadmin/filelist/documenten/Guides_and_Manuals/Community_Empowerment_in_East_Africa/special_brief_-_civil_society_responses_ to_the_kenyan_crisis.pdf. Accessed 13 February 2009.
48. GJLOS is a Kenyan government programme but the procurement systems and finances are managed by the accounting giant KPMG. The programme envisages an ideal-type relationship between the state and civil society whereby non-state actors implement reforms under priority areas that have been identified by the state and agreed by contributing donors.
49. Authors' interview. SIDA. Nairobi. 18 January 2007.
50. Authors' interviews. USAID. Nairobi. 20 July 2006; DFID. Nairobi. 19 July 2006.
51. Authors' interview. European Commission. Nairobi. 2 February 2007.
52. Authors' interview. Human rights lawyer. Nairobi. 5 June 2007.

53. Authors' interview. SIDA. Nairobi. 18 January 2007.
54. 'Interview: President Kibaki Talks About MDG Progress in Kenya.' *Mail and Guardian* (South Africa). 22 October 2008. http://kenvironews.wordpress.com/2008/10/22/interview-president-kibaki-talks-about-mdg-progress-in-kenya/. Accessed 13 February 2009.
55. Authors' interview. USAID. Nairobi. 20 July 2006.
56. Round-table discussion on 'Civil Society and the Securitisation of Aid in the EU'. London. 8 November 2006.
57. Authors' interview. International Commission of Jurists. Nairobi. 20 January 2007.
58. Authors' interview. Kenya National Commission on Human Rights. Nairobi. 17 July 2006.
59. Comment at the round-table discussion on 'Civil Society, Security and Aid in Eastern Africa Since 2001'. Nairobi. 4 December 2007.
60. Authors' interview with head of an unregistered human rights organisation. Nairobi. 6 December 2007.
61. Comments by Lawrence Mute. In 'Civil Society Responses to Counterterrorism Measures in Kenya'. Muslim Human Rights Forum. September 2008, p. 6.
62. Comment at the round-table discussion on 'Civil Society, Security and Aid in Eastern Africa Since 2001'. Nairobi. 4 December 2007.
63. Ibid.
64. Authors' interview. Institute for Security Studies. Nairobi. 22 January 2007.
65. 'Shame in the Horn of Terror'. *The East African*. 31 July 2007.
66. Authors' interview. Northern Aid. Nairobi. 16 January 2007.
67. Authors' interview. Muslim Human Rights Forum. Nairobi. 31 January 2007.
68. Authors' interview. Young Muslims Association. Nairobi. 19 July 2006.
69. Authors' interview. Northern Aid. Nairobi. 16 January 2007.
70. Authors' interview. Young Muslims Association. Nairobi. 19 July 2006.
71. Authors' interview. Northern Aid. Nairobi. 16 January 2007.
72. Reflections by participants, Roundtable on 'Civil Society and the Securitisation of Aid in Kenya', 19 January, 2007, Fairview Hotel, Nairobi.
73. Ibid.
74. Authors' interview. Northern Aid. Nairobi. 16 July 2007.

7
Civil Society, Security and Aid in India

> Whether it likes it or not, India is now at the centre of the global war on terror.
>
> Indrani Bagchi, *Times of India*, 7 December 2008, p. 1

Unlike Kenya, India is not a country where Al Qaeda attacks on US targets have been carried out. Unlike Afghanistan, it is not a country where Al Qaeda or affiliated organisations have cells from which they have organised jihadi attacks. Nor is it a country where military intervention has occurred in pursuit of the War on Terror. Still, India has a lengthy history of terrorism and social violence. From the US perspective the terrorist attacks in India have been viewed as domestic concerns. The US regards India as strategically important in South Asia. The US–India '123' nuclear agreement in 2007 was further confirmation of India's strategic importance to the US. Although it is has not been regarded as a front line state in the War on Terror, India's rivalry with Pakistan is thought to have distracted Pakistani military and security agencies away from fighting militants along its long, porous border with Afghanistan.

In other respects, India was relatively unimportant to the prosecution of the War on Terror. Compared with Kenya, there was little pressure on New Delhi to introduce new counter-terrorism structures. The US did not object to the repeal of the Prevention of Terrorism Act 2002 (POTA) by the Congress-led coalition government in 2004. The Indian government has not regarded Islamic extremism to be a significant security threat. Militant activity in Kashmir has been viewed as an exception and unconnected to communal divisions and social violence elsewhere in the country.

The audacious, well-co-ordinated attacks in Mumbai in November 2008 challenged assessments of the nature and threat of terrorism in

India. Mumbai was lumped with Madrid, London, Bali and New York as a victim of global jihadi terrorism. It was thought that the nature of the Mumbai attacks was qualitatively different and that the state required new powers to fight a virulent new strain of terrorism. Fearing an outbreak of hostilities between two nuclear powers, and alarmed at the apparent targeting of American and British passport holders in the attacks, Washington and London offered their expertise and advice to the Indian authorities on strengthening their counter-terrorism infrastructure. Although India was never a front-line state in the War on Terror, its politics and civil society, as well as its bilateral relations with the US and the UK, have not been wholly immune to the War on Terror regime. Rather, the regime has subtly infiltrated political debate and social attitudes in India.

This chapter will examine the various domestic and international drivers and political and social aspects of counter-terrorism in India. The influences of the War on Terror are apparent in discussions on India's counter-terrorism responses, including the passing and later repeal of POTA as well as government efforts to address the social marginalisation and exclusion of Muslims. Specifically, right-wing Hindu nationalist politicians have advocated a hard-line stance on fighting terrorism and have manipulated the War on Terror discourse in pursuit of their political interests. They have reverted to the polarising language of the War on Terror and a related notion of global Islamic extremism to justify their position for more restrictive security legislation. Their arguments have depended on questioning the nationalist credentials of Indian Muslims, who, they suggest, sympathise with global jihadi elements. US and UK assessments of the threat of terrorism in South Asia and Afghanistan have influenced foreign and aid policy towards India as well. This is reflected in experimental, security-oriented aid projects targeting Muslims in India as well as support for the Indian government's efforts to fight money-laundering and terrorist financing. More recently, the US has sought India's co-operation in its efforts to stabilise Pakistan as part of a grander military strategy encompassing the war in Afghanistan.

The chapter begins by tracing how Hindu right-wing nationalist politicians have manipulated the War on Terror discourse to fuel suspicions of Indian Muslims as sympathising, if not supporting, global jihadists. The following section examines US and UK diplomacy and aid to India against the backdrop of shifting global politics since the 9/11 attacks. The chapter then assesses the intersection of these global politics with political and social divisions in India, focusing on the suspicion of Muslim institutions, the impacts of terrorist legislation on minorities, heightened regulation of CSOs by their grantees and the negotiation of regulations governing NGOs. The final section examines civil society responses in India to counter-terrorism in the shifting global, regional and national political contexts.[1]

Pushing for counter-terrorist legislation: Manipulating the War on Terror

Before the terrorist attacks in Mumbai in November 2008, India did not feature prominently in the prosecution of the War on Terror. The US took little noticeable interest in India's internal security and then only when incidents threatened to disturb regional stability, such as those following the attack on the Indian Parliament in December 2001. Rather, the centre of concern was relations between Pakistan and India, both nuclear powers.[2] Still, the language of the War on Terror has circulated in political debates on counter-terrorism and the position of India's large Muslim minority population. In this and the next section we examine the various security threats facing India and how right-wing Hindu nationalist politicians exploited the War on Terror discourse and post-9/11 global political climate to press for tighter security arrangements and to raise suspicions of Indian Muslims.

Until recently, the Indian government has not regarded global jihadi terrorism as a primary security concern. Rather, India's post-independence security agenda has centred on three main threats: the conflict in Kashmir, secessionist movements in north-east India and the Maoist-inspired Naxalite movement, which began in 1967 and has spread over large parts of the country. In a speech to security officials in November 2008, days before the attacks in Mumbai, the Indian Prime Minister Manmohan Singh cited left-wing extremism as the most serious security threat facing India.[3] Latterly, security officials and agencies have indicated concern surrounding the status and position of Indian Muslims. Some view Muslims as a security risk and as disloyal to India.[4] This in turn has informed contrasting official approaches towards Muslims, on the one hand increasing surveillance of Muslim communities but on the other hand addressing the disadvantage of Muslims in education and employment.

The first of these conflicts is embedded in the complex history and politics of Indo-Pakistan relations and in a much broader geo-strategic politics involving other major powers, which have included in different periods the US, the former Soviet Union and Iran. Whilst there are cross-border politics pertaining to the north-east conflict and to the

Maoist insurgency that is spreading across India, the Kashmir conflict has become increasingly internationalised. Until the late 1980s the conflict in Jammu/Kashmir was treated primarily as an internal security issue, though it clearly had an international dimension through the interest and support emanating from diaspora groups in the UK and the US. From the late 1980s onwards the conflict became enmeshed in Indo-Pakistan bilateral relations and regional politics in South Asia.

Whilst the Jammu and Kashmir Liberation Front was an indigenous initiative, seeking independence from both Pakistan and India, after 1989 it was gradually overtaken by other groups that infiltrated the province and sought to make Kashmir part of Pakistan (Luce, 2007, p. 233). The collapse of the Soviet Union and the subsequent withdrawal of Soviet troops from Afghanistan left a legacy of jihadi fighters who were sponsored variously by the US, Pakistan, Iran and Saudi Arabia. Al Qaeda and ex-mujahedin fighters set up base-camps in Kashmir with the backing of Pakistani ISI officers to launch attacks on government and warlord troops in Afghanistan and to fuel the insurgency in Kashmir. In this way the conflict in Kashmir became Islamicised as the axis of conflict extended beyond a dispute over territorial control and sovereignty to encompass divisions around religion and communal identity. This in turn intensified government suspicion of Muslims as somehow disloyal to India and preferring allegiance to Pakistan. Nevertheless, as Nussbaum (2007) points out, the Kashmir conflict was always seen as an exceptional issue inside India. It was not used to mobilise Indian Muslims nor did it seemingly increase the terrorist threat facing India from global jihadi groups.

Up until the attacks on Indian cities in 2008 the Indian government tended to blame terrorist attacks on Pakistan as a reflex to their long-standing dispute over Kashmir. This changed in the aftermath of the bombings in Ahmedabad and Delhi in 2008. A previously unknown home-grown terrorist outfit, the Indian Mujahedin, claimed responsibility for the attacks, referring to both familiar global jihadi tropes as well as distinctly domestic grievances, especially the anti-Muslim attacks in Gujarat in 2002, which are examined later.[5] Similarly, the terrorists involved in the Mumbai attacks in November 2008 appropriated global jihadi discourses to justify their assaults on a Jewish centre, on US and British nationals, and on symbols of 'Western' wealth and lifestyles. The terrorists sought to gain maximum publicity value by entering the city through the Gateway of India as well as first attacking and then establishing a logistics base inside the iconic Taj Hotel. In other respects, the attacks bore the hallmarks of an Al Qaeda–inspired plot even though there was no evidence that Al Qaeda was directly involved in the planning or in financing the attacks. The Indian media played into the drama of the violence by depicting the events as 'India's 9/11', thereby catapulting Mumbai onto the international stage of Al Qaeda victims alongside Madrid, Bali, London and New York.

Public debate ensued over the institutional failures and lack of co-ordination that marred the initial response of the security services. In response to a groundswell of public anger at politicians concerning administrative and policing incompetence, the government hastily initiated discussions on reforming its counter-terrorism institutional framework alongside other policing reforms. Both Condoleeza Rice and Gordon Brown visited India in the aftermath of the attacks to offer technical expertise and assistance. The Mumbai attacks changed perceptions of the nature of the terrorist threat facing India as being qualitatively different and separate from the terrorism threat facing the US, the UK, Spain and other countries where militants had launched attacks. In this way, the attacks gave leverage to the Indian government to act robustly in pushing the Pakistani government to crack down on militant groups based in the country.

Whilst the events of Mumbai drew India deeper into international co-operation on counter-terrorism, even before this the effects of the War on Terror regime were being felt. The War on Terror added greater complexity to how the Kashmir conflict was framed and underlined the urgency to seek a resolution. It also provided a political opening for Hindu nationalist groups and political parties, notably the Bhartiya Janata Party (BJP), to take up issues of security instrumentally by passing POTA in 2002.

India's first anti-terror law, the Terrorist and Disruptive Activities (Prevention) Act (TADA), was passed in 1985 upon the assassination of former Prime Minister Indira Gandhi by her Sikh bodyguard and was used to crack down on Sikh militancy in the Punjab (Singh, 2004, p. 149). Previously, the Indian government used special military powers granted under the 1958 Armed Forces (Special) Powers Act to curb the secessionist struggles in Kashmir and the north-east. TADA was renewed again in 1987 and thereafter every two years. The provisions of the law were effectively diluted over time through court rulings. Reports that the law was misused against workers in Gujarat, farmers' movements and Muslims led to public outcry and the law was allowed to lapse in 1995. There was then a legal hiatus between 1995 and 2000 when no specific anti-terrorist law was in place.

By 2000 the BJP-led government and the Law Commission called for the introduction of a new anti-terror law, which was opposed by some parliamentarians who feared the law would target members of minority and disadvantaged groups. Significantly, the Law Commission's 173rd Report took a partial view of the perceived threats within the country, omitting any mention of threats from Hindu fundamentalists such as the Shiv Sena (Singh, 2004, p. 150). This in turn reflected the way that TADA was used against Muslims during outbreaks of communal violence. Hence, when the Prevention of Terrorism Ordinance (POTO) was introduced in October 2001 following the 9/11 attacks in the US, many interpreted this as a crackdown on Islamic militants, although the official rationale made no such specific reference (Singh, 2004, p. 150).[6] The idea of a bill on terrorism was further debated in parliament, a debate that was peppered with references to a global fight against terrorism and the presumed role of Pakistan in hosting and supporting militant groups that threaten India's security. As Parliament was adjourned following the December 2001 attacks on Parliament in Delhi, a second ordinance was then promulgated which laid the basis for a bill on terrorism. Parliamentary and presidential approval for the bill was given in March 2002 and the Prevention of Terrorism Act (POTA) became law. As is explained below, POTA, as with preceding anti-terror laws, was used to target individuals from disadvantaged backgrounds and against political opponents.[7]

When the United Progressive Alliance government led by the Congress Party came to power in September 2004, it made good on a campaign pledge to repeal POTA. However, this did not apply retrospectively and those detained under the Act continue to be incarcerated. Moreover, several of the provisions in POTA exist in other legislation such as the Armed Forces (Special Powers) Act, the Disturbed Areas Acts applying in the north-east and Jammu and Kashmir, the Maharashtra Control of Organised Crime Act (MCOCA)[8] and the Unlawful Activities Prevention Act (UAPA 1967, 2004; PUDR, 2005b). In 2004, several key amendments were made to UAPA incorporating provisions from POTA. Other loopholes in the law have meant that in practice the state has relinquished very few powers. These amendments thus had the effect of making permanent extra-ordinary anti-terror provisions in law (PUDR, 2005b, p. 8).

In December 2008, in the aftermath of the Mumbai attacks, the lower house of the Indian parliament passed the Unlawful Activities (Prevention) Amendments Bill. It increased the period of detention of suspects from 90 to 180 days. The bill evoked debate around safeguarding constitutional rights, the targeting of Muslims and the need for new legislation with a multitude of security laws already in place. Yet, there was a strong political imperative to be seen to be acting and the bill passed easily. BJP leader L.K. Advani criticised the Congress Party for repealing POTA (Lakshmi, 2008). The government emphasised the importance of reforming also the police, criminal law and justice system. The communalisation of police forces in some states and police handling of the Delhi bomb blasts in September 2008 raised legitimate concerns over whether greater powers could be entrusted to police and judicial forces that had in the past targeted Muslims.[9]

Right-wing Hindu nationalists, security and the demonisation of Muslims

Hindu nationalist groups and political parties have appropriated the 'War on Terror' discourse to raise suspicions of Indian Muslims as somehow being untrustworthy and sympathising with global jihadist struggles. These poisonous claims have gained traction and legitimised historical prejudices and fear of Muslims, especially among the burgeoning Hindu middle classes. As an employee at the Dalit Foundation commented, 'the War on Terror is affecting more Muslims. Dalits are never considered as traitors to the country so they can't easily be blamed.'[10]

Suspicion of Indian Muslims was heightened when a Muslim medical student originally from India was convicted in the attack on Glasgow. The terrorist attacks in Mumbai in November 2008 put a cap on the idea that terrorism in India was purely a domestic affair albeit with connections to Pakistan. Widespread sympathy for India in the aftermath of the Mumbai attacks enabled India to reframe its conflict with Pakistan as part of a global struggle against extremism and jihadist terror. This framing has not gone unquestioned. Some analysts argued that the attacks had little to do with Al Qaeda–inspired jihadi terrorism[11] and were instead the latest in a series of hostilities by Pakistan.[12] Still, the potent symbolism of these attacks has drawn India more wholly into the fold of global counter-terrorism co-operation. Indian politicians, led by the BJP, have sought to exploit the new links for their own political agendas.

Since the launch of the War on Terror, the BJP has built upon a background of communal unrest stretching back to the riots in Ahmedabad in the late 1960s to fuel suspicion of Muslims, to attribute violent incidents to Muslim groups and to link Muslims to global jihadism. By communalising the police force and other government institutions, especially in Mumbai and Gujarat, the BJP and related right-wing Hindu forces have been able to perpetuate this discourse and give it literally greater force through the coercive apparatus of the state. To understand how the BJP has managed to manipulate the discourse of the War on Terror to cast suspicion on Muslims in India, we need to first briefly outline the rise of right-wing Hindu fundamentalist politics in India.[13]

The intense communalism and specifically anti-Muslim rhetoric and action that spiralled in Mumbai and Gujarat over the last decade built upon the tensions engendered through the promotion of Hindu fundamentalist politics by the BJP (Yagnik, 2002; Independent People's Tribunal, 2007). The BJP-led National Democratic Alliance formed the government between 1999 and 2004, when it was ousted by the Congress-led United Progressive Alliance. The BJP has dominated Gujarat state politics since 1998. Gujarat Chief Minister Narendra Modi was resoundingly re-elected in 2007. The destruction of the Babri Masjid in 1992 was a key moment in the deepening of communal politics in India, spinning a cycle of revenge and avenge amongst sections of the Hindu and Muslim populations (Luce, 2007, pp. 251–252). The BJP established deep inroads into the social consciousness of many Hindus through its social partner organisation the Rashtriya Swayamsevak Sangh (RSS), a highly trained quasi-military organisation with both ideological and coercive functions. The RSS set up schools for young people, inculcating in them the beliefs and practices of Hinduism and the idea that India was a solely Hindu nation. They have held disturbing sway over the police in cities such as Mumbai and over government and educational institutions in Gujarat. Funded, inter alia, by diaspora groups in the UK and the US, the RSS has become a global enterprise dedicated to Hindu supremacy.

The BJP and the RSS[14] have played a key role in constructing and promoting an image of Muslims as would-be terrorists. Three days after the attack on the Twin Towers in September 2001, the Chief Minister of Gujarat, Narendra Modi, participated in a debate on Star News TV, an Indian news channel, on the provocative topic 'Is Islam the Cutting Edge of Terrorism?' In the debate he stated that 'All Muslims are not terrorists but all terrorists are Muslims', a refrain that had appeared in the US and Europe and had now found its way via the global media to India.[15] Modi's statement sought to project the link between terrorism and Muslims beyond India and beyond the India–Pakistan axis into a global context.

The implications of the anti-Muslim politics of the Hindu right in India were laid bare in the widespread violence against Muslims in Gujarat following the Godhra train incident in February 2002. On 27 February 2002 over 58 passengers travelling on the Sabarmati Express train were burned to death in carriage S-6 as the train pulled out of

Godhra station. Passengers on the train included a large group of supporters of the Vishwa Hindu Parishad (VHP), who had travelled to the site of the demolished Babri Masjid to protest in support of the construction of a temple dedicated to Lord Rama on the site of the former mosque. Although the exact circumstances of Godhra have still to be established, it is alleged that scuffles broke out between these Hindu supporters and Muslim vendors and within 15 minutes carriage S-6 was ablaze. There is considerable controversy surrounding the events that morning and court cases were still pending in 2008.

The BJP framed the event not only as a terrorist incident but more specifically as being linked to Muslims who were conspiring to commit terrorist attacks. The Gujarat BJP government arrested those accused of being involved in the Godhra incident under POTA (Grover, 2002, p. 380). By rehearsing the refrain that 'all terrorists were Muslims' Modi added to a repertoire of tropes, phrases and associations that could be used to shape the understanding of the Godhra event. According to Varadarajan (2007, p. 5), both the central and Gujarat BJP governments claimed that the attack on the train was a premeditated, terrorist act ordered by Pakistan with the aim of inciting communalism and destabilising India. Modi sought to explain the tragedy in these terms by claiming the incident was guided by a 'jihadi mentality' and was 'a preplanned conspiracy of collective terrorism' (Varadarajan, 2002; footnote 17, p. 36). Home Minister Lal Krishna Advani in a briefing to journalists in early March 2002 went further by linking the incident to the attack on the Indian Parliament in December 2001[16] whilst Jana Krishnamurthy, President of the BJP, claimed Pakistan and the ISI in particular were behind the Godhra incident.[17] Advani later denied any link of the Godhra tragedy to terrorism and, moreover, that any BJP leaders had suggested such a link. However, these initial remarks by leading BJP politicians subtly reinforced a discourse that associates terrorism, fundamentalism and extremism with Muslims, who are portrayed as an undifferentiated whole. Thus, it neatly serves the Hindu nationalist agenda of the BJP. In a speech to the BJP national executive meeting in Goa in April 2002, the Prime Minister of the then BJP-led government, Atal Bihari Vajpayee, linked terrorism to militant Islam[18] and the desire of Muslims across the world to 'spread their beliefs by terror'.[19] Vajpayee reportedly had wanted Modi to resign but was persuaded otherwise after discussing with other Asian leaders who were dealing with Islamic terrorism (Nussbaum, 2007, p. 66).

The War on Terror gave legitimacy and cover to the anti-Muslim attitudes of the Hindu right in India, personified in Modi's demagoguery.

Modi appropriated the discourses of the War on Terror to propose that local security incidents were embedded in a wider global Islamic terrorist agenda. In this way, BJP leaders could frame the Godhra tragedy and its aftermath in terms of a global threat of terrorism. Modi's reference to a Newtonian logic of 'action–reaction' to justify the killings of Muslims after the Godhra incident contributed further to the simplistic rendering of Muslims as being culpable. The attribution of the Godhra tragedy to 'Islamic terrorism' provoked violence across Gujarat and as a result 2,000 Muslims were killed and 200,000 displaced (Varadarajan, 2007, p. 9).

The communalisation of the police in Mumbai and Gujarat (Sundar 2002, pp. 99–102; Setalvad, 2002, pp. 177–213) coupled with the global circulation of the idea of 'Islamic terrorism' has played itself out in local politics. A series of car bomb blasts in Mumbai in 2003 was allegedly carried out by the Gujarat Muslim Revenge Force, which sought to avenge the attacks upon Muslims the previous year (Luce, 2007, p. 252). Following the bombing of a commuter train in Mumbai in July 2006, the police raided predominately Muslim slums and arrested over 400–500 youth.[20] This echoed a similar pattern after the Gujarat riots when the Anti-Terrorist Squad in the Gujarat police reportedly detained illegally 300 Muslim youth under POTA, some of whom were allegedly tortured.[21] Though local activists launched a national campaign around some of these cases, taking the matter to the National Human Rights Commission, many of the detainees are still being held under POTA.

At issue here is the way that a polarising global discourse such as the War of Terror feeds into and exacerbates domestic social and political divisions. Given the gradual communalisation of the police forces and other parts of the state, particularly in Gujarat and Maharashtra, the polarising effects of the War on Terror discourse do little to improve democratic governance in India. Instead of a state that protects its citizens regardless of religion, the state too becomes mobilised by politicians in a politics of hate.

Given the increasing construction of Muslims in India as associated with global terrorism, it is noteworthy that in 2006 the Government of India set up a commission to investigate the socio-economic position of Muslims in India. The report confirmed claims long made by Muslim leaders and social justice advocates that Muslims are particularly disadvantaged in access to public sector positions and education but significantly over-represented in prisons.[22] This was the first time in 20 years that a special commission had been established for this purpose.[23] What prompted this initiative is unclear but no doubt the reasons are complex. Nevertheless it occurs at a time when Muslims in India are being constructed as problematic and when Western governments are trying to analyse the causes of radicalisation and establish preventive programmes. Although the report found that only 4 per cent of Muslim youth attend madrassas, dispelling the impression that Muslims attend madrassas in large number,[24] a UK Foreign Office official in India indicated that the Sachar Committee report was being used as 'a peg for madrassa reforms'.[25] Apparently the Indian government had been offering substantial sums for the reform of madrassas, provoking, however, stiff resistance from Muslim clerics.[26] However, other actors are also using it to push other agendas. For example, DFID has indicated support to the Ministry of Education to collect data on school enrolment by Muslim boys and girls and also Scheduled Caste and Scheduled Tribal children, thereby promoting further work on social exclusion.[27]

The Sachar Committee recommended, inter alia, establishing an Equal Opportunities Commission, establishing procedures to ensure fair representation of minorities in government, and moving madrassa pupils into mainstream education. Though the government announced an action plan to implement these recommendations in August 2007,[28] there has been only minimal follow-up since then. As a prominent Muslim leader stated, '[The report] is symbolically important. It is the first time since Independence that it has been officially recognised as a problem. ... In 1988 the Gopal Singh Report was issued but everyone forgot about it and this might be the fate of this report. It is the first time you have official recognition and some follow-up.'[29]

The next section explores how international forces have transmitted aspects of the global War on Terror regime into India.

India, aid and counter-terrorism

As India is not dependent on aid, we propose that the leverage of the US and its allies to influence the design and implementation of CTMs would be less. In other countries, aid is an important tool that donors have used to pressurise aid-recipient governments to undertake various counter-terrorism reforms, as we saw in Kenya. This section examines the relative importance of post-9/11 security objectives in changing aid policy and practice to India since 2001, focusing on US and UK foreign assistance.

Several contextual factors are important in understanding the effects of post-9/11 global security imperatives on American and British aid to India. First, Indian leaders tried to steer a route of neutrality through the Non-Aligned Movement in the choppy waters of the Cold War. As India was not solidly positioned in either of the superpower camps, it received development and military aid from both the West and the Soviet Union.

Second, as a former British colony, India has for decades been a major recipient of UK aid, ranking at or near the top of UK aid-recipients. Third, even though India has been a major benefactor of British aid and Japanese assistance,[30] donor policy influence has been minimal and the Indian government has been increasingly assertive in its foreign relations. For example, in recent years it has declined assistance from some donors, including Australia.[31]

Aid flows since 2001 from different donors have varied. British aid flows to India have remained high owing to historical ties between the two countries. India has been the leading recipient of DFID assistance, though for a time in 2003/2004 Iraq overtook India (DFID, 2007a). In recent years India was a top recipient of net UK bilateral ODA (OECD-DAC, 2007).[32] Overall aid flows to India have increased sharply since 2001 and British aid accounts for one-third of foreign development assistance to India (DFID, 2008). In January 2008 UK Prime Minister Gordon Brown announced a further three-year package of aid, amounting to £825 million, so that India met the Millennium Development Goals (DFID, 2008). In South Asia, security concerns have influenced increased British aid flows to Pakistan and development aid programming focussed on achieving counter-radicalisation objectives such as reform of madrassa curricula. Still, UK foreign assistance to India dwarfs its assistance to Pakistan. In 2005–2006, UK development aid to Pakistan amounted to £97 million, not considering other substantial UK economic and security assistance (www.dfid.gov.uk/Documents/publications/sid2006/table-7.xls, accessed 5 June 2009).

Post-9/11 security objectives in the region have not trumped the continuing emphasis of UK development aid on poverty reduction. It is interesting, therefore, that some DFID staff have sought to tie their work into security concerns as a way to give higher profile to otherwise more marginal issues. One DFID official in New Delhi commented, 'security can be a useful stick and it can work both ways. You can use it opportunistically.'[33] The same official explained, 'We need to use the space that security creates regarding its links with social exclusion and conflict.... I have been successful in pushing social exclusion because of the security issue.'[34] It is noteworthy that the logic of supporting work on the socially excluded as a way of addressing the causes of terrorism is also apparent in US foreign assistance to India. US aid has been directed to the poorest segments of India's population in order to mitigate the economic and social conditions that are thought to contribute to radicalisation and extremism (Lum, 2008).

The UK government has, however, pursued an anti-radicalisation agenda in India through its foreign policy arm. The key FCO initiative – the 'Engaging with the Islamic World' programme – was created after 2001 but built on existing work done by other units within FCO. The unit supports projects that seek to better understand the causes of radicalism. India has been a focal point for this new unit influenced by several factors. Concern over India's location in an unstable region and porous borders was one such factor. Another concern was perceived social inequalities in India and the low socio-economic position of Indian Muslims, which was confirmed in the findings of the Sachar Committee. There was also concern that growing investment ties between India and the UK had opened opportunities for organised crime, especially in a context of poor checks and balances and government inefficiencies in India (FCO, December 2006). Another significant concern was disapora links and funding of radical groups in the region. The November 2008 attacks in Mumbai raised the spectre that members of the South Asia diaspora in the UK were financing militant groups, including Lashkar-e-Taiba, which was accused of planning and carrying out the attacks.[35]

Within the overarching framework of the Engaging with the Islamic World, the British High Commission in New Delhi has supported initiatives aimed at fostering greater understanding of Indian Muslims. However, Indian academics and civil society activists have criticised these efforts, citing the failure of UK multicultural policies in comparison to the success of India's emphasis on diversity. Critics have also accused the British government of 'co-opting civil society or co-opting the Muslim population as part of the US alliance'.[36] The Engaging with the Islamic World programme highlights the increasing intersection between foreign policy, domestic policy and global political agendas. For example, FCO analysts have considered the importance of the South Asian diaspora in the UK in radicalising Muslims in India. The FCO has encouraged the new Department for Communities and Local Government to undertake complementary work in the UK. In this way global, foreign policy and domestic agendas become interwoven with the effect of 'securitising' strands of public policy. Ties between DFID, FCO and the Ministry of Defence have increased since 2001. In India it is thought that the FCO wants to set policy through the Engaging With the Muslim World programme but have it implemented by DFID[37].

Whilst long-standing historical ties and regional influence have been the main influences on UK aid to India, the War on Terror regime and regional stability have been driving forces behind US assistance to India since 2001. US assistance to Asia decreased throughout the 1990s following the end of the Cold War and because of nuclear proliferation sanctions on Pakistan and India (Lum, 2008). The 9/11 attacks precipitated a dramatic reversal of US policy and a re-engagement with the region. In particular, Bush waived US sanctions in September 2001, re-opening US assistance channels, and cleared more than $2 billion in debt owed by Pakistan.

Although India was the largest recipient of US bilateral assistance in South Asia before 2002, it has subsequently fallen well behind Pakistan, which has received significant politically determined assistance from the US for its contribution to Operation Enduring Freedom in Afghanistan. In sum, Pakistan received more than $10 billion in military, economic and development assistance from the US between 2002 and 2007, including an estimated $2.3 billion between 2005 and 2007 (Cohen and Chollet, 2007). By comparison, India received an estimated $265 million between 2005 and 2007 (Lum, 2008). Notably, US foreign assistance to India peaked in 2006 but fell in 2007 and 2008 after the US State Department re-classified India as a 'transforming' country.[38] Further, even though US assistance to India pales in comparison to the substantial assistance to Pakistan, overall US aid to India increased significantly in FY2002 and FY2003 for its regional counter-terrorism co-operation (Lum, 2008). At the operational level the USAID has set up some new projects focussing on Muslim communities and madrassas, themes that reflect War on Terror objectives. However, the bulk of programming remains directed at poverty reduction in general, even though at the strategic level USAID has sought to link its poverty reduction objectives to global security and transforming the conditions that terrorist groups are alleged to exploit.

Thus, US foreign assistance to India after 9/11 has been determined by consideration of India's strategic importance in South Asia and its contribution to the War on Terror. Following the attacks in Mumbai in November 2008, concern that the pattern of terrorist violence in India was merging with the discourses and practices of global jihad led the US to offer its technical expertise to the Indian government in reforming its counter-terrorism and intelligence structures. Further, the designation of India as strategically important to US national interests has also entailed greater security co-operation and military ties, which were concretised through the New Framework for the US–India Defense Relationship (2005) outlining a ten-year programme of shared objectives. For example, in 2002 Indian paratroopers and US special operations forces participated in the largest-ever joint army and air exercises since

India's independence (Rocca, 2002). They also have established a Joint Working Group on Counter-terrorism, which predates 9/11. The signing of the '123' civilian nuclear agreement between the US and India in October 2008 was the clearest demonstration of their deepening bilateral ties.

In summary, the significance of the War on Terror regime in shaping aid flows to India varies according to the discrete security, social and economic concerns of different donors. For the UK, its counter-terrorism agenda has not significantly influenced DFID programming in India. However, counter-radicalisation objectives linked to its counter-terrorism efforts have seeped in through UK foreign policy structures in India. In contrast, the War on Terror regime coupled with broad geo-strategic interests and concern over China's rising status as a rival to American hegemony have renewed US interest in South Asia, leading to enhanced aid flows and a new strategic partnership that was cemented in the '123' nuclear agreement. Importantly, greater US assistance flows to both Pakistan and India since 2001 need to be viewed against US sanctions on both countries in the 1990s for conducting nuclear tests. By and large, at the operational level, neither USAID nor DFID have established any specific programmes or projects aimed at preventing terrorism or developing counter-terrorist capacity in India. Rather, the goals of the War on Terror have been pursued through various military, security and diplomatic ties.

Tracing the effects of the War on Terror regime on civil society

There has not been a general crackdown on Indian civil society under the banner of the War on Terror, or in pursuit of other security objectives. Still, CTMs have been used selectively with respect to increased monitoring and surveillance of Muslim communities and any groups that are perceived to threaten the union state. Moreover, aspects of the War on Terror regime have intersected with state–civil society relations, especially in regard to foreign assistance of civil society groups. These points are explored in greater detail below.

The association of Indian Muslims with global jihadi terrorism, which Hindu nationalists have claimed as discussed previously, has cast suspicion over Muslim community organisations including madrassas and mosques. These suspicions have been greatest in north-east India along the Bangladesh and Nepal borders, where the union government has investigated several mosques and madrassas (Alam, 2004). Secessionist and political movements in the north-east and groups in areas affected by the Naxalite insurgency have been tarred as terrorist organisations. This labelling has provided justification for states to act against these groups and undermine their possible wider appeal. What has changed since 2001 is that earlier these various movements and groups had been labelled as 'extremist' or 'radical'. However, since 2001 the 'terrorist' label has been added as a way of further delegitimising their claims.

As of 2007, 32 organisations have been listed under the Schedule of Terrorist Organisations. Most of these are linked to secessionist causes, such as the Khalistan Zindabad Force, the Jammu and Kashmir Islamic Front or the Manipur People's Liberation Front, to ideological causes, such as the Communist Party of India (Marxist–Leninist), or to religious fundamentalism, such as the Students Islamic Movement of India (SIMI), Al Qaeda or Al-Umar-Mujahideen. Agreement to ban a particular organisation has also factored in the efforts of the Indian government to build alliances with regimes in neighbouring states. At the behest of the Nepalese government, New Delhi banned Akhil Bharatiya Nepali Ekta Samaj (ABNES), a Nepali migrants' welfare organisation with no apparent background of involvement in terrorism in India. This case highlights the partial and political use of the POTO/POTA (Singh, 2007, pp. 146–147). However, it is noteworthy that extremist Hindu nationalist groups were not banned under POTA. In response to the ban on SIMI through the POTO in October 2001, then Madhya Pradesh Chief Minister Digvijay Singh and Samajawadi Party leader Mulayam Singh Yadav in Uttar Pradesh demanded similar bans on Hindu fundamentalist groups such as Bajrang Dal, Shiv Sena and the Vishwa Hindu Parishad (Singh, 2007, p. 145).

It is noteworthy that the police and courts have misused counter-terrorism provisions to target certain communities. Relating to this is the tendency of regimes to play on the threat of terrorism to push through restrictive security measures, as typified in the demonising of Muslims by the BJP preceding the passing of POTA. As previously noted, TADA and POTA were adhered to selectively to target particular minorities and political opponents. In Gujarat, Rajasthan and Jammu and Kashmir, the majority of those arrested under TADA were Muslims, whilst in Delhi and Uttar Pradesh Sikhs formed a large part of those arrested under the act (Singh, 2007, p. 53). A fact-finding mission by lawyers and human rights activists in 2003 found there were over 3,200 cases lodged under the POTA. Of these, most accused were illiterate, poor, landless and/or Dalit and adivasis. In one instance a 16-year-old woman was arrested under POTA in Jharkhand for organising women in her village around gender issues (Gonsalves, 2004, p. 2). In 2003, over 287 people were detained in Gujarat alone under POTA. Most of these were Muslims who were arrested in the aftermath of the Godhra tragedy. Just under a third of these were charged with conspiracy to commit a terrorist act rather than any specific crime (Mander, 2004). Thus counter-terrorist legislation was being used selectively and politically against particular communities, who were being arrested merely because they were the subject of causes around which militant groups had formed.

The vagueness of the definition of terrorist activities under POTA had enabled states such as Tamil Nadu, Gujarat and Uttar Pradesh to apply the legislation widely to a range of activities and people, who were then labelled as 'terrorists' or 'anti-national' (People's Union for Democratic Rights, 2005a, p. 1). In both Tamil Nadu and Uttar Pradesh the incumbent governments invoked POTA against leading political critics and opponents.[39] In Uttar Pradesh, the state government and police were alleged to have misused security legislation and criminal codes to quell resistance to mining operations after coming under pressure from the World Bank and mining companies.[40] Furthermore, in December 2005 the BJP-dominated Chhattisgarh state assembly passed its own Special Public Safety Act, which widened the net of civil society groups vulnerable to accusation of being 'unlawful' or engaging in 'terrorist' activities beyond the ban on Naxal groups that already existed under the Unlawful Activities Prevention Act (UAPA) 2004 (Singh, 2007, p. 310).

Although specific actors in Indian civil society have been targeted under anti-terror provisions in law, generally counter-terrorism responses have had a minimal impact on relations between the union state and the organisations registered under the Societies Act. The Registration of the Societies Act (1860) came into force under the British Raj as a way of regulating and monitoring new organisations that were emerging then. The Act was inspired by particular concerns surrounding the new Gandhian-inspired self-help organisations and various social and religious reform groups with anti-colonial roots (Sheth and Sethi, 1991, pp. 50–51). India's new leaders not only fashioned a state that made some commitment to state-provided education, health and social welfare but also allowed voluntary organisations, charities and religious bodies to flourish. After independence in 1947, the charitable and welfare-oriented part of civil society – referred to variously as the 'voluntary sector', 'social action groups', 'people's organisations' or 'NGOs' – has continued to grow and thrive. These groups are required to register under the Societies Act and related legislation. The diversity and size of this organised sector of voluntary organisations has burgeoned, especially since the mid-1970s. It is estimated that by 2000 there were over 1.2 million NGOs in India, only half of which were registered (Bal, 2006, p. 17). Of these an estimated 85 per cent are 'one-man NGOs', raising doubts around the transparency and accountability of NGOs in general.[41] According to the umbrella organisation, Voluntary Action Network India (VANI), the majority of registered organisations are religious in nature.[42]

Both union and state governments have related ambivalently with civil society. On the one hand, CSOs have been viewed with suspicion. During the Emergency period between 1975 and 1977 NGO leaders who participated in anti-government protests were imprisoned. It was during this time that Indira Gandhi introduced the Foreign Contributions Regulation Act (FCRA) to monitor and tighten control over external funding of NGOs. While harbouring suspicions of civil society, the Indian government has also regarded it instrumentally as a cost-efficient way of delivering welfare. NGOs and Gandhian groups particularly were supported by the state through the 1950s (Sen, 1999, p. 334). NGOs were also encouraged to contribute to development projects during the period of Janata rule from 1977 to 1980. However, during the 1980s and 1990s, the ruling Congress Party, suspicious of the political threats posed by some NGOs, followed a dual-pronged strategy of not only extending control over NGOs but also encouraging service-delivery–oriented NGOs (Sen, 1999, pp. 341–343).[43] In 1994 under the Congress government of Narasimha Rao the first steps were taken to revise the tax and regulatory frameworks governing voluntary organisations. However, momentum was lost following the 1998 elections, which brought to power the BJP-led National Democratic Alliance. Relations were tense between the BJP and voluntary organisations. Though the BJP worked on a new policy, its vision of charitable regulation was at odds with what voluntary organisations were advocating, especially concerning restrictions on foreign funding.[44] Further advances were made on the policy in 2004 when the Congress Party returned to power leading a new coalition government. Since then, relations have warmed somewhat between the union state and voluntary organisations. The National Planning Commission, which oversees voluntary organisations in India, drafted a new policy framework in consultation with key voluntary sector actors. The Prime Minister approved the final policy in 2007.

NGOs were satisfied with amendments made to the final policy, which included the removal of the word 'control' from the proposed Foreign Contributions (Management and Control) Bill (Interview, VANI, December 2006). However, tensions remain between the government and NGOs, which have voiced concern over the decentralisation of registration requirements that NGOs re-register every five years.[45] The Indian government has also introduced new due diligence requirements affecting NGOs under anti-money–laundering legislation.[46] Still, the government and donor agencies hold considerable concerns about the probity and accountability of the sector, reflecting trends more broadly in scrutinising civil society, as examined in Chapter 2. A European diplomat explained some of the concerns of European donors: 'We have a lot to do with NGOs because of our programme and project funds. We are disappointed with NGOs here. It is too territorial and self-interested. It is charismatic individuals and all about money.'[47] The pursuit of funds, as in Afghanistan and Kenya, leads to competition for resources amongst NGOs and a consequent lack of co-operation. The same diplomat emphasised that 'It is hugely competitive. Human rights groups compete for money and refuse to co-operate. There is fragmenting and frequently an unwillingness to co-operate.'[48]

Within the government itself there are also different approaches to this sector. Whilst the National Planning Commission under Congress governments has sought a more conciliatory and instrumental approach to NGOs, government officials within the Ministry of Home Affairs, which is responsible for security, continue to analyse the world through the lens of the Cold War. They view foreign-funded NGOs with suspicion, either as pawns of external governments seeking to lever influence over internal politics or as terrorist front groups.[49] Indeed, one interviewee from the donor community suggested that the Indian government has used the threat of terrorism to restrict foreign contributions to NGOs.[50] Part of this is also informed by the government's determination to channel resources to state coffers rather than to NGOs.[51] The Indian government has been more permissive of foreign funding of NGOs that focus on service-delivery in health and education. Negotiation between the government and NGOs over the proposed Foreign Contributions (Management and Control) Bill thus invoked concerns from the security-related institutions about purposes of foreign-funded NGOs. The global War on Terror regime was no doubt one of several contextual factors shadowing these negotiations.

As discussed previously, the War on Terror regime has not led to significant changes in how donor agencies have engaged with civil society in India. Nonetheless, to a limited extent, post-9/11 security concerns have seeped into donor engagement with civil society in India. This is apparent, for instance, in efforts to cultivate new engagement with Muslim communities, as USAID has done. It is also apparent in how DFID officials have used the discourses of the War on Terror to seek support for Indian organisations working on socially excluded communities.

Similarly, international foundations working in India have not re-oriented their work with civil society, even though the new anti-terror clauses in the standard grant agreement letters for foundations such as Ford and Rockefeller pertain to grantees in India. As elsewhere, the inclusion of these new clauses has raised eyebrows among Indian civil society groups, some of whom have voiced their opposition. To our knowledge, only one Indian NGO has refused to sign a Ford Foundation grant letter of agreement because of the anti-terrorism clause (Sidel, 2008, p. 18), though it later withdrew this refusal after reassurances from Ford.[52]

Civil society responses

Indian civil society is often caricatured as diverse, active and vibrant and this is regarded as being a reflection of India's pluralistic, mature democracy. Hence, it might be expected that Indian civil society would resist CTMs that impinge on its work and act more assertively in defence of its own interests than a civil society in an authoritarian regime. However, it is also true that civil society in India is divided and fragmented. The relationship of the union and state governments with civil society is also contradictory and complex, as explained earlier. Secessionist movements in north-east India and Kashmir, for example, have preoccupied the union state and have been sharply repressed, constraining the spaces for collective action of any sort in these regions. Indeed, there is little non-governmental activity in either region compared with the rest of the country. The head of a foundation in New Delhi explained that NGOs working in these areas also contend with the suspicion of armed groups: 'The insurgents do not welcome NGOs. They might welcome civil society but they have their own idea of how this should be. In the north-east, NGOs have neither the confidence of the state nor of the militants.'[53]

Divisions within civil society mirror social segmentation that is seen more broadly in India. There is a historical precedent to communalist politics playing out within civil society but this became more of an issue in the 1980s paralleling the rise of the Hindu far right. Since then, Hindu nationalist groups have sought to mobilise tribals and Dalits as a way of undermining the work of Christian missionaries in tribal areas (Sabrang Communications Private Limited, 2002, pp. 70–73). As explained previously, these groups have fomented hatred of Muslims and led efforts to socialise youth in Hindu nationalist ideology. More worrying is that right-wing Hindu groups were implicated in terrorist attacks in Malegaon in 2008. The Indian media has reported that the killing of the Anti-Terrorist Security Chief Hemant Karkare in the Mumbai attacks was the work of the RSS, VHP and Bajrang Dal. Karkare was thought to have evidence implicating Hindu nationalist groups in the Malegaon attacks (*Times of India*, 7 December 2008, p. 2). This is an important rejoinder to the fixation on links between Indian Muslims and global jihadi networks.

Given the segmented nature of civil society in India, it is instructive to explore how different civil society actors have responded to counter-terrorism measures, practices and discourses. As in Kenya, the UK and the US, human rights organisations, lawyers and individual activists have led opposition to counter-terrorism practices and advocated for the rights of terror suspects. Human rights lawyers who sought to defend terror suspects have been labelled by politicians and the media as 'sympathising with terrorists'. The People's Union for Democratic Rights (PUDR) and the Human Rights Network India have documented the arrest and interrogation of suspects under anti-terror provisions in law, highlighting the tendency for poor and marginalised groups to be detained without trial for long periods despite a lack of evidence (PUDR, 2005a). In one case, Syed Abdul Rahman Geelani, a lecturer from the University of Delhi and an activist on Kashmir, was arrested for planning the attack on the Indian parliament in December 2001. He was repeatedly tortured during his imprisonment before being released after several years. His co-accused is still detained and Geelani requires constant protection.

Formally registered, service-delivery-type voluntary organisations have generally been silent on the state's counter-terrorism responses, including on issues of public debate such as the targeting of Muslims and the government's security co-operation with the US. Two features of the Indian voluntary sector help to explain their failure to speak out. First, some NGOs are masked, profit-making ventures by individuals and do not aspire to work on issues of social justice. Second, many mainstream service-delivery-type organisations depend on donors or the Indian government for funding to provide welfare. As Sheth and Sethi (1991) explain, they have become 'instrumental appendages' of the state. Intense competition for funds means that many groups are reluctant to stake a position on political issues and have lost sight of the larger political picture. The political blindness of many Indian civil society groups is apparent in other areas. For example, developmental and welfare NGOs have not taken up the social exclusion of Dalits. Instead, these issues have been addressed mainly by human rights groups, as well as more recently established Dalit rights organisations.[54] The depoliticised nature of mainstream civil society in India is also evident in their lack of engagement and work within conflict areas. Although there is much rhetoric around poverty and development, it is as though these 'difficult' parts of India are somehow not relevant to the debate.

The depoliticisation of Indian civil society has had clear implications for the protection and promotion of human rights and the rights of disadvantaged groups. This was poignantly revealed in the weak response of voluntary sector agencies to the conflagration of violence in Gujarat in 2002, particularly compared to their responses to the devastating earthquake in Kucch in 2001. The head of a human rights group in Ahmedabad argued, 'It is interesting to compare the poor response (of civil society) to the violence and the earthquake response, which was exemplary. There was violence on a huge scale and massive displacement. You see the number of groups that were providing relief in response to the violence dwindling to 10 or 12. It was such a contrast with the earthquake response.'[55] The Gujarat state government, which itself was implicated in orchestrating the anti-Muslim attacks, provided little relief or rehabilitation for Muslim victims. Even so, very few civil society organisations offered assistance leaving the bulk of the responsibility to Muslim religious trusts and organisations such as the Islamiya Relief Committee (Luce, 2007, pp. 161–162) and to Muslim-dominated panchayats.[56] A well-known human rights activist stated, 'there were no international NGOs there (responding to the violence)... It was not only the government that abdicated its responsibility (to protect). Civil society did so, as well.'[57]

There were some smaller initiatives led by non-Muslim organisations as well as organising efforts by human rights and social justice organisations. For example, two months after the violence, the Society for the Promotion of Rational Thinking, along with Action Aid, Citizen's Initiative, Janpath and the Gujarat Sarvajanik Relief Committee, organised a rally in Ahmedabad involving over 3,000 people to pay tribute to the victims of the violence (*Hindustan Times*, 13 September 2002, reprinted in Varadarajan, 2002, pp. 352–355). The Citizen's Initiative brought together a number of local, national and international groups under an umbrella to distribute food and grains in relief camps that were mainly serviced by Muslim organisations.[58] It is noteworthy that the violence in Gujarat was widely condemned at the national level. Journalists, social and political activists, NGOs, lawyers, human rights groups and students denounced the state-led pogrom. As Nussbaum (2007, p. 31) explains, many individuals horrified at the events of 2002 flocked into Gujarat to organise relief work and to document the deaths, attacks and rapes and disseminate their findings on the Internet. One of the most detailed records was provided by the Concerned Citizens Tribunal, which was organised by Teesta Setalvad from Maharashtra state. Setalvad also played a key role in the legal NGO 'Communalism Combat' and was pivotal in seeking justice for the victims in the Best Bakery Case, in which over 20 Muslims were killed during the attacks in March 2002. However, BJP politicians allegedly pressurised the key witness to renounce her statement and Chief Minister of Gujarat Narendra Modi called for public scrutiny of NGOs (Nussbaum, 2007, p. 40).

The failure of voluntary sector agencies, development-oriented NGOs and trades unions in Gujarat to speak out against the anti-Muslim violence relates to at least four factors. First is the dependency of many civil society organisations in the state on government contracts. This would also explain the extraordinary growth of the voluntary sector in Gujarat in recent decades, which otherwise would attest to the strength of civil society. A human rights official commented, 'civil society is growing on state largesse to provide services, not because of a record of protest and providing alternatives'.[59] The head of an organisation that worked in the relief camps added to this view: 'Many mainstream NGOs did not want to be part of it (the relief response) because they are running huge government schemes.'[60] A second and related factor was that, as is true of mainstream civil society groups elsewhere in India, voluntary sector and service-delivery-type organisations in Gujarat were blind to processes of marginalisation and exclusion affecting Muslims. They focussed on poverty alleviation and delivering welfare to the poor without appreciating the exclusionary processes and power relations that were leading to peoples' social exclusion.

A third factor was the increasing fragmentation and polarisation of civil society in Gujarat since the 1980s. The loss of jobs in the textile industry following its mechanisation was particularly damaging since the trade unions for textile workers previously brought together Hindu and Muslim workers. Moreover, textile factory owners were alleged to have fomented Hindu nationalist sentiment to drive a wedge between the workers and break the collective resolve of the workers. The loss of jobs and diminishing power of the unions saw the rise of Hindu nationalists who filled the void. What was also especially painful for the small human rights organisations that did respond to the violence was the silence of the Gandhian groups, who were alleged to have been 'saffronised' – in other words, to have come under the influence of Hindu nationalists. Thus, they were less inclined to show support for Muslims and more so in a context in which Muslims had been linked with terrorism. Finally, another factor was the intimidation of civil society by Modi. He campaigned for chief minister on a populist platform that was anti-Pakistan and against human rights groups. Specifically, he positioned himself as the nemesis of the National Human Rights Commission (NHRC). So, for example, his campaign literature and advertisements in local newspapers questioned, 'Who is the NHRC for?' and 'Who is civil society for?', the implication being that they pandered to the interests of Muslims. A prominent social justice activist in Gujarat explained, 'He spoke about civil society in the language of "five stars." The hidden meanings of his rhetoric were that civil society is foreign-funded, they travel widely and stay in posh hotels. He called them "pseudo-secular." Few NGOs challenged him, as many of them depend on the state's largesse.'[61] Therefore, the reticence of mainstream NGOs and voluntary welfare-delivery organisations to respond in the aftermath of the violence was fitting the nature of these organisations to be 'instrumental appendages' of the state, as Sheth and Sethi (1991) observe.

The November 2008 Mumbai attacks stimulated intense public debate on terrorism and how the government should respond and frame its policies with respect to domestic legislation, police reforms and relations with Pakistan. Human rights groups cautioned against passing any hastily crafted laws and warned against increasing the powers or resources of the police and intelligence agencies when they had failed to win the public trust and proved themselves to be so incompetent in preventing and responding to the attacks. It was also notable that many ad-hoc groups emerged to protest policing and administrative incompetence and voice outrage at their politicians. Vigils and protests were held throughout India. Muslims held their own demonstrations against the attacks, with protesters waving placards calling for war on Pakistan. The heads of prominent Muslim organisations including the Vice-Chancellor of Jamia Millia Islamia, the All-India Babri Masjid Reconstruction Committee and the Shahi Imam of Jama Masjid in Delhi condemned the attacks as 'un-Islamic' (Dash, 2008; Raha, 2008). Jamiat Ulama-I-Hind along with secular groups organised a peace march in 12 cities that had been the site of terrorist violence in 2008 (Raha, 2008). However, when Jamia Millia Islamia, a government-funded public university, established a fund to provide legal assistance to two of its students who were arrested in the September 2008 Batla House police raid in Delhi, BJP politicians accused the university of using public funds to support terrorism, thus once more trying to link Indian Muslims with global jihad.[62] Some Muslim commentators have lamented the way that some Muslim leaders have felt compelled to publicly denounce the Mumbai attacks, as they perceive such public denunciations to reinforce the idea of Muslims as a separate and suspect population.[63]

Conclusion

This chapter has highlighted aspects of the War on Terror regime that have intersected with political tensions, social violence and insurgency in India. Right-wing Hindu nationalist groups and politicians have drawn upon War on Terror discourses to demonise Muslims as untrustworthy and disloyal to the union state. Anti-Muslim demagoguery by the BJP has been an important device for advancing their political agenda, including strengthening security institutions and practices. Although POTA was repealed in 2004 by the Congress Party–led coalition government, in practice the state retained most of its security powers in a raft of other anti-terror provisions in law.

India has a long history of terrorism. Up until the November 2008 Mumbai attacks, the US and the UK viewed terrorist attacks in India as relating to domestic concerns, particularly long-running hostilities between India and Pakistan. However, the attacks in Mumbai in November 2008 were depicted by the Indian media in shocking terms and in a way to demonstrate that the terrorist threat facing India is the same as that facing other countries where terrorist atrocities have occurred, including the US, the UK, Spain, Morocco and Indonesia.

The attacks in Mumbai in November 2008, the latest in a series of terrorist violence to hit Indian cities in 2008, ultimately highlighted the failure of the War on Terror as a template to guide security policy in South Asia. Professor Mohammed Ansari, the former head of the Indian National Commission on Minorities, notes that the War on Terror policies pursued subsequent to the 9/11 attacks in the US have failed to address problems of violence and communal tensions in India: 'there cannot be a uniform response to difference incidents of violence'.[64] The 'sledgehammer' approach adopted by the US to terrorism has not effectively addressed the roots of violence in India, which are deeply lodged in its colonial past, the legacy of partition, communal tensions and inequalities linked to its economic transition and inadequate social policies, and wider instability in South Asia.

Despite this complex framing of terrorism in India, the government of India proposed major counter-terrorism reforms in the aftermath of the Mumbai attacks. Within this context the US and the UK have offered to share their expertise in establishing structures to strengthen co-ordination among and between various security and intelligence agencies. However, what was absent from the debate on reforming India's counter-terrorism structures in the aftermath of the Mumbai attacks was any serious deliberation on how to incorporate human rights and civil liberties protections for minorities. Furthermore, there was no debate surrounding the failures of India's social policies. This was in spite of past experience of anti-terror responses being targeted at marginalised groups.

The chapter uncovered how the War on Terror has influenced aid flows and policy in India. Whilst the War on Terror along with geo-strategic interests underpinned increases in US aid to South Asia, long-standing historic ties and poverty reduction objectives are more significant factors shaping British aid flows to India. Operationally, DFID has not introduced specific counter-terrorism capacity-building pro-grammes in India. However, diplomatic, military and security ties have been more significant in transmitting elements of the War on Terror regime.

The main effects of all this on civil society relates to the construc-tion of Muslims as implicated in global jihadi terrorism, the casting of suspicion over Muslim organisations, the labelling of other political movements as 'terrorist' as a delegitimising tactic, the abusive treatment of selective groups under counter-terrorist legislation, and some very limited internationally funded projects on the ground aimed at Mus-lim communities. In terms of civil society responses to these processes, the picture is complex and differentiated. Resistance to the excesses of security legislation and its effects on marginalised groups has come predominantly from human rights networks. Funded voluntary sector groups and international development organisations have, apart from a few exceptions, been remarkably uninterested in how security legisla-tion impacts poor and vulnerable groups or in the conflicts grinding on in the North East and in Kashmir. Though there was a national out-cry over the pogrom against Muslims in Gujarat in 2002, and some national activism around the situation of Muslims there, there were few responses from civil society actors in Gujarat. Rather, Muslim organisa-tions carried out the bulk of relief and rehabilitation as well as mounted protests at the treatment of Muslims.

The precursor to the Mumbai attacks was the series of assaults on Indian cities in 2008, allegedly by the Indian Mujahedin, a domestic terrorist group. This raised alarm bells within Muslim communities in India to break the cycle of attack and revenge. Indian Muslims have consciously sought to establish their nationalist credentials through various peace marches and statements by influential Indian Muslims in the press in the aftermath of the Mumbai and Delhi bombings. But the terrorist attacks also exposed the abject failure of the Indian government to address the situation of Muslims. In particular, the government has failed abysmally to press the judicial cases stemming from the anti-Muslim attacks in Gujarat in 2002 or to address the needs of Gujarati Muslims still residing in 'relief colonies' (Amnesty International, 2007). Some Muslim activists have also expressed concern about the pressure on Muslim leaders to openly denounce the terrorist attacks on the grounds that this inadvertently assigns some responsibility for these events to Muslims in India.

In the final concluding chapter we draw together the key findings of the book and reflect on their implications for governments, international development institutions and civil society actors in unravelling the global War on Terror regime.

Notes

1. This chapter is based on documentary research and fieldwork carried out between 2006 and 2008. Altogether, over 58 interviews were conducted in India between May 2006 and December 2008 with key informants in human rights groups, developmental NGOs, voluntary sector groups, civil servants, bilateral aid agencies, contributors to the Sachar Committee report, Muslim leaders and commentators, journalists, researchers and faith-based groups. An LSE/VANI round-table involving government officials, NGOs, community leaders and researchers was held in Delhi in December 2006 on the theme of the research.

2. As Martha Nussbaum (2007, p. 4) commented, 'During the ascendancy of the Hindu right, when intelligent diplomatic pressure could have achieved change, US foreign policy was largely indifferent to internal tensions in India, focusing only on the threat of nuclear conflict with Pakistan.'

3. Prime Minister's speech at DGP conference. 23 November 2008. New Delhi. Text of speech. http://pmindia.nic.in/lspeech.asp?id=758. Accessed 30 November, 2008.

4. For an insightful personal account about the fact that an identity as Muslim is in part given by non-Muslim behaviour and attitudes see Razzack (1991).

5. 'Blasts After Blasts'. *The Economist*. 31 July 2008; 'India Faced with Home-Grown Terrorism'. *Christian Science Monitor*. 26 September 2008.

6. As Singh (2004, p. 150) points out, it is noteworthy how the POTO/POTA, unlike the TADA, does not refer to 'threatening harmony between communities' as an act of terror, suggesting that the POTO/POTA legislation is cast within a Hindu nationalist framework that effectively links Muslims to terrorism.

7. By 30 June 1994 over 76,000 people had been arrested under TADA, of which only 1 per cent were actually convicted (Singh, 2003).
8. The MCOCA has been applied in Maharashtra since 1999 and Delhi since 2002. The Gujarat assembly passed a similar bill in June 2004, which also contained provisions similar to those in POTA. So if POTA was repealed, the Gujarat government could through this law continue to detain people in the state arrested under POTA (Singh, 2007, pp. 288; 293–295). MCOCA was used in the parliamentary debate on the Prevention of Terrorism Bill in 2002 as a model for the new law, primarily on the basis of its high conviction rate.
9. The police responded swiftly to the blasts, engaging in a dramatic shoot-out with suspected terrorists in a Muslim neighbourhood of Delhi. Two suspects were killed, both students from Jamia Millia Islamia University (Authors' interview. Media co-ordinator, Jamia Millia Islamia. Delhi. 8 December 2008). However, the official account given by police was discredited by the press and rights groups and revealed fundamental mistrust of the police forces ('Indians Question Police Response to Recent Bombings.' *The New York Times*, 3 October 2008).
10. Authors' interview with Dalit Foundation. Delhi. 6 December 2006.
11. Authors' interview. Executive Director, Institute of Conflict Management. Delhi. 13 December 2008.
12. Interview. Executive Director, Institute of Conflict Management. Delhi. 13 December 2008.
13. For an excellent treatment of the rise of Hindu fundamentalist politics in India see Corbridge and Harriss (2007).
14. As Varadarajan (2002, p. 3) explains, the RSS serves as an umbrella organisation linking the BJP to more violent, right-wing Hindu elements such as the VHP and Bajrang Dal.
15. Varadarajan (2002, p. 7). And authors' interview. Siddharth Varadarajan. Delhi. 4 December 2006.
16. 'Advani Clean Chit to Modi', *Telegraph*, 4 March 2002, in Varadarajan (2002, footnote 9, p. 36).
17. Koppikar, Smruti, 'BJP Chief Reads Riot Act to Muslims'. *Indian Express*, 13 April 2002, in Varadarajan (2002, footnote 10, p. 36).
18. In his speech Vajpayee slips between linking terrorism with Islamic militants specifically and with Muslims generally, who he presents as having a predilection to terrorism.
19. This speech caused national controversy. When a privilege motion was raised in Parliament, the Prime Minister was forced to admit that the word 'such' had later been inserted into versions of the speech that were officially published, so that the reference would be only to Islamic militants and not all Muslims (Varadarajan, 2007, p. 26).
20. Authors' interview with investigative journalist. New Delhi. 4 December 2006.
21. Authors' interview with Action Aid employee. Ahmedabad. 8 December 2006.
22. 'Report Shows Muslims Near Bottom of Social Ladder.' *The New York Times*. 29 November 2006.
23. Authors' interview. Member of Sachar Committee. Delhi. 5 December 2006.

24. 'Sachar Nails Madrasa Myth: Only 4% of Muslim Kids Go There.' *Indian Express* (Delhi). 1 December 2006.
25. Authors' interview with UK FCO official. New Delhi. 6 December 2008.
26. Ibid.
27. Authors' interview. UK DFID. Delhi. 30 November 2006.
28. 'Government Unveils Action Plan on Sachar Committee report in Parliament.' *The Financial Express* (Delhi). 31 August 2007.
29. Authors' interview. Vice-Chancellor, Jammia Millia Islamia. Delhi. 12 December 2008.
30. However, most of Japan's aid takes the form of development loans rather than grant aid, such as the US$4.6 billion loan as part of its ODA to India to help build a Mumbai–Delhi freight rail connection.
31. Authors' interview with UK FCO official. New Delhi. 6 December 2006.
32. 'Aid Statistics, Donor Aid Charts: United Kingdom'. Organisation for Economic Cooperation and Development. http://www.oecd.org/dataoecd/42/53/40039127.gif. Accessed 31 October 2008.
33. Ibid.
34. Authors' interview with UK DFID official. New Delhi. 30 November 2006.
35. According to Bruce Riedel, a terrorism expert at Brookings Institution and advisor to President Obama, Al Qaeda operational activities in the last few years have drawn increasingly from Pakistani diasporas in UK, Denmark, Germany and Spain (*Times of India*, 6 December 2008).
36. Ibid.
37. Authors' interview. DFID India. Delhi. 30 November 2006.
38. 'US Slashes Aid to India by 35%.' *The Financial Express* (Delhi). 25 July 2007.
39. In Uttar Pradesh Chief Minister Mayawati invoked POTA against Raja Bhaiyya, an independent Member of the Legislative Assembly and Minister in the BJP–BSP coalition government and his 80-year old father, a move that was widely seen as an act of political revenge. Similarly, in Tamil Nadu the Jayalalitha government arrested the MDMK leader Vaiko under POTA (for further details see PUDR, 2005b, p. 7).
40. Author' interview with senior human rights activist. New Delhi. 12 December 2005.
41. According to the Income Tax Act voluntary organisations raise over US$60 billion domestically, a further US$6 billion coming from government and international agencies. It is noteworthy that the bulk of this funding is channelled to fee-charging hospitals and schools and to religious organisations.
42. Authors' interview. VANI. Delhi. 28 November 2006.
43. On the one hand, it tried to establish National and State Councils for rural NGOs, amended the FCRA in 1985 and removed tax exemptions from income-generating NGOs (Sen, 1999, pp. 341–343). On the other hand, it increased government funding to NGOs, incorporating service-delivery NGOs more fully into state development plans.
44. Another issue of concern was that the BJP wanted staff in voluntary organisations to work voluntarily, without salaries (Authors' interview. VANI. Delhi. 14 December 2006).
45. Authors' interview. VANI. 14 December 2006.
46. Authors' interview. Representative and programme officer. Ford Foundation. Delhi. 11 December 2008.

47. Authors' interview. UK FCO official. New Delhi. 6 December 2006.
48. The interviewee pointed out, however, that their engagement with particular human rights groups had been positive.
49. Ibid.
50. Authors' interview. DFID official. New Delhi. 30 November 2006.
51. Ibid.
52. The date of the interview is 11 December 2008.
53. Authors' interview. Head of National Foundation Institute. Delhi, 5 December 2006.
54. It should be noted that Christian Aid has taken the lead in championing the causes of Dalits and adivasis, though in doing so it has to deal with the suspicion that as a Christian organisation its primary purpose is religious conversion (Authors' interviews. DFID India. Delhi. November 2006. And Christian Aid. Delhi. 28 November 2006).
55. Authors' interview. Managing Trustee. Janvikas. Ahmedabad. 8 December 2006. For an excellent, textured analysis of the violence in Gujarat and discrimination in earthquake relief see Simpson (2006, 2008).
56. For a detailed account of the failure of Gujarat state to provide adequate relief for those displaced in the riots see Varadarajan, 2002, chapter 9 (pp. 307–330), which provides a substantial extract from the People's Union for Democratic Rights (PUDR), 'State, Society and Communalism in Gujarat'. New Delhi. May 2002.
57. Authors' interview with Harsh Mander. Centre for Equity Studies. New Delhi. 30 November 2006.
58. Authors' interview. Samerth. Ahmedabad. 7 December 2006.
59. Authors' interview. Managing Trustee. Janvikas. Ahmedabad. 8 December 2006.
60. Authors' interview. Samerth. Ahmedabad. 7 December 2006.
61. Authors' interview. Managing Trustee. Janvikas. Ahmedabad. 8 December 2006.
62. Authors' interview. Media and cultural co-ordinator, Jamia Millia Islamia. Delhi. 7 December 2008.
63. Ibid.
64. Authors' interview. Chair, National Commission on Minorities. New Delhi. 14 December 2006.

8
Conclusion

If the US administration changes, security measures and laws won't change. It will require a new civil rights movement
Observation of security analyst, December 2007

We are not going to continue with a false choice between our safety and our ideals ... The message that we are sending to the world is that the United States intends to prosecute the ongoing struggle against violence and terrorism ... And we are going to do so vigilantly, we are going to do so effectively, and we are going to do so in a manner that is consistent with our values and our ideals
Remarks by President Barack Obama after signing executive orders to overhaul US national security policy, 22 January 2009

This book set out to examine critically the effects of the post-9/11 global security regime on development policy and practice and civil society. In the immediate years after 9/11 anecdotal evidence emerged of the suspected diversion of aid to address global and national security concerns defined by the West, of the potential vulnerability of charities to misuse by terrorist networks and of the demonisation of Muslims as being somehow linked to terrorism by virtue of their religion as illustrated by references of politicians to 'Islamic fascism' and 'Islamic extremism'. Recent works have examined the effects of the political suspicion of charities on the spaces and actors of civil society to organise as well as the impacts of post-9/11 security imperatives on development engagement with non-governmental actors. This book has sought to add to this burgeoning area of work by providing detailed empirical evidence of some of the direct and indirect outcomes of the global War on Terror regime for development and civil societies in different parts of the world. This chapter identifies the significant findings and common themes of the book as well as the significance of these for aid and civil society.

This book set out three propositions to examine the impacts of the post-9/11 global security regime on development and civil society. First, we proposed that the War on Terror regime has intensified the convergence of development and security actors around the shared pursuit of a presumably agreed notion of global security. This has led to the increasing securitisation of aid, by which we mean the absorption of global and national security interests into the framing, structuring and implementation of development and aid. This convergence has become generalised beyond the narrower domain of conflict and post-conflict settings to development and aid policy more broadly. This process has been observed in a number of phenomena: increasing aid flows to countries deemed pivotal to the achievement of the political and military objectives of the War on Terror; the greater focus on national and global security objectives in official aid policies and discourses, based on normative assumptions around the positive links between development and security and the negative links between poverty, alienation and vulnerability to terrorist recruitment; the newly important emphasis on counter-terrorism assistance and the concomitant creation of new programming to strengthen core security institutions and prevent radicalisation; promotion of whole-of-government approaches that institutionalise ties between military, foreign policy, defence and aid departments in closer, strategic ways; expanding military intervention in development and increasing linkages, though controversial, between military and civilian actors.

Second, we argued that the deepening and extending relations between development and security actors had significant impacts on the spaces and actors of civil society that were worth analysing in their own right. The War on Terror regime, drawing on a framework that defines the world in stark contrasts, has bifurcated civil society into 'good' and 'bad' parts. This has drawn civil society further into the gaze of security, police and intelligence institutions, a process that was underway already in the 1990s. Whilst governments have relied on 'hard', coercive measures to rein in and control 'bad' civil society, they have also used 'soft' measures to nurture parts of civil society viewed instrumentally as helping states to achieve their security objectives and interests. The War on Terror regime has thus also created opportunities for certain parts of 'good' civil society to engage more directly with government departments and agencies through which they acquire resources and authority although not necessarily grass-roots legitimacy. It has also, in some contexts such as Kenya, galvanised parts of civil society and given it renewed direction and purpose during a period of political instability and uncertainty. However, the engagement of states with civil society around post-9/11 security imperatives has also revealed the costs to civil society of its increasing instrumentalisation. The reticence of mainstream CSOs to respond to the targeting of Muslim groups and others representing 'suspect' communities such as asylum-seekers and migrants shows that parts of civil society have lost sight of their role in encouraging public dialogue and deliberation, as well as holding states and markets to account, demanding transparency and working towards social justice.

Finally, we suggested that how the greater convergence between development policies and practice and security objectives and interests affects civil society actors would be contextually specific. As shown throughout the book, the impacts of the War on Terror regime are contradictory, creating both threats and opportunities for civil societies in different places. This is evident not only in the cases of Afghanistan, Kenya and India detailed here but also in the US, the UK, continental Europe, the Middle East and Latin America[1]. Finally, we stress that the location of a country on the democratic/authoritarian spectrum, its relative importance to US geo-strategic, economic and political interests, the character and history of state–civil society relations, and the response of civil society actors to counter-terrorism initiatives are all important factors in determining the particular effects of the War on Terror regime in different contexts.

Key findings

How the War on Terror unfolds varies according to political, economic, historical and social context

This book shows that outcomes of the War on Terror regime for development and civil society vary across contexts according to the nature of state–civil society relations; the responses of non-governmental public actors to CTMs; the character of the political regime and in particular whether the regime is an established democracy, a new democracy, authoritarian or democratic and whether it is stable or in conflict; the geo-strategic significance to the US; and dependence on aid. However, there have also been some counter-intuitive outcomes of the War on Terror regime for civil societies in different parts of the world. One outcome that is notable for being unexpected is the significant impact of CTMs on civil society in the US. As an established democracy with an extensive, multi-layered and vocal civil society, we expected that advocacy groups would robustly oppose the implementation of measures and bureau-cratic practices of control that have disproportionately affected Muslim organisations. Instead, many mainstream groups were reluctant to speak out. As Sidel (2007) explains, they hoped that by staying beneath the parapet and adapting to new due diligence requirements they would be spared the harshest scrutiny. It is only when it became clear that the government intended to step up pressure on the voluntary and founda-tion sectors as a whole that a greater array of groups spoke out. However, responses have continued to be muted relative to the intense pressure and climate of fear engendered by the changing regulatory regime for civil society. By comparison, in Kenya, which has a rather new democ-racy that has been significantly tested by recent political conflict and ethnic tensions, civil society has been alert to and organised against proposed anti-terror measures and laws that affect their work.

At the front line of the War on Terror, Afghanistan demonstrates the complex intertwining of global, regional and local politics and the encapsulation of development practice in security and political strate-gies and goals to build a liberal democracy that will co-operate in the new global security regime. Western attempts at stabilisation and state re-building have cast civil society in a contractual role as deliverer of educational, health and welfare services. In the process, any notion of civil society as a watchdog on the state, as an advocate for the inter-ests of marginalised communities or as an arena for public deliberation and debate has been pushed to the margins. Developmental NGOs are heavily dependent on aid funding whilst other parts of civil society including religious organisations, trade and professional associations rely on community support or members' fees for their sustainability. Further, military intervention and insurgency are defining the field of non-governmental public action with implications for civil society's claims to independence, impartiality and neutrality. With US forces engaged in OEF and ISAF troops in counter-insurgency, human secu-rity has been made secondary to the prioritisation of strengthening and shoring up the authority of the feeble Afghan government.

The military's increasing foray into development work as part of a broader politico-military strategy to simultaneously secure territory and dominate the ideological battlefield has created tensions with human-itarian workers who argue that the military's involvement infringes on the neutrality, independence and impartiality of civilian aid actors. This has in turn uncovered the fallacy of international NGO claims to be independent and neutral since most development NGOs directly or indirectly implement government social welfare programmes and are thus perceived by local populations as contributing to the state's agenda. While humanitarian actors in Afghanistan have tried to link the insecurity of aid workers to the military's involvement in the same sort of activities that NGOs undertake, the continuing attacks on aid workers suggest that insurgents recognise that NGOs have been absorbed into the project of constructing a neo-liberal state. Non-governmental actors in Afghanistan are participants in the politics and processes of state-building. This implies a different understanding of civil society as well, since there is a blurred divide between the state and civil society in Afghanistan. Thus, secular non-governmental actors in the post-Taliban period have been important in helping guarantee the legitimacy of the fledgling state under foreign tutelage.

In the case of Kenya, a newly democratising state, the War on Terror security regime has played out differently. In particular, debates on counter-terrorism and regional security have reinvigorated civil society, leading to new networking and political activity and renewing the sense of purpose of civil society following the election of a reform-minded government in 2002, which co-opted the top civil society leadership. Like Afghanistan, Kenya has been the target of international terrorism, notably the 1998 US embassy bombing in Nairobi. However, it was only after the 9/11 attacks that the US pressured the Kenyan government to strengthen its counter-terrorist framework. Unlike Uganda or Tanzania, civil society activists in Kenya working with parliamentarians succeeded in preventing a proposed counter-terrorist bill from being enacted. This success was in part due to a concerted civil society campaign, the resistance of some parliamentarians and also the diminishing importance of aid in the Kenyan government's expenditures, which meant it was able to resist some aspects of the counter-terrorism juggernaut. Despite this victory, various extrajudicial CTMs have been adopted, such as the establishment of a dedicated ATPU and the government's participation in a regional rendition programme in the Horn of Africa, involving the rendition of terror suspects to Ethiopia, Somalia and Guantanamo Bay. This has led to claims by civil society members that the government was seeking to introduce CTMs through the back door. But it has also revealed the difficult task for civil society in opposing the government's counter-terrorism agenda. This is because of both the secrecy of the government's intelligence and policing operations as well as the divisions and discord within civil society itself. The main civil society opponents to the counter-terrorist bill comprised Muslim leaders and the democracy and governance groups that had roots in the aid-supported democracy movement of the 1990s. As in other countries, Muslim communities and organisations in Kenya have borne the brunt of the War on Terror security regime and have also led opposition to its implementation whilst leading civil society acolytes, including prominent activists and church leaders, have been reticent to speak out against the targeting of Muslims. Aid agencies have established counter-radicalisation programmes in predominately Muslim coastal areas, following the misguided logic that Muslims are somehow predisposed towards terrorism. This funding has proved divisive within Muslim civil society, with some groups accepting the funds while other organisations have refused Western aid funding as a matter of principle.

The dynamics of the War on Terror and civil society have played out differently still in the case of India. It has a long experience of terrorist-type attacks related to the dispute with Pakistan in Kashmir and secessionist struggles in the north-east. The discourses of the War on Terror have intersected with security discussions on Pakistan and the status of India's large Muslim minority population. Al Qaeda cells or related international jihadist groups have not been active in India, at least until recently. Like many other states India was quick to declare itself an ally in the War on Terror. Political leaders have used this discourse to condemn political opponents and social movements such as secessionist struggles in Kashmir and the north-east and class-based movements such as Maoists in Chattisgarh and Naxalites. Geopolitically, the stability of India is crucial for the region and the US has established military and political ties to keep India on board, the nuclear deal being the clearest evidence of this. India has over the past two decades introduced a raft of counter-terrorist legislation that predates the War on Terror. Problems of poor governance in security institutions has meant that marginalised social groups such as dalits, adivasis, the poor, the landless and Muslims have been most vulnerable to the misuse of counter-terrorist legislation, as well documented by Indian human rights networks and lawyers. Police responses to attacks in recent years, notably following the Delhi bomb blasts in September 2008, have encouraged popular mistrust of law enforcement agencies and the sense of discrimination and bias in policing practices. As in most other countries, resistance to these human rights violations committed under the rubric of counter-terrorism has come from human rights groups, lawyers and activists. The provisions of counter-terrorist legislation have thus extended beyond their specific remit to cover social movements such as the Maoist and Naxalite insurgencies in rural areas and secessionist struggles in the north-east. Jihadist groups claimed responsibility for a series of bombings in India in 2007 and 2008, building upon the rising tensions in some states between Muslims and Hindus. These daring attacks reflect the global circulation of jihadist discourses and the institutional learning that is happening within jihadist networks as militants in different parts of the world become increasingly bold in their actions. In particular, since the anti-Muslim attacks in Gujarat in 2002, and subsequent attacks that have been blamed on Muslims seeking retribution, Hindu nationalist leaders, such as BJP leader L.K. Advani, have discursively linked Muslims with terrorism and extremism. The War on Terror has intensified communal divisions by giving legitimacy to views that Muslims are somehow connected to terrorism by virtue of their religious identity. India has a large Muslim population which is relatively marginalised in terms of numerous social, economic and political indicators as the Sachar Committee documented in its influential report released in December 2006.

The detailed case studies presented in this book are part of a larger picture illustrating the global spread of the post-9/11 War on Terror security regime. Allies in the War on Terror have been rewarded with foreign assistance for military and development purposes. Across the world countries have complied with new FATF recommendations on counter-terrorism financing and moved to introduce or strengthen counter-terrorist legislation. There has been greater global co-operation in the exchange of passenger information, surveillance, renditions and interrogation of suspect terrorists. At the same time it has been mainly human rights groups, scholars and activists in most countries who have mounted significant challenges to the introduction of new counter-terrorism structures. Muslim communities have come under suspicion whether in the UK, Indonesia, Tanzania or China. Despite attempts by the UK government to shift the language of debate away from phrases such as 'Islamic fascism' and the War on Terror, this language has gained currency across the world. Bilateral donor agencies such as AusAID, USAID, CIDA and DANIDA have to varying degrees absorbed the War on Terror security agenda into mission statements and programming. Donor countries have also begun to reach out to Muslim organisations and religious leaders, both domestically as well as in countries where they have aid programmes. How the War on Terror regime unfolds thus varies according to political, social and economic contexts.

The post-9/11 War on Terror regime has led to increasing convergence of security and development

Security is not new to development but its position and place in aid has been concretised and generalised in the post-9/11 context. The convergence of security with development was already underway in the 1990s in conflict areas such as Kosovo and Sierra Leone. Military actors were venturing not only into humanitarian work and quick-impact development projects but also into areas of law and governance. At the same time bilateral development agencies were advancing into the terrain of security through security sector reforms which aimed to improve the transparency, accountability and overall governance of security-related institutions. Civil society actors were drawn into the web of security both through their encounter on the ground with militaries 'doing development' and through donor efforts to involve them in bolstering the demand side of governance in relation to security institutions and preventing conflict. From the perspective of humanitarian workers this increased involvement of UN peace-keeping forces and national militaries in development work not only blurred the boundaries between the military and the civilian agencies and organisations but also undermined their own claims to neutrality, impartiality and independence.

This earlier experience and institutional learning in development and aid agencies around issues of security sector reform, conflict prevention and peace-building has informed new expansive efforts at harnessing the contribution of development to new security imperatives. Since September 11 development–security ties have been increasingly formalised and institutionalised through military planning as well as the formulation of new national security strategies and development frameworks. Flowing from this, there has been significant experimental activity around combining military and development competencies and resources in the exercise of power to achieve the security objectives of the War on Terror. Military leaders in the UK and the US view development as being a crucial part of their work going forward. AFRICOM, the new US combatant command covering Africa, has a civilian in the position of deputy head and incorporates social development as a strategic objective (Ploch, 2007). In Afghanistan and Iraq, the military has become engaged in development work through PRTs as a way to dominate the ideological battlefield by delivering development to communities. Development donors and other aid actors are also adapting to the formulation of a new global security regime that states unequivocally the importance of development. Underlying this is the implicit assumption that international terrorism has its roots in poverty, alienation and a lack of democracy. This line of reasoning is reflected in the statements of the heads of bilateral development agencies, which emphasise global security concerns as a justification for doing development. Development actors are contributing to the shaping of this new strategic role for development through the formulation of new strategy frameworks, the creation of specialised offices, positions and co-ordinating roles, as well as programming to work on security.

A common concern within aid circles is that development assistance has been diverted towards battlegrounds in the War on Terror and that the poverty focus of development has been diluted as greater assistance is devoted to security-oriented activities. This book has found mixed and contradictory evidence in respect to these concerns. There has not been a systematic shift in development resources away from core development commitments in areas of health and education. It is accurate that there are significant new aid flows to areas that are of strategic value in view of new security imperatives. For example, since 2001 aid flows have increased to front-line states in the War on Terror, including Afghanistan, Iraq and Pakistan. This increased support is emblematic of the newly important emphasis on fragile states, which are thought to be breeding grounds for extremism and terrorism. However, donor governments have come up with these funds through various complex ways and there is no easily identifiable, universal trend of aid shifting away from lower-income countries to fragile states. Even in non-front-line states such as Uganda and the Philippines, development aid has been used as an incentive to encourage countries to comply with the demands of the War on Terror through instituting their own counter-terrorist structures.

The newly important emphasis on security in the field of development has resulted in new programming and resource commitments to security-oriented activities. An example of this is resources that have been devoted to strengthening state competencies in areas of counter-terrorism in aid-recipient countries, such as through supporting procurement of new communications hardware, offering technical assistance in devising counter-terrorist legislation or training prosecutors and intelligence officials in conducting investigations of suspected terrorists. Development aid has been used as a complement to these types of security assistance. Anti-radicalisation initiatives have targeted youth thought to be vulnerable to terrorist recruitment. Support has also been extended to madrassas to reform curricula and train teachers.

Even though volumes of aid committed to security activities are miniscule relative to the large proportion of aid spent on health and education initiatives, they are nonetheless significant as experimental activities that test the latest institutional thinking on how to use development in achieving the political and military objectives of the new global security regime. Given that, as mentioned earlier, the US and UK militaries see development as an increasingly standard part of their work, such experimentation is of crucial significance for how military–civilian boundaries develop in future. Moreover, they present new challenges for both militaries and civil societies. Thus, the importance of these experiments is that they may indicate the future orientation of development and its relation to security. Security and development thinkers and planners alike are closely following the implementation of these experimental, security-focussed development initiatives.

In observing this deepening convergence of development and security we do not suggest that aid has become wholly subservient to security, that development agencies have no field of autonomous action or that aid flows have been diverted away from low-income countries. The processes are much more complex and subtle than such a bald interpretation would suggest. There are differences in how development institutions have responded to the incursions of the War on Terror regime that are informed in part by their institutional independence from and historical relation to foreign policy departments. For example, the UK DFID, which is a separate government department to the FCO, has absorbed the security concerns of the government but has maintained an emphasis on poverty reduction as its core mandate. This contrasts with Danish, Australian and US bilateral aid agencies, which are more subordinated in relation to their respective foreign ministries and have given far greater attention to post-9/11 global security in their mission statements. Moreover, in some aid-recipient countries the securitisation of aid has not extended into programming, remaining at the rhetorical level of country strategy statements. However, it is also not the case that the War on Terror regime has had no impact on development and aid; such a conclusion would be empirically incorrect.

The global War on Terror has affirmed the strategic importance of civil society to global, regional and national security

The intensifying convergence of development and security since 9/11 reflects recognition of the dynamics of a new generation of warfare and the distinctiveness of a new international security threat. Recent security thinking has clearly established civil society as a key battleground in contemporary conflict. The continuing restructuring of Western militaries, the emphasis on civil–military co-operation, and institutionalised ties between security and development actors are a harbinger of future directions for the military and the centrality of civil society in fighting New Wars. Development–security ties will become further embedded as the legal, policy and institutional groundwork is completed for new state–society and civil–military relations. This book shows that co-operation around security objectives is emerging as a significant new field for non-governmental public action and that civil society futures are inextricably tied up in the agendas of state-building and international security.

In particular, there has been a thickening of connections between states and 'good' civil society, especially in the realm of service provision but also as part of counter-radicalisation initiatives. Governments have identified civil society as a significant contributor to 'soft' responses to new security threats focussing on governance and social policy interventions. The objective of these is to win the ideological battle for hearts and minds. Governments in the US, the UK and Denmark have sought to absorb 'moderate' civil society actors into strategic networks to fight terrorism. In the UK these efforts have ranged from neighbourhood-level efforts to combat extremist influences to consultation with national Muslim leaders on key problems facing Muslim communities and a global initiative within the FCO on 'Engaging with the Muslim World'. In the field of development, donors have sought to fund interfaith dialogue as well as various Muslim interest groups that have been encouraged to form by the possibility of receiving aid funding. Recognising the importance of the Internet in propagating extremist ideologies, governments have also promoted moderate views through chatrooms, blogging and placing stories on regional news websites.

These measures have entailed a greater focus on Muslims and raised awareness about the charitable work of Muslim organisations. The post-9/11 imperative of securing support for the War on Terror exposed the relative inattention to the concerns of Muslims in aid as well. Donors have sought to gain the trust of Muslim populations in aid-recipient countries by initiating dialogue with Muslim representative bodies and religious leadership as well as by supporting Muslim groups. Western aid flows have increased to Muslim organisations and groups as they have come under the gaze of donors whose remit is to pursue the political objectives of the War on Terror. However, Muslims have been viewed through the prism of counter-terrorism rather than social policy as such.

Notably, although bilateral donors have extended their engagements and funding for Muslim groups, charitable giving by Muslims has diminished due to concerns of running foul of anti-terror laws and banking regulations. Although this is difficult to quantify, there is ample qualitative evidence from small Muslim organisations which claim a reduction in funding received from small, individual donors. It has also become more difficult for Muslim community groups in aid-recipient countries to receive funding and form partnerships with donors in Gulf states, Saudi Arabia and Iran. Post-9/11 anti-terrorism financing regulations and provisions in law have put pressure on Muslim organisations to institute transparency and accountability reforms to make it easier to trace money flows and ensure funds are not being diverted to terrorist activities. Western donors and aid agencies have worked with Muslim organisations and charity regulators in Muslim countries through initiatives such as the Montreux Initiative and the Humanitarian Forum.

The greater engagement of the state with 'good' civil society for security purposes has also engendered trade-offs between security and civil society. Civil society is the embodiment of civil liberties such as freedom of association and freedom of speech. However, civil society is not an even playing field; it reflects and reproduces power relations and inequalities that permeate society. It provides an arena for both conservative and progressive forces and for powerful and marginalised groups. In its bifurcation of civil society into 'good' and 'bad' parts the War on Terror regime constructs some groups as suspect and problematic, and others as innocuous or useful in countering terrorism. In many countries it is poor, vulnerable and marginalised groups who experience most the sharp end of counter-terrorist legislation and practices when these are misused, as seen in the chapters on India, Kenya and Afghanistan. In India the media and politicians have branded human rights lawyers and groups, who take up the rights of people detained under counter-terrorist legislation and/or extrajudicial CTMs, as sympathetic to terrorism. This trade-off has implications for the work of civil society around poverty and social justice such that 'good' civil society that co-operates with governments and militaries in pursuing the War on Terror is encouraged and financed by states, whereas 'bad' civil society that seeks to defend the rights of terrorist suspects or to represent the interests of 'suspect' communities is restricted, audited and proscribed.

Civil society has come under greater suspicion in the post-9/11 context, resulting in the merging of the regulatory regime of civil society with counter-terrorism structures

The War on Terror has heightened a climate of fear and suspicion that accelerated moves already underway for various reasons to tighten up the regulation of civil society. The prioritisation of fighting terrorism crystallised the concerns of development donors around the transparency, probity and representativeness of civil society that were emerging in the 1990s. Civil society became a specific focus of concern in post-9/11 security discourses that sought to define the new terrorist threat as networked and transnational. As a way of organising, civil society was seen to embody certain characteristics that made it vulnerable to misuse by terrorist networks seeking cover to plan and mobilise support for attacks. Political leaders claimed that CSOs could be used for money-laundering and transferring funds to extremists and, further, that members of terrorist groups could more easily gain travel documents under cover as charitable workers.

In practice there is no evidence that CSOs have been widely or regularly misused to support terrorism, as argued throughout this book. This raises questions of how and why these suspicions have gained such wide currency in policy and practice towards civil societies around the world as there is no systematic or verifiable proof. In part it could be that this suspicion arises from the experience of US security agencies that worked through Muslim charitable organisations as a way of channelling support to mujahedin factions fighting Soviet forces in Afghanistan in the 1980s (Wright, 2007). It also reflects the awareness, but inadequate understanding, of groups that are involved in both social welfare activity and militancy, such as Hamas, Hezbollah and Lashka-e-Taiba. Still another possible reason is the intention of regimes to crack down on their political opponents and, hence, their need to identify a basis on which to act. For example, opposition groups in Malawi and Zambia have been labelled as 'terrorists'. Rebels in Congo and Rwanda have been branded terrorists as well and beyond negotiation.[2] In Uganda, the government passed new legislation in 2006 that requires NGOs to re-register on an annual basis. The law also created representation for security agencies on the government's NGO registration board but not for NGOs themselves. The Ugandan government has also misused anti-terror legislation to target its political opponents.[3] Other governments in the region have adopted similar restrictive civil society legislation ostensibly as a security measure but also as a tactic to undermine foreign influence in their countries' political affairs. In 2009 the Ethiopian government passed the Charities and Societies Proclamation law, which includes a provision stating that any organisation which receives over 10 per cent of its funding from abroad is a 'foreign NGO' and bans such designated groups from working in areas of democracy and human rights, conflict resolution and criminal justice.[4]

Suspicion of the association between civil society and terrorism has become generalised in the context of the War on Terror. However, some groups have been more affected than others. Unsurprisingly, Muslim organisations have been the focus of most concern, as was seen in the stigmatisation and demonisation of Muslim populations and groups in the US, the UK, India and Kenya. Nearly all of the non-profit groups shut by the US government since 9/11 have been Muslim organisations, including the Holy Land Foundation, which was the largest Muslim charitable organisation in the US before 2001 (Sidel, 2007). The assets of these organisations were seized and their personnel were detained and charged with criminal offences of providing material support to terrorists. In Kenya as well, Muslim NGOs were closed following the US embassy bombing in Nairobi in 1998 and since then several other Muslim groups have come under intense scrutiny, forcing many to scale back their humanitarian work. Other Muslim advocacy groups have been reluctant to register or have desisted from using the word 'Muslim' or Arabic names to avoid coming under suspicion.

This suspicion of civil society has led governments around the world to merge their regulatory regimes for civil society with structures for fighting terrorism. Thus, charitable regulation by governments is not solely about enabling the contribution of non-governmental actors to social services delivery and welfare provision but also to ensure these spaces are not misused by terrorist and criminal networks. Political claims that civil society is an uncontrolled realm where terrorists recruit support and plot attacks have led governments around the world to introduce a raft of legislative restrictions and regulatory controls on non-governmental actors and spaces. These range from the special recommendations of the FATF on anti-terrorism financing, which governments have used to formulate new anti–money-laundering laws, to central bank directives that make it more difficult for groups to open bank accounts, stricter registration requirements for NGOs and societies, increased auditing of CSOs by internal revenue authorities, limits on foreign funding of CSOs and due diligence requirements that organisations ensure their funds are not misused directly or indirectly in support of terrorism. Safeguarding national security has been the rationale for the surveillance of peace groups by US intelligence agencies as well as the inspection of student groups and societies on US campuses. The Israeli government has long claimed that Islamic social welfare groups in the Occupied Palestinian Territories support Hamas, which it designated a 'terrorist organisation' in 1989, and used this as a basis to close these charities. In Uganda, the government branded the opposition leader a 'terrorist'. Playing the counter-terrorism card has become a favoured tactic by autocrats around the world. Thus, the effects of the crackdown on civil society are not limited to actual 'terrorist' groups.

This heightened regulation has had an impact on how development donors support and engage with their grantees as well. The due diligence provisions of post-9/11 anti-terror legislation require donor agencies to ensure that no aid funds are inadvertently diverted to or otherwise misused by terrorist groups. This legal requirement has induced more conservative and cautious grant-making practices by aid donors, particularly in contexts where designated terrorist groups operate, such as Sri Lanka, Palestine, Afghanistan and Iraq. Donor agencies and private grant-makers have introduced new background checks and certification requirements that their grantees abide by various anti-terrorism laws, regulations and bank directives. Large private philanthropies in the US such as the Ford and Rockefeller Foundations have introduced new language in their standard grant agreement letters that requests grantees to certify they do not support terrorism and violence. Among bilateral donors, USAID has gone the furthest in requiring its grant recipients to sign ATCs as well as to check the personal details of their staff and the staff of their partner organisations in the South against an intelligence database. This type of partner vetting was piloted by USAID in its programme in Palestine and is subsequently being scaled up to cover other partner countries, even though no single grantee was subsequently denied funding based on counter-terrorism intelligence checks.

In general, mainstream civil society has failed to respond robustly to the War on Terror regime

The effects of the War on Terror regime on civil society depend on how non-governmental actors perceive and respond to the tendency of governments to engage with civil society actors as 'bad' and 'good'. Mainstream civil society has in general been quiescent in the War on Terror regime. Key civil society actors, including NGO umbrella bodies and other representative organisations, in many countries have failed to speak out against the targeting of Muslims. The implementation of anti-terrorism measures has disproportionately affected Muslim organisations even though they can be used against groups of any type, orientation, background or purpose. Further, by casting a shadow over Muslim civil society, the global War on Terror regime has put a chill on their activities and networking, regardless of their aims and associations. The reticence of mainstream civil society to speak out and act reflects the perception that civil society begins and ends with the funded non-profit sector and blindness to other parts of civil society, especially Muslim organisations and other non-Western groups. It also reinforces the idea that Muslims are the 'other' and, hence, share little in common with non-Muslim and/or secular groups. In aid-recipient contexts, the failure of donor-funded civil society to speak out points to the depoliticising effects of aid regimes. Donor funding of mainstream CSOs that do not rely on dues from members has made these groups blind to their essential foundations in promoting basic democratic freedoms, civil liberties and group rights. Instead, they have sought to stay beneath the parapet in the hope of not being lumped with groups that have been designated as 'bad'.

There is evidence of a nascent push-back by civil society to the introduction of counter-terrorism structures affecting the work of civil society. In Europe, Cordaid has chaired an information-sharing network that has sought to monitor and document the impact of anti-terror laws and new civil society regulation in different countries. In the US a coalition of lawyers and pressure groups – including OMB Watch, Grantmakers Without Borders and Urgent Action Fund – have lobbied politicians and government agencies concerning the impacts of compliance with anti-terror guidelines and directives on their work. Encouragingly, secular groups, rather than Muslim organisations, have led these efforts following the pioneering resistance by Muslim groups. Similar advocacy efforts have been undertaken in the UK by civil liberties groups such as Liberty as well as by new grass-roots groups that have formed to oppose counter-terrorism efforts by the government. UK-based organisations such as Reprieve, Caged Prisoners and Human Rights Watch have documented the culpability of governments in rendition programmes and have partnered with human rights groups in detainees' countries of origin in Africa and the Middle East.

The global War on Terror has galvanised a new field of political action and actors

While many mainstream civil society actors in different political contexts have failed to respond to the institution of new regulatory and registration restrictions on civil society, as well as to resist the targeting of certain civil society actors, it has also been true that the global War on Terror has galvanised a new field of political action and actors. In particular, the introduction of counter-terrorism legislation, measures and practices as part of the War on Terror has renewed the purpose of human rights organisations, civil liberties groups and activists. In Kenya, debates on proposed counter-terrorism legislation have reinvigorated sections of civil society, which was rudderless following the election of a reform-minded government in 2002 and after the demise of the umbrella NGO Council. As explained before, there has been new networking within civil society in both Europe and the US in response to governmental counter-terrorism and anti–money-laundering measures that restrict non-governmental actors. International NGOs have come late to these debates but have also recently begun assessing the impacts of the War on Terror on their own operations, including their relations with partners in developing countries. In Afghanistan, civil society actors have documented abuses of foreign militaries as well as encouraged adjustments in military practices. For example, they have requested military personnel to stay in uniform when carrying out development projects and have also asked for regularised contact with military actors so as to better co-ordinate development interventions in general and to more capably look after the safety and security of their own staff.

The global War on Terror has also resulted in a new emphasis on Muslim organisations and groups that were previously ignored. This relates to the logic of 'good' and 'bad' civil society that has meant governments seek partnerships and co-operation with 'good' organisations while adopting a cautious stance towards non-governmental actors that are unknown or that operate in areas of conflict. As mentioned earlier, the imperative to win the ideological battle against terrorists has led donors to seek out groups that can help deliver new assistance being channelled in front-line areas as well as build relation of trust within suspect communities. Thus, working with Muslim organisations and groups has been an important element of strategies to garner legitimacy and build bonds within Muslim communities. These groups have been identified through the very fact of their Muslim identity as opposed to necessarily any consideration that they might be able to more effectively address the poverty, marginalisation and social exclusion of some Muslim populations.

Since 2001 there has been new interest and support for peace and security programming in CSOs as well as for dedicated security analysis NGOs. Conflict prevention and peace-building became important programmatic areas of work in many NGOs in the 1990s on the heels of the turn to conflict in development strategies. This has been followed up by the emergence and growth of NGOs that look specifically at security policy. Security analyst NGOs have been courted by development donors to advise on security sector reforms as well as to provide independent insight and perspective on conflict situations and militant groups.

At the same time, debates on the root causes of terrorism have benefited some development actors that claim a link between poverty, alienation and the threat of terrorism. While we do not suggest that development donors and NGOs have exaggerated these linkages to get funding, they have been sensitive to the political prioritisation of counter-terrorism and the need to rationalise their own roles in relation to the shifting imperatives of governments.

Implications of our findings

Theoretically, this book raises important issues around how we conceptualise civil society. Two key issues stand out, namely the contradictory treatment of civil society by states and the fundamental purposes of civil society. As governments and donors have increased their engagement with civil society over the past three decades, certain parts of civil society have entered into contractual relations with states to provide services and social welfare. The increased flow of resources to civil society that has resulted from these ties has helped to make some NGOs and voluntary sector agencies financially stable. There is also evidence here of institutional learning in efforts by states to seek the co-operation of civil society actors in security-related governance and social policy work. Through outsourcing the provision of public services to civil society, states have grown familiar with different forms of partnership with non-governmental actors. Crucially, contractual relations between states and CSOs are about expanding the state's legitimacy by demonstrating its competencies in delivering social welfare and security. Thus, these ties are ultimately about strengthening the power of states, not necessarily about promoting an independent space for political deliberation and action on social justice.

In some respects, the co-operation states are pioneering with 'good' civil society in the War on Terror is an extension of this logic and strategic thinking that non-governmental actors can be co-opted into strengthening and building states. The implementation of the post-9/11 global security regime has not implied a straightforward restriction of civil society. The pursuit of the War on Terror has not been solely about circumscribing civil society. Political leaders around the world have sought to exert greater control over civil society and it is true that the War on Terror has given cover to governments to do this for their own domestic political reasons. However, implicit in the prosecution of the War on Terror is a continuation and extension of the logic that civil society can strengthen the legitimacy of political regimes. States have sought to nurture ties with 'good' civil society in part because they recognise the need to dominate the ideological battlefield and to this end seek popular approval of their responses to the perceived threat of terrorism. This suggests an extended role for civil society – not only as a sub-contractor, but also as a type of social guarantor that works to promote the legitimacy of states. However, the engagement of states with non-governmental actors in this vein has typically been limited to building and formalising ties with a particular stratum of organisations focussed on service-delivery and welfare provision as well as a handful of 'figure-head' NGOs that governments consult as representing the voices of discrete communities. In this way the values that civil society embodies have been co-opted in serving the political and social needs of the state with the result that civil society has been emasculated.

Moreover, there is less attention to civil society's other purposes, such as serving as an arena for public deliberation, contestation and debate and promoting values of solidarity and justice, as was seen in the civil society approaches of donor agencies in the 1990s (Howell and Pearce, 2001). The implications are evident in the reticence of many mainstream CSOs across different countries to protest the targeting of Muslim communities and organisations. This was the case not only in newly established democracies such as Kenya but also in long-established democracies such as the US. There is thus a process of depoliticisation taking place as states redefine the role of civil society.

The book also has implications for how we conceptualise the links between civil society, security and development. Whilst in the 1990s security and development began to converge in conflict/post-conflict situations, the War on Terror regime has accelerated and generalised this process of convergence to development policy more broadly. These processes need to be observed and explained for they begin to alter the boundaries of the domains of development and security.

Furthermore, the absorption of security concerns into development has subtly altered how aid and donor agencies view and engage with civil society partners. The golden era for civil society in the 1990s has now passed. The War on Terror regime draws on a framework of thought that works with the dichotomy of 'good' and 'evil' and thus instinctively bifurcates civil society into 'good' and 'bad' elements. The idea of 'uncivil' society has received little attention in writings on civil society. However, the suspicion cast over a spectrum of civil society groups as threatening and abetting violence and terror raises theoretical questions about the normative features of 'civil' society or 'good' civil society and the politics of these designations, as well as how civil society becomes mired in situations of warfare, militancy, extremism and counter-insurgency.

Questions also remain about the relative positions of state security and human security: Is one always at the expense of the other? Is state security a precondition for human security? Moreover, does increasing security always carry the price of diminishing rights and liberties? Or is there a way of strengthening security based on principles of inclusion, respect for human rights and safeguarding the interests of minorities and marginalised groups?

At the policy and practical level there are important issues to debate around the legitimate scope of activity of development and security actors. Where are the boundaries between development and security policies and activities? Should, for example, development statistics include the contributions of militaries, whether or not the source of that funding is a development or military agency? Similarly, where development agencies embark upon security sector reforms, should this be considered part of ODA? How do humanitarian workers reclaim the veil of neutrality and impartiality in conflict settings such as Afghanistan and Iraq, where militaries have become deeply involved in development? Or is the attainment of neutrality illusory anyway? Rather, is to be open and clear about their positions as well as the politics of their involvement in delivering aid the task for humanitarian actors? There is a clear need for a space for humanitarian actors to operate safely and securely in situations of warfare and counter-insurgency. However, aid and development actors need to think strategically with respect to their own politics and ways of operating in contexts where the civil–military, public–private and governmental–non-governmental boundaries are blurring. These old conceptual dichotomies on which non-governmental aid actors defined their own identities have become inadequate in the context of contemporary warfare in which states are building new ties with civil society actors to achieve certain security and political goals. There are also important questions to be addressed by mainstream, government-funded civil society around how they engage with other civil society actors in maintaining and defending the autonomy and values of civil society. There is a need to re-insert the politics back into funded civil society, which has become sanitised and depoliticised under the weight of government funding. CSOs need to recognise their own part in political contexts and recover some of the passion and moral drive that once energised their activities.

There are also issues to be addressed concerning the increasingly contractual relations between civil societies and states. The future for civil societies in many contexts is inextricably linked with the political agendas of state-building and reconstruction being pursued in post-war and conflict situations as diverse as Sierra Leone and Afghanistan, where the role of civil society is seen to implement a development agenda, but one over which it has minimal input or influence. The notion of civil society as an independent actor, and as a force for accountability in governance, is undermined in this arrangement. On the one hand, the space for civil society has expanded enormously in areas of technical concern and implementation. On the other hand, the space for civil society to organise and advocate around an independent stance on matters of political and/or economic substance has been constrained by post-9/11 counter-terrorism structures.

Ultimately, a strategic, considered and calm response to the real threat of terrorism is required. A commitment to preserving and upholding democratic processes, civil liberties and spaces for civil society actors is integral to this. It is also important that such responses seek a more genuine and less self-interested dialogue with 'suspect' communities and groups acting on their behalf. Terrorists seek to distance democratic states from their citizens by pushing them to become more repressive, more authoritarian and so more unpopular. At the same time they also seek to drive a wedge between communities they claim to be fighting on behalf of and the rest of the population; in this instance, between Muslims and non-Muslims. The international Islamic threat has been hugely exaggerated and the US and coalition forces have overreacted to the spectacular nature of terrorist acts. This not only has diverted attention away from what might be argued to be more compelling and acute threats, such as rising poverty and climate change, but has also left in its wake a legacy of laws, institutions and practices that will not be simply undone.

Within days of assuming the mantle of US President in January 2009, President Obama began to disassemble some of the most disputed and excessive aspects of the War on Terror regime. Not only did he abandon the phrase War on Terror but he also announced the imminent closure of the Guantanamo Bay detention facility and introduced restrictions on interrogation techniques such as water-boarding. He also unequivocally stated that the US does not torture. However welcome these preliminary steps are, we argue that greater legal, policy and institutional reform will be required to undo the most damaging aspects of the War on Terror regime as well as to frame a more strategic and measured response to the threat of terrorism. The War on Terror is not just about the ideologies and political interests of a particular administration and, hence, it will not simply vanish with the change of political leadership in the US and other leading countries prosecuting the War on Terror. Rather, as emphasised throughout the book, the War on Terror is a regime constituting a set of institutional arrangements, policies, bureaucratic procedures and practices, discourses and legislation that have become deeply entrenched in governance, political discourse and culture.

Shifting responses to the threat of terrorism will require amending and/or repealing counter-terrorist legislation, measures and practices; dissolving specialist structures established for War on Terror purposes; changing a range of discourses, including not just the phrase War on Terror but also essentialist language that links Islam and terrorism; establishing priorities and core principles that are relevant and integral to a just and responsible democratic society; and re-thinking the complex relations between aid, development and security. This needs to take place both in specific country and regional contexts and also at the global level. As key sponsors of the War on Terror, the oft-described 'beacons of democracy', the US and its closest allies, the UK in particular, have an important and perhaps leading role to play in bringing about these changes. However, this will not occur in a political void. It will require the ubiquitous will and commitment of political leaders and parties and a serious and thorough assessment of the gains and losses from the War of Terror for democracy; a strategic rethink of how to provide and maintain security, both narrowly and broadly defined, in a way that preserves civil liberties and the spaces for civil society players; reflecting critically on the securitisation of aid and crafting more resolutely a development strategy that, whilst recognising the nested and complex intersection of security and development interests, ensures some autonomy to give priority to issues of social justice and poverty elimination.

Though this will require political capital, none of this can be achieved if there is not simultaneous action and strategic reflection by civil society actors. The role of such a movement would be not only to press for such changes but also to rethink ways to ensure security without disposing of civil liberties and restricting the spaces for civil society actors. The experience of groups opposing post-9/11 counter-terrorism structures has drawn attention to some of the forces that can be built upon to effect such a change, such as human rights and civil liberties groups, organisations for and by marginalised groups and other concerned non-governmental public actors. Whilst these seeds are already fertilising the ground for change, it will also require mainstream civil society to critically review its responses to the War on Terror regime in different contexts. In particular, mainstream civil society will need to consider seriously whether it wants to play a role in such a movement or rather if it wants to remain peripheral in these political debates and preserve its own contractual relations with governments and donors by not taking a stand. In the end it is about rescuing parts of civil society from the processes of technicisation, instrumentalisation and depoliticisation, which have led these to forget the fundamental role of civil society in a democratic society. At the heart of such a role are public dialogue, deliberation, citizen engagement and democratic vigilance. Whether or not governments, international institutions and civil society actors make these critiques and take steps for systemic change will be pivotal in whether the War on Terror regime does unravel or whether we remain with only minimal, though important, adjustments to the worst aspects of the regime. In its detailed review of how the War on Terror regime has unfolded in different contexts and its effects on aid policy and civil societies, we hope that this book makes a contribution towards moving on from the War on Terror regime.

Notes

1. For detailed studies of the Middle East and continental Europe see Mansour (2009), Lind (2009) and Colas.
2. 'Africa's Year of Terror Tactics'. *BBC News online.* 2 January 2007. http://news.bbc.co.uk/go/pr/fr-/1/hi/world/africa/6217895.stm; Rubongoya (2009).
3. 'The Politics of Uganda's Anti-Terrorism Law'. Presentation by Joshua Rubongoya. Round-table meeting on 'East Africa Post 9/11: The Impact of Counterterrorism Measures on Civil Society'. Centre for Civil Society (London School of Economics) and Chatham House. London. 17 July 2008.
4. 'Ethiopia Curb on Charities Alarms Human Rights Activists.' *Guardian.* 26 January 2009.

Bibliography

ActionAid Afghanistan and ELBAG, 2007, *Gaps in Aid Accountability. A Study of NSP Finances*, Action Aid, Afghanistan.

ActionAid India, 2007, 'Scrap Communal Violence Bill Says Bhartiya Muslim Mahila Andolan', Press Release, ActionAid India, New Delhi, 26 April 2007.

Africa Confidential, 2005, 'Smashing the Fruit Bowl', 2 December 2005.

Alam, Md. Muktar, 2004, *Madrasa and Terrorism. Myth or Reality*, Indian Social Institute, New Delhi.

Almond, G. and S. Verba, 1989, *The Civic Culture: Political Attitudes and Democracy in Five Nations*, Sage, London.

Amnesty International, 2005, 'Kenya: The Impact of "Anti-Terrorism" Operations on Human Rights', 23 March 2005.

Amnesty International, 2007, *Amnesty International Annual Report 2007*, Amnesty International, London.

Anderlini, Sanam Naraghi and Camille Pampell Conaway, 2004, 'Security Sector Reform', pp. 31–40, in Initiative for Inclusive Security and International Alert, *Inclusive Security, Sustainable Peace: A Toolkit for Advocacy and Action*, International Alert, London, UK and Women Waging Peace, Washington, DC, USA, November 2004.

Anderson, David, 2003, 'Briefing: Kenya's Elections 2002 – the Dawning of a New Era?', *African Affairs*, 102, pp. 331–342.

Anderson, Mary B., 1999, *Do No Harm: How Aid Can Support Peace and War*, Lynne Rienner Pubs Inc., US.

Arulanantham, Ahilan, 2008, ' "A Hungry Child Knows No Politics": A Proposal for Reform of the Laws Governing Humanitarian Relief and "Material Support" of Terrorism', American Constitution Society for Law and Policy, June.

Australian Government/AusAID, 2003, *Counter-Terrorism and Australian Aid*, August.

Bal, Hartosh Singh, 2006, 'Image Boost for NGOs', *Civil Society*, August, pp. 15–19.

Ball, N. and M. Brzoska with Kingma, K. and H. Wulf, 2002, 'Voice and Accountability in the Security Sector', Bonn: International Centre for Conversion, Paper 21, July.

Barkan, Joel, 2004, 'Kenya after Moi', *Foreign Affairs*, 83(1), pp. 87–101.

Barkan, Joel, 2008a, 'Kenya's Great Rift', *Foreign Affairs*, 87(1), www.foreignaffairs.com/articles/63212/joel-d-barkan/kenyas-great-rift.

Barkan, Joel, 2008b, 'Will the Kenyan Settlement Hold?', *Current History*, April, pp. 147–153.

Beall, Jo, 2006, 'Cities, Terrorism and Development', *Journal of International Development*, 18(1), pp. 105–120.

Bebbington, A. and J. Farrington, 1993, 'Governments, NGOs and Agricultural Development – Perspectives on Changing Interorganisational Relationships', *Journal of Development Studies*, 29(2), pp. 199–219.

Belgrad, Eric and Nitza Nachmias (eds), 1997, *The Politics of International Humanitarian Aid Operations*, Praeger Publishers, Westport.

Belloni, R., 2001, 'Civil Society and Peace-building in Bosnia and Herzegovina', *Journal of Peace Research*, 38(2), pp. 163–180.

Billica, Nancy, 2006, 'Philanthropy and Post-9/11 Policy Five Years Out', Report for the Urgent Action Fund. December 2006. Mimeo.

Blair, Tony, 2003, Prime Minister's Speech to Congress, Office of the Prime Minister, 17 July, downloaded from www.ppionline.org/ppi_ci.cfm on 6 September 2005.

Booth, David (ed.), 2003, *Fighting Poverty in Africa: Are PRSPs Making a Difference?* Overseas Development Institute, London.

Borchgrevink, Kaja and Arne Strand, 2007, 'Religious Actors and Civil Society in Post-2001 Afghanistan', International Peace Research Institute, Oslo, November.

Branch, Daniel and Nicholas Cheeseman, 2006, 'The Politics of Control in Kenya: Understanding the Bureaucratic-Executive State, 1952–1978', *Review of African Political Economy*, 107, pp. 11–31.

Breen, Oonagh B., 2008, 'EU Regulation of Charitable Organisations: The Politics of Legally Enabling Civil Society', *International Journal of Not-for-Profit-Law*, 10(3), June, pp. 50–78.

Briggs, Rachel, Catherine Fieschi and Hannah Lownsbrough, 2006, *Bringing It Home: Community-Based Approaches to Counter-Terrorism*, Demos Council of the European Union, 2005, 'The European Union Counter-Terrorist Strategy', 14469/4/05, 30 November, Brussels.

Burke, Jason, 2004, *Al-Qaeda. The True Story of Radical Islam*, Penguin, London.

Buzan, Barry, 1991 (revised 2007), *People, States and Fear. An Agenda for International Security Studies in the Post-Cold War Era*, ECPR Press, Colchester, UK.

Buzan, Barry, 1993, 'Societal Security, State Security, and Internationalisation', pp. 41–58, in Ole Waever *et al.* (eds), *Identity, Migration and the New Security Agenda in Europe*, Pinter, London.

Caparini, Marina, 2005, 'Enabling Civil Society in Security Sector Reconstruction', pp. 69–94, in Alan Bryden and Heiner Hanggi (eds), *Security Governance in Post-Conflict Peace-Building*, Yearbook 3, Geneva Centre for Democratic Control of Armed Forces (DCAF), Geneva.

Cardoso, Fernando Henrique and Enzo Faletto, 1979, *Dependency and Development in Latin America*, University of California Press, Berkeley, CA.

Carothers, Thomas, 2006, 'The Backlash Against Democracy Promotion', *Foreign Affairs*, 85(2), March/April, pp. 55–68.

Cassen, Robert, 1994, *Does Aid Work? Report to Intergovernmental Task Force*, Clarendon Press, Oxford.

Chandhoke, Neera, 2003, *The Conceits of Civil Society*, Oxford University Press, Oxford.

Charity Commission, 2009, *Inquiry Report. Palestinians Relief and Development Fund (Interpal)*, Charity Commission, London.

Christian Aid, 2004, *The Politics of Poverty. Aid in the New Cold War*, Christian Aid, London.

Citizens for Global Solutions, 2006, 'The Nethercutt Provision: Cutting Off Our Nose to Spite Our Face', Briefing Paper, http://www.globalsolutions.org/files/general/nethercutt_impact.pdf, accessed 15 June 2007.

Clayton, Andrew (ed.), 1996, *NGOs, Civil Society and the State: Building Democracy in Transitional Societies*, INTRAC, Oxford.

Cohen, Craig and Derek Chollet, 2007, 'When $10 Billion Is Not Enough: Rethinking US Strategy Toward Pakistan', *The Washington Quarterly*, 30(2), 7–19.

Colas, Alex, 2009, 'Madrid Bombings, Counter-Terrorism and Civil Society', in Jude Howell and Jeremy Lind, *Civil Society Under Strain: The War on Terror Regime, Civil Society and Aid Post-9/11*, Kumarian press, Stirling, Virginia.

Commission of Human Security, 2003, *Report of the Commission on Human Security*, New York.

Con Omore, Osendo and Wambui Gachucha, 2003, 'Harambee: Patronage Politics and Disregard for the Law', *Adili*, Issue 50, December, Transparency International Kenya, Nairobi, http://www.tikenya.org/documents/Adili50.pdf, accessed 1 March 2009.

Cooper, Helene and Thom Shanker, 'Aides say Obama's Afghan Aims Elevate War', *New York Times*, 28 January.

Cooperation for Peace and Unity (CPAU), 2007, *The Role and Functions of Religious Civil Society in Afghanistan*, CPAU, Kabul.

Corbridge, Stuart and John Harriss, 2007, *Reinventing India*, Polity Press, Cambridge.

Cornea, G. A., Richard Jolly and Frances Stewart (eds), 1987, *Adjustment with a Human Face. Volume 1: Protecting the Vulnerable and Promoting Growth*, Oxford University Press, Oxford.

Cortright, David, 2005, 'A Critical Evaluation of the UN Counter-Terrorism Program. Accomplishments and Challenges', Conference paper to the Transnational Organised Crime, International Terror and Money Laundering, Transnational Institute, Amsterdam.

Corvalan, C. S., 1992, 'A Seminar to Reflect the Role of Development NGOs', *Development in Practice*, 2(1), pp. 55–57.

Cosgrave, John, 2004, *The Impact of the War on Terror on Aid flows*. Report for ActionAid.

Cosgrave, John and Rie Andersen, 2004, *Aid Flows to Afghanistan*, December, DANIDA, Belgium.

Council of the European Union, 2005, 'The European Union Strategy for Combating Radicalisation and Recruitment to Terrorism', 14781/1/05, 24 November, Brussels.

Cramer, Christopher, 2006, *Civil War Is Not a Stupid Thing. Accounting for Violence in Developing Countries*, Hurst and Company, London.

Curtis, Polly, 2008, 'Terror Code Tells Teachers to Watch Pupils', *The Guardian*, 8 October, p. 8.

Dalacoura, Katerina, 2005, 'US Democracy Promotion in the Arab Middle East Since 11 September 2001: A Critique', *International Affairs*, 81, pp. 963–979.

Dash, Dipak Kumar, 2008, 'Pak Attacked at Eid Prayers, Subdued Celebrations', *Times of India*, 10 December, p. 4.

Davis, Bruce, 2005, 'Aid and Security after the Tsunami', archived speech delivered on 27 October, Australia.

De Tocqueville, Alexis, 1994, *Democracy in America*, Everyman, London.

Development Assistance Committee (DAC), 2007, *European Community (2007), DAC Peer Review: Main Findings and Recommendations*, DAC, see www.dochas.ie/documents/DAC_Review_of_EU_aid.pdf.

DFID, 1997, *Eliminating World Poverty: A Challenge for the 21st Century*, White Paper on International Development.

DFID, 2000, *Eliminating World Poverty: Making Globalisation Work for the Poor*, White Paper on International Development.

DFID, 2005a, *Fighting Poverty to Build a Safer World. A Strategy for Security and Development*, London.

DFID, 2005b, *Why We Need to Work More Effectively in Fragile States*, London.

DFID, 2007a, *Statistics on International Development 2007*, Table 7, www.dfid.gov.uk/aboutdfid/statistics.asp, accessed November 2008.

DFID, 2007b, *Statistics on International Development: 2002/3–2006/7*, accessed on website

DFID, 2008, 'UK Prime Minister Announces Aid Package for India', Press Release, January, DFID.

Dobbins, James *et al.*, 2005, *The UN's Role in Nation-Building. From the Congo to Iraq*, Rand Corporation, Santa Monica, CA.

Duffield, Mark, 2001, *Global Governance and the New Wars: The Merger of Development and Security*, Zed Books, London.

Duffield, Mark, 2007, *Development, Security and Unending War. Governing the World of Peoples*, Polity Press, Cambridge.

Dunn, Alison, 2008, 'Charities and Restrictions on Political Activities: Developments by the Charity Commission for England and Wales in Determining the Regulatory Barriers', *International Journal of Not-for-Profit Law*, 11(1), November, pp. 51–66.

El-Bushra, Judy, 2007, 'Feminism, Gender and Women's Peace Activism', *Development and Change*, 38(1), pp. 131–147.

Elliott, Larry, 2006, 'Brown to Use Classified Intelligence in Fight to Cut Terrorist Funding', *The Guardian*, 11 October, p. 14.

'Environment for Civil Society: A Comparative Analysis of "War on Terror" States', *International Journal of Not-for-Profit-Law*, 10(3), June, pp. 7–49.

Escobar, Pepe, 2001, 'The Roving Eye. Anatomy of a "Terrorist" NGO', *Asia Times Online*, 26 October.

Fickling, David, 2006, 'Islamic Charity Target of Anti-Terror Raids', *The Guardian*, 24 May.

Filkins, Dexter and Souad Mekhennet, 2006, 'Pakistani Charity Under Scrutiny in Financing of Plot', *New York Times*, August 14.

Fowler, A., 1988, 'NGOs in Africa: Achieving Comparative Advantage in Relief and Microdevelopment', *IDS Discussion Paper*, no. 249.

Fowler, A., 1991, 'The Role of NGOs in Changing State–Society Relations', *Development Policy Review*, 9(1), pp. 53–84.

Fowler, Alan, 2005, 'Aid Architecture. Reflections on NGO Futures and the Emergence of Counter-Terrorism', *INTRAC Occasional Papers*, 1 January, Oxford.

Fox, Jonathan and L. David Brown (eds), 1998, *The Struggle for Accountability: The World Bank, NGOs and Grassroots Movements*, MIT, Cambridge, Mass. and London.

'Fragile States Strategy', January 2005, USAID, Washington D.C.

Frank, Andre Gunder, 1966, 'The Development of Underdevelopment', *Monthly Review*, 18, September.

Frantz, T. D., 1987, 'The Role of NGOs in Strengthening Civil Society', *World Development*, 15(supplement 1 autumn), pp. 121–127.

Gearty, Conor, 2003, 'Reflections on Civil Liberties in an Age of Counter-Terrorism', *Osgoode Hall Law Journal*, 31, pp. 185–210.

Gearty, Conor, 2007a, 'Terrorism and Human Rights', *Government and Opposition*, 42(3), pp. 340–362.

Gearty, Conor, 2007b, *Civil Liberties*, Clarendon Law Series, Oxford University Press, Oxford.

Gellner, Ernst, 1994, *Conditions of Liberty. Civil Society and Its Rivals*, Hamish Hamilton, London.

German, T. and J. Randel, 1995, *The Reality of Aid 95. An Independent Review of International Aid*, Earthscan, London.

Ghali, Boutros Boutros, 1992, 'An Agenda for Peace, Preventive Diplomacy, Peace-Making and Peace-Keeping', Report of the Secretary-General pursuant to the statement adopted by the Summit Meeting of the Security Council, 31 January 1992, UN Document A/47/277-S/24111.

Ghali, Boutros Boutros, 1995, 'Supplement to An Agenda for Peace', position paper of the Secretary General on the occasion of the Fifth Anniversary of the UN, UN Doc. A/50/60-S/1995/1, 3 January.

Ghani, Ashraf and Clare Lockhart, 2008, *Fixing Failed States. A Framework for Rebuilding a Fractured World*, Oxford University Press, Oxford.

Giustozzi, Antonio, 2007, *Koran, Kalashnikov and Laptop. The Neo-Taliban Insurgency in Afghanistan*, Hurst and Company, London.

Gonsalves, Colin, 2004, 'POTA- A Movement for Its Repeal', unpublished report, pp. 1–2.

Gonsalves, Colin, 2007, 'More Teeth to Police, Not Victims', *Combat Law*, 6(4), July–August, pp. 1–8, www.combatlaw.org, accessed 13 November 2008.

Goodhand, Jonathan and Mark Sedra, 2007, 'Bribes or Bargains? Peace Conditionalities and "Post-Conflict" Reconstruction in Afghanistan', *International Peace-keeping*, 14(1), pp. 41–61.

Gordon, Stuart 2006, 'The Changing Role of the Military in Assistance Strategies', in Victoria Wheeler and Adele Harmer (eds), *Resetting the Rules of Engagement: Trends and Issues in Military-Humanitarian Relations*, HGP Report 21, Overseas Development Institute, Humanitarian Policy Group, London.

Gordon, Stuart 2009, 'Civil Society, the 'New Humanitarianism' and the Stabilisation Debate: Judging the Impact of the Afghan War', chapter 7, in Jude Howell and Jeremy Lind, (eds), Civil Society under Strain. Counter-Terrorism policy, Aid and Civil Society, Kumarian Press, Stirling, Virginia.

Government of Canada, 2002, 'Freedom from Fear: Canada's Foreign Policy for Human Security', Department of Foreign Affairs and International Trade.

Government of Sweden, 2003, 'Shared Responsibility: Sweden's Policy for Global Development', Government of Sweden.

Gramsci, Antonio, 1971, *Selections from the Prison Notebooks*, Lawrence and Wishart, London.

Gramsci, Antonio, 1978, *Selections from Political Writings, 1921–1926*, Lawrence and Wishart, London.

Grover, Vrinder, 2002, 'The Elusive Quest for Justice. Delhi, 1984, to Gujarat, 2002', Chapter IX, pp. 356–388, in Varadarajan, 2002.

Habermas, Juergen, 1992, *The Structural Transformation of the Public Sphere*, Polity Press, Cambridge.

Hanggi, Heiner, 2005, 'Approaching Peacebuilding from a Security Governance Perspective' in Alan Bryden and Heiner Hanggi (eds), *Security Governance in Post-Conflict Peace-Building*, Yearbook 3, Geneva Centre for Democratic Control of Armed Forces (DCAF), Geneva.

Hann, Christopher and Elizabeth Dunn (ed.), 1996, 'Introduction: Political Society and Civil Anthropology', *Civil Society: Challenging Western Models*, Routledge, London.

Harmony Project, 2007, *Al Qa'idas (mis) Adventures in the Horn of Africa*, Combating Terrorism Center, West Point.

Hendrickson, Dylan *et al.*, 2005, *A Review of DFID Involvement in Provincial Reconstruction Teams (PRTs) in Afghanistan*, DFID, London, July.

HM Government, 2006, *Countering International Terrorism: The United Kingdom's Strategy*, July, pp. 1–33.

House of Commons Home Affairs Committee, 2005, *Terrorism and Community Relations. Sixth Report of Session 2004–2005*, 1(6), April.

Howell, Jude, 2000, 'Making Civil Society from the Outside – Challenges for Donors', *The European Journal of Development Research*, 12(1), June, pp. 3–22.

Howell, Jude, 2006, 'The Global War on Terror, Development and Civil Society', *Journal of International Development*, 18(1), pp. 121–135.

Howell, Jude and Jeremy Lind, 2009, 'The Global "War on Terror" Regime and Development Policy and Practice Post-9/11', *Third World Quarterly*, 30(7), October.

Howell, Jude and Jenny Pearce, 2001, *Civil Society and Development. A Critical Exploration*, Lynne Rienner Publishers, Boulder and London.

Howell, Jude, Armine Ishkanian, Marlies Glasius, Hakan Seckinelgin and Ebenezer Obadare, 2007, 'The Backlash Against Civil Society in the Wake of the Long War on Terror', *Development in Practice*, 18(1), pp. 82–93.

Hughes, Lotte, 2004, 'Fight for the Forbidden Land', *The Sunday Times*, 4 January 2004, http://www.timesonline.co.uk/tol/life_and_style/ article837474.ece.

Huntington, Samuel, P., 1991, *The Third Wave: Democratisation in the Late Twentieth Century*, University of Oklohoma Press, Norman and London.

Huntington, Samuel, P., 1992, *The Third Wave: Democratization in the Late Twentieth Century*, University of Oklahoma Press, Norman.

Hurwitz, Agnes and Gordon Peake, 2004, 'Strengthening the Security–Development Nexus: Assessing International Policy and Practice since the 1990s', Conference Report, International Peace Academy, April, New York, pp. 1–11.

Independent People's Tribunal, 2007, 'Rise of Fascism in India, Victims of Communal Violence Speak', Human Rights Law Network, Delhi.

IRIN News.Org, 2006, *Afghanistan: Growing Insurgency and Booming Opium Trade Major Challenges – Security Council*, 17 November.

IRIN News.Org, 2007, *Afghanistan: UN Highlights Conflict's Impact on Civilians*, 17 August.

Islamic Relief, 2006, 'British Aid Worker Arrested in Israel', *Islamic Relief*, 17 May, 2006, Hiroshima University.

Israel Ministry of Foreign Affairs, 2006, 'British National Arrested for Assisting Hamas', *Israel Ministry of Foreign Affairs*, 29 May, www.mfa.gov.il.

Jacobs, Susan, Ruth Jacobson and Jenny Marchbank (eds), 2000, *States of Conflict: Gender, Violence and Resistance*, pp. 45–65, Zed Books, London.

Jakobsen, Peter Viggo, 2005, *PRTs in Afghanistan: Successful but not Sufficient*, DIID Report 2005–2006.

Jenkins, Rob, 2007a, 'Civil Society versus Corruption', *Journal of Democracy*, 18(2), April, pp. 55–69.

Jenkins, Rob, 2007b, 'NGOs and Indian Politics', pp. 1–35, in pre-publication draft for Niraja Gopal Jayal and Pratap Bhanu Mehta (eds), *The Oxford Companion to Indian Politics*, Oxford University Press, Oxford.

Johnson, Chris and Jolyon Leslie, 2004, *Afghanistan. The Mirage of Peace*, Zed Books, London.

Keefe, Patrick Radden, 2008, 'State Secrets: A Government Misstep in a Wiretapping Case', *The New Yorker*, 28 April, 2008.

Keane, John (ed.), 1988, 'Despotism and Democracy', *Civil Society and the State: New European Perspectives*, University of Westminster Press, London.

Keenan, Jeremy, 2006, 'Security and Insecurity in North Africa', *Review of African Political Economy*, 108, pp. 269–296.

KNCHR, 2003, 'Suppression of Terrorism Bill, 2003. Critique by the Kenya National Commission on Human Rights', Mimeo, Nairobi.

Lafer, Gordon, 2004, 'Neoliberalism by Other Means: The "War on Terror" at Home and Abroad', *New Political Science*, 26, pp. 323–346.

Lakshmi, Rama, 2008, 'Lower House of Indian Parliament Passes Tough New Anti-Terror Laws', *Washington Post Foreign Service*, 17 December 2008.

Landim, L., 1987, 'NGOs in Latin America', *World Development*, 15(supplement 1 autumn), pp. 29–38.

Latif, Aamir, 2007, 'Pakistanis Hail Charity Re-Opening', *IslamOnline.net*, 27 April.

Laville, Sandra, 2007, 'Anti-Terrorism Strategy Needs Overhaul, Says ex-MI6 Chief', *The Guardian*, 16 May.

Wright, Lawrence. 2007, *The Looming Tower: Al Qaeda's Road to 9/11*. London: Penguin.

Leader, Nicholas and Mohammed Haneef Atmar, 2004, 'Political Projects: Reform, Aid and the State in Afghanistan' in Antonio Donini, Norah Niland and Karin Wermester (eds), *Nation-Building Unraveled? Aid, Peace and Justice in Afghanistan*, Kumarian Press, Bloomfield.

Lind, Jeremy, 2009, 'The Changing Dynamics of Civil Society and Aid in the Israel-Palestine Conflict Post-September 11 2001', chapter 10 in Jude Howell and Jeremy Lind (eds), *Civil Society Under Strain. Counter-Terrorism Policy, Aid and Civil Society Post-9/11*, Kumarian Press, Stirling, Virginia.

Luce, Edward, 2007, *In Spite of the Gods. The Strange Rise of Modern India*, Doubleday, New York.

Lum, Thomas, 2008, 'US Foreign Aid to East and South Asia: Selected Recipients', CRS Report for Congress, 16 May 2008, Congressional Research Service, Washington, DC.

Macrae, Joanna and Adele Harmer (eds), 2003, 'Humanitarian Action and the "Global War on Terror": A Review of Trends and Issues', HPG Report No. 14, Humanitarian Policy Group, Overseas Development Institute, London.

Macrae, Joanna and Adele Harmer. 2004. 'Beyond the Continuum: An Overview of the Changing Role of Aid Policy in Protracted Crises' in Adele Harmer and Joanna Macrae (eds), *Beyond the Continuum: The Changing Role of Aid Policy in Protracted Crises*, HPG Report 18, Humanitarian Policy Group, Overseas Development Institute, London.

Maley, William, 2006, *Rescuing Afghanistan*, Hurst and Company, London.

Mamdani, Mahmood, 2005a, *Good Muslim, Bad Muslim: America, the Cold War and the Roots of Terror*, Three Leaves Press Edition, Doubleday, New York.

Mamdani, Mahmood, 2005b, *Good Muslim, Bad Muslim: Islam, the USA and the Global War Against Terror*, Permanent Black Press, New York. Delhi.

Mander, Harsh, 2004, 'POTA and Its Phantom Limbs', *Hindustan Times.com*, 24 September.

Mansour, Nisrine, 2009, 'Only "Civilians" Count: The Influence of GWOT Discourses on Humanitarian Responses to "Terror"-Related Conflicts', chapter 11 in Jude Howell and Jeremy Lind (eds), *Civil Society Under Strain. Counter-terrorism policy, aid and civil society post-9/11*, Kumarian Press, Stirling, Virginia.

Matrix Insight, 2008, *Study to Assess the Extent of Abuse of Non-Profit Organisations for Financial Criminal Purpose at EU Level*, 3 April, pp. 183

Mazrui, Ali A., 2003, 'Terrorism and the Global Image of Islam: Power, Passion and Petroleum', Public Lecture, Nairobi, 13 July 2003.

McGreal, Chris, 2006, 'Israel Accuses British-Funded Islamic Charity of Being Front for Terrorists', *The Guardian*, 31 May.

McHugh, Gerard and Lola Gostelow, 2004, *Provincial Reconstruction Teams and Military–Humanitarian Relations in Afghanistan*, Save the Children Fund Report, London.

McNerney, Michael J., 2006, 'Stabilisation and Reconstruction in Afghanistan: Are PRTs a Model or a Muddle?', *Parameters*, Winter, 2005–2006, pp. 32–46.

Meyer, C. A., 1995, 'Opportunism and NGOs: Entrepreneurship and Green North–South Transfers', *World Development*, 23(8), August, pp. 1277–1290.

Moore, Mick (ed.), 1993, 'Introduction', *Good Government?, IDS Bulletin*, 21(1), January, pp. 1–6.

Morris, Debra, 2002, 'Charities and Terrorism: The Charity Commission's Response', *The International Journal of Not-for-Profit Law*, 5(1), September.

Morris, Nigel, 2007, 'Smith in New Push to Extend Terror Detention Beyond 28-Day Limit', *The Independent*, 25 July.

Moss, Todd, David Roodman and Scott Standley, 2005, 'The Global War on Terror and U.S. Development Assistance: USAID Allocation by Country, 1998–2005', Center for Global Development, Washington, DC.

Muslim Human Rights Forum, 2007, 'Horn of Terror: Report of US-Led Mass Extra-Ordinary Renditions from Kenya to Somalia, Ethiopia and Guantanamo Bay January–June 2007', July 2007, Nairobi.

Mustapha, Said Ben, 2001, 'Statement by the President of the Security Council', UN Doc. S/PRST/2001/5, UN Security Council, 20 February.

Ndegwa, Stephen, 1994, 'Civil Society and Political Change in Africa', *International Journal of Comparative Sociology*, 35(1/2), pp. 19–36.

Norrell, Magnus, 2005, 'Swedish National Counter-Terrorism Policy after "Nine-Eleven": Problems and Challenges', Swedish Defence Research Agency, Stockholm.

Norton-Taylor, Richard, 2009, 'Hutton Admits Iraq Suspects Were Handed to US', *The Guardian*, 27 February 2009, p. 4.

Noxolo, Patricia, 2006. 'Riding, Re-Focusing, Challenging: NGOs and the Politics of Security Around Immigration and Asylum Post 9/11', Draft paper for the Migration, Democracy and Security project. Paper available at: http://www.midas.bham.ac.uk/riding%20refocusing%20challenging.pdf.

Nussbaum, Martha C., 2007, *The Clash Within. Democracy, Religious Violence and India's Future*, The Belknap Press of Harvard University Press, Cambridge, Massachusetts and London.

O'Connor, Tim, Sharni Chan and James Goodman, 2006, 'The Reality of Aid. An Independent Review of Poverty Reduction and Development Assistance', accessed online 4 February 2008, www.ccic.ca/e/docs.

OECD, 2001, 'Security Issues and Development Cooperation: A Conceptual Framework for Enhancing Policy Coherence', *DAC Journal*, 2(3).

OECD, 2006, *Survey on Monitoring the Paris Declaration. Afghanistan*, OECD.

OECD-DAC, 2007, 'Aid at a Glance Chart. UK', *Development Corporation Directorate*, OECD, www.oecd.org, accessed November 2008.

OMB Watch, 2005, 'Safeguarding Charity in the War on Terror', October 2005, Washington, DC, Mimeo.

OMB Watch and Grantmakers without Borders, 2008, 'Collateral Damage: How the War on Terror Hurts Charities, Foundations, and the People They Serve', July 2008, Washington, DC, and Boston, Mimeo.

Organisation for Economic Cooperation and Development (OECD), 2005a, 'Sweden (2005), DAC Peer Review: Main Findings and Recommendations', Development Assistance Committee.

Organisation for Economic Cooperation and Development, 2005b, *DAC Peer Review. Australia. Development Assistance Committee*, www.oecd.org/dac, accessed February 2008.

Parliamentary Library, Department of Parliamentary Services, 2004, *Research Note. The Changing Focus of Australia's Aid Program: Budget 2004–2005*, number 59, 1 May.

Pearce, J., 1993, 'NGOs and Social Change: Agents or Facilitators?', *Development and Practice*, 3(3), pp. 222–227.

Pearce, Jenny, 2006, 'A Case-Study of IDRC-Supported Research on Security Sector Reform in Guatemala', Final Report for IDRC Peace, Conflict and Development Programme, Department of Peace Studies, Bradford.

People's Union for Democratic Rights (PUDR), 2005a, *Why the AFSPA Must Go. A Fact-Finding Report*, February.

People's Union for Democratic Rights (PUDR), 2005b, 'Obsessive Pursuit. The Unlawful Activities Prevention Act, 2004. Reinforcing a Draconian Law', Delhi, PUDR, January.

Perito, Robert, 2005, *The US Experience with Provincial Reconstruction Teams in Afghanistan: Lessons Identified*, Special Report No. 152, US Institute of Peace, Washington, DC.

Perito, Robert, 2007, *The US Experience with Provincial Reconstruction Teams in Iraq and Afghanistan*, Briefing and Congressional Testimony, US Institute of Peace, Washington, DC.

Perkins, Emily, 2006, *Navigating Politics: A Comparison of INGO Approaches in Afghanistan*, Japan Afghan NGO Network, unpublished report.

Ploch, Lauren, 2007, 'Africa Command: US Strategic Interests and the Role of the US Military in Africa', CRS Report for Congress, Congressional Research Service, Washington, DC.

Potts, Deborah and Chris Mutambirwa, 1998, ' "Basics Are Now a Luxury": Perceptions of Structural Adjustment's Impact on Rural and Urban Areas in Zimbabwe', *Environment and Urbanization*, 10(1), pp. 55–75.

Putnam, Robert, 1993a, *Making Democracy Work: Civic Traditions in Modern Italy*, Princeton University Press, Princeton.

Putnam, Robert, 1993b, 'The Prosperous Community: Social Capital and Public Life', *The American Prospect*, 13, pp. 35–42.

Quigley, Nolan and Belinda Pratten, 2007, *Security and Civil Society. The Impact of Counter-Terrorism Measures on Civil Society*, NCVO report, 11 January.

Raha, Ashirbad, 2008, 'Sombre Sunday: City Marches for Peace', *Times of India*, December, p. 5.

Ramesh, Randeep, 2008, 'Yahoo Worker Accused of Role in Indian Terror', *The Guardian*, 8 October, p. 24.

Rashid, Ahmed, 2000, *Taliban: The Story of the Afghan Warlords*, Pan, London.

Rashid, Ahmed, 2008, *Descent into Chaos. How the War Against Islamist Extremism Is Being Lost in Pakistan, Afghanistan and Central Asia*, Allen Lane, London.

Razzack, Azra, 1991, 'Growing up Muslim', *Seminar 387*, November, pp. 30–33.

Regan, Tom, 2006, 'Britain Drops Phrase "War on Terror" ', *The Christian Science Monitor*, 11 December.

The Reality of Aid, 2006, *The Reality of Aid 2006: Focus on Conflict, Security and Development*, Quezon City, IBON Books, Philippines.

Republic of Kenya, 2003, 'Suppression of Terrorism Bill', Government Printer, Nairobi.

Reusse, Eric, 2002, *The Ills of Aid. An Analysis of Third World Development Policies*, University of Chicago Press, Chicago.

Rocca, Christina B., 2002, 'Transforming US–India Relations', Speech by Christina B. Rocca, US Assistant Secretary of State for South Asian Affairs, 14 May 2002, India Ministry of External Affairs. http://meaindia.nic.in/jk/christinarocco-14may2002.htm. Accessed 29 October 2008.

Rubin, Barnett, R., 2002, *The Fragmentation of Afghanistan*, Yale University Press, New Haven and London.

Rubin, Barnett R., 2004, 'Crafting a Constitution for Afghanistan', *Journal for Democracy*, 15(3), July, pp. 5–19.

Rubongoya, Joshua, 2009, 'Counter-Terrorism Legislation and Civil Society in Uganda', in Jude Howell and Jeremy Lind (eds), *Civil Society Under Strain: The War on Terror Regime, Civil Society and Aid Post-9/11*, Kumarian press, Stirling, Virgina.

Sabrang Communications Private Limited, 2002, *The Foreign Exchange of Hate. IDRF and the American Funding of Hindutva*, Sabra Communications Private Limited, pp. 1–88, 20 November.

Saeed, Abdul Baseer, 2004, 'Minister Scorns NGOs' Work', *Institute for War and Peace Reporting*, 11 November.

Saikal, Amin, 2006, *Modern Afghanistan. A History of Struggle and Survival*, I. B. Tauris, London and New York.

Salamon, Lester M. and Helmut Anheier, 1992, 'In Search of the Non-Profit Sector. The Questions of Definitions', *Voluntas*, 3(2), pp. 125–151.

Salamon, Lester, M. and Helmut Anheier, 1999, *The Emerging Sector Revisited: A Summary*, Johns Hopkins University, Institute for Policy Studies, Centre for Civil Society Studies, Baltimore.

Sen, Siddhartha, 1999, 'Some Aspects of State–NGO Relationships in India in the Post-Independence Era', *Development and Change*, 30, pp. 327–355.

Setalvad, Teesta, 2002, 'When Guardians Betray. The Role of the Police in Gujarat', Chapter V, pp. 177–213, in Varadarajan, 2002.

Shabi, Rachel, 2004, 'Guantanamo in Our Backyard', *The Guardian Weekend*, 11 September, pp. 38–44.

Shepherd, Jessica, 2007, 'The Rise and Rise of Terrorism Studies', *The Guardian*, 3 July.

Sheth, D. L. and Harsh Sethi, 1991, 'The NGO Sector in India: Historical Context and Current Discourse', *Voluntas*, 2(2), November, pp. 49–68.

Sidel, Mark, 2004, *More Secure, Less Free?: Anti-Terrorism Policy and Civil Liberties after September 11*, The University of Michigan Press, Ann Arbor.

Sidel, Mark, 2007, *More Secure, Less Free?: Anti-Terrorism Policy and Civil Liberties after September 11*. University of Michigan Press, Ann Arbor.

Sidel, Mark, 2008, 'Counter-Terrorism and the Enabling Legal and Political Environment for Civil Society: A Comparative Analysis of "War on Terror" States', *International Journal of Not-for-Profit Law*, 10(3), June. Available on website www.icnl.org/knowledge/ijnl/vol10iss3/special_2.htm

Simpson, Ed, 2006, 'The State of Gujarat and the Men Without Souls', *Critique of Anthropology*, 26(3), pp. 313–330.

Simpson, Ed, 2008, 'Was There Discrimination in the Distribution of Resources after the Earthquake in Gujarat? Imagination, Epistemology and the State in Western India', *NGPA Research Paper 23*, LSE.

Singh, Ujjwal Kumar, 2003, 'Democratic Dilemmas. Can Democracy Do Without Extraordinary Laws?', February, pp. 1–6, unpublished paper.

Singh, Ujjwal Kumar, 2004, 'State and Emerging Interlocking Legal Systems. "Permanence of the Temporary" ', *Economic and Political Weekly*, 39(2), January 10, pp. 149–154.

Singh, Ujjwal Kumar, 2007, *The State, Democracy and Anti-Terror Laws in India*, Sage Publications, New Delhi.

Sorderberg, Mimmi and Thomas Ohlson, 2003, 'Democratisation and Armed Conflicts', Swedish International Development Agency.

Sparks, Chris, 2003, 'Liberalism, Terrorism and the Politics of Fear', *Politics*, 23(3), pp. 200–206.

Starr, S. Frederick, 2006, 'Sovereignty and Legitimacy in Afghan Nation-Building' in Francis Fukuyama (ed.), *Nation-Building: Beyond Afghanistan and Iraq*, The John Hopkins University Press, Baltimore.

Stevens, Daniel and Kanykey Jailobaeva, 2009, 'False Choice? The War on Terror and Its Impact on State Policy Towards Civil Society in Uzbekistan and Kyrgyzstan' in Jude Howell and Jeremy Lind (eds), *Civil Society Under Strain: Civil Society, Security and Aid Post-9/11*, Kumarian Press, Stirling Virginia.

Stewart, Frances, 2003, 'Development and Security', in *QEH Working Paper Series*, Centre for Research on Inequality, Human Security and Ethnicity, Queen Elizabeth House, Oxford.

Stewart, Patrick and Kaysie Brown, 2007, *Greater than the Sum of Its Parts? Assessing 'Whole of Government' Approaches to Fragile States*, Center for Global Development.

Sundar, Nandini, 2002, 'A License to Kill. Patterns of Violence in Gujarat', Chapter III, pp. 75—134, in Varadarajan, 2002.

Swedish International Development Agency (SIDA), 2005, 'Promoting Peace and Security Through Development Cooperation'.

Swedish International Development Agency (SIDA), 2006, 'SIDA's Direction. Where We Are. Where We Are Going'.

Taylor, Charles, 1990, 'Modes of Civil Society', *Political Culture*, 3(1), Fall, pp. 95–118.

Thier, J. Alexander, 2004, 'The Politics of Peace-Building. Year One: From Bonn to Kabul' in Antonio Donini, Norah Niland and Karin Wermester (eds), *Nation-Building Unraveled? Aid, Peace and Justice in Afghanistan*, Kumarian Press, Bloomfield.

Timmons, Heather, 2006, 'British Study Charitable Organisation for Links to Plot', *New York Times*, 24 August.

Travis, Alan, 2008a, 'Revealed: Britain's Secret Propaganda War Against Al-Qaida', *The Guardian*, 26 August 2008.

Travis, Alan, 2008b, 'Terror: Secret MI5 Report Challenges Views on Extremists', *The Guardian*, 21 August, p. 1.

Tujan, A., A. Gaughran and H. Mollett, 2004, 'Development and the "Global War on Terror" ', *Race and Class*, 46(1), pp. 53–74.

Uesugi, Yugi, 2006, *Provincial Reconstruction Teams (PRTs) in Afghanistan: Filling the Gaps in Peacebuilding*, Hiroshima University.

UN, 2004, 'We the Peoples: Civil Society, the United Nations and Global Governance', UN Report of Panel of Eminent Persons, June.

UNDP, 1994, 'New Dimensions of Human Security', Chapter II, pp. 22—46, in UNDP, *Human Development Report*, New York.

UNDP, 1995, 'UNDP and Organisations of Civil Society', Unpublished paper.

United States, 2003, 'National Strategy for Combating Terrorism', US Government, Washington, DC.

United States, 2004, 'US Foreign Aid: Meeting the Challenges of the Twenty-First Century', Bureau for Policy and Program Coordination, United States Agency for International Development, Washington, DC.

USAID, 2005, 'At Freedom's Frontiers. A Democracy and Governance Strategic Framework', pp. 1–28, December, PD-ACF-999, Washington DC, USAID.

USIG, 2007, 'Country Information Afghanistan', April, United States International Grantmaking Council on Foundations, accessed on www.usig.org/countryinfo/afghanistan.asp in August 2007.

USIP, 2006, 'Terrorism in the Horn of Africa', Special Report, United States Institute of Peace, Washington, DC.

Van Rooy, Alison, 1997, 'The Frontiers of Influence: NGO Lobbying at the 1974 World Food Conference, The 1992 Earth Summit and Beyond', *World Development*, 25(1), pp. 93–114.

Van Rooy, Alison (ed.), 1998, *Civil Society and the Aid Industry*, Earthscan, London.

Van Rooy, Alison. 1998. *Civil Society and the Aid Industry: The Politics and Promise*, Earthscan, London.

Varadarajan, Siddharth (ed.), 2002, *Gujarat. The Making of a Tragedy*, Penguin Books, India.

Wadham, John, 2002, 'Terror Law Takes Liberties', *The Observer*, 10 March.

Waldman, Matt, 2008, 'Falling Short. Aid Effectiveness in Afghanistan', *ACBAR Advocacy Series*, March, Kabul.

Wallerstein, Immanuel, 1979, *The Capitalist World Economy*, Cambridge University Press, Cambridge.

The Weekly Brief, 2003, 'Kenya Under Attack! Is the Anti-Terrorism Bill a Tool of Terror?' Nairobi.

Weinstein, Jeremy, M., John Edward Porter and Stuart E. Eizenstat, 2004, *On the Brink, Weak States and National Security*, Center for Global Development.

Weiss, Martin, 2005, 'Terrorist Financing: The 9/11 Commission Recommendation', CRS Report for Congress. Congressional Research Service. Washington, DC.

Whitaker, Beth Elise, 2007 'Exporting the Patriot Act? Democracy and the "War on Terror" in the Third World', *Third World Quarterly*, 28(5), pp. 1017–1032.

White, Gordon, 1994, 'Civil Society, Democratization and Development (I): Clearing the Analytical Ground' *Democratization*, 1(3), pp. 375–390.

Wintour, Patrick 2006, 'Blair: Middle East Strategy Is Not Working', *The Guardian*, 2 August.

WMD and ICNL, 2008, 'Defending Civil Society', World Movement for Democracy (National Endowment for Democracy) and the International Centre for Not-for-Profit Law, February 2008, Mimeo.

Woods, Ngaire, 2005. 'The Shifting Politics of Foreign Aid', *International Affairs*, 81(2), pp. 393–409.

World Bank, 1996, *The World Bank's Partnership with Nongovernmental Ogranisations*, Washington, DC, World Bank.

Worldwide, 18 May, www.islamic-relief.com.

Wright, Lawrence, 2007, *The Looming Tower: Al-Qaeda's Road to 9/11*, Penguin, London.

Yagnik, Achyut, 2002, 'The Pathology of Gujarat', pp. 408–415, in Varadarajan, 2002.

Zagaris, Bruce, 2002, 'The Merging of the Counter-Terrorism and Anti-Money Laundering Regimes', *Law and Policy in International Business*, 34(1), pp. 45–77.

Index

Note: Page reference with *n* notation refer to a note on that page

Risk Matrix for the Charitable Sector
    (US Treasury), 55
Rocca, C. B., 179
Rockefeller Foundation, 55–6, 184
Rousseau, J. J., 33
Rubin, B. R., 106, 113, 114
Rubongoya, J., 16 *n*10, 49, 217 *n*2, *n*3

Sachar Committee, 175, 177
Saeed, A. B., 120
Said, B. M., 44 *n*5
Saikal, A., 106, 113, 132 *n*6, 133 *n*19
Salamon, L. M., 33
Sanabel Relief Agency, 62
Sanayee Development
    Organisation, 128
SCA (Swedish Committee for
    Afghanistan), 114, 123
securitisation of aid
    Afghanistan, 111–12, 124–8
    Australia, 80–5
    background, 78–9
    concept analysis, 4
    Duffield, 8
    Kenya, 142, 148
    macro-level observations, 77–8
    meso-level observations, 78
    micro-level observations, 78
    patterns and distinctions, 99
    Sweden, 96–9
    United Kingdom, 89–96
    United States, 85–9
security, 148
    mutual reinforcement of
        human/state, 25–6
    post-Cold War concept expansion,
        24–5
    role of civil society, 37
'Security and Civil Society' (shadow
    report), 66
security of the poor, 93–4, 100
security sector, importance of good
    governance, 20–1, 23
security sector reforms
    and conflict prevention, 23
    donor influence, 20–1
    institutional programmes, 26–7
Sen, S., 182, 193 *n*43
Setalvad, T., 174, 187

Sethi, H., 185, 188
Shabi, R., 60, 61
Shepherd, J., 16 *n*11
Sheth, D. L., 185, 188
shuras, 112, 115–16, 118–19, 122
SIDA (Swedish International
    Development Agency), 24, 29, 77,
    97–9, 153
Sidel, M., ix, 16 *n*10, 53, 54, 55–6, 58,
    62, 69, 72–3, 74 *n*17, 75 *n*24, 89,
    184, 198, 208
Sierra Leone, 8, 19, 92
SIMI (Students Islamic Movement of
    India), 180
Simpson, E., 194 *n*54
Singapore, 28
Singh, U. K., 169, 170, 180, 181, 191
    *n*6, 192 *n*7, *n*8
social capital, Putnam's work, 33
Solomon Islands, 82–3
Somalia, 39, 50, 99, 136
SOT (Suppression of Terrorism Bill
    (Kenya, 2003)), 139–40, 147,
    154–7, 159
South Korea, 28
Sparks, C., 74 *n*1
Spy Files Project (ACLU), 57
Stabilisation Unit, 92
Starr, S. F., 132 *n*6
state sponsors of terror, US list, 136
Stevens, D., 16 *n*10, 49, 51
Stewart, F., 18
Stewart, P., 93
Strategy on Conflict Management and
    Peacebuilding (SIDA, 1999), 24
Strategy on Conflict Prevention and
    Management (SIDA, 1999), 27
Straw, Jack, 64
structural adjustment programmes,
    impact of IMF-sponsored, 39
sub-Saharan Africa, 31
Sudan, 94, 99, 136
Sundar, N., 174
'Supplement to an Agenda for Peace'
    (1995), 21
sustainable development,
    requirements, 109
Sweden, 68, 80, 91, 96–100
Swisspeace, 118